BLACK YANKS IN THE PACIFIC

A volume in the series

The United States in the World

Edited by Mark Philip Bradley and Paul A. Kramer

A list of titles in this series is available at
www.cornellpress.cornell.edu.

BLACK YANKS IN THE PACIFIC

Race in the Making of American Military Empire after World War II

Michael Cullen Green

Cornell University Press
Ithaca and London

First published 2010 by Cornell University Press

Printed in the United States of America

Library of Congress Cataloging-in-Publication Data

Green, Michael Cullen, 1977-
  Black Yanks in the Pacific : race in the making of American military empire after World War II / Michael Cullen Green.
      p. cm.—(The United States in the world)
  Includes bibliographical references and index.
  ISBN 978-0-8014-4896-6 (cloth : alk. paper)
  1. United States—Armed Forces—African Americans—History—20th century.   2. African American soldiers—Japan—History—20th century.   3. African American soldiers—Korea—History—20th century.   4. Japan—History—Allied occupation, 1945–1952.   5. Korean War, 1950–1953—Participation, African American.   6. United States—Race relations—History—20th century.   I. Title. II. Series: United States in the world.

E185.63.G725 2010
940.54'03—dc22
                                        2010008556

Cornell University Press strives to use environmentally responsible suppliers and materials to the fullest extent possible in the publishing of its books. Such materials include vegetable-based, low-VOC inks and acid-free papers that are recycled, totally chlorine-free, or partly composed of nonwood fibers. For further information, visit our website at www.cornellpress.cornell.edu.

Cloth printing   10 9 8 7 6 5 4 3 2 1

For my parents,
Dan and Andrea Green

Contents

Acknowledgments

I incurred many debts as I pondered, researched, and wrote this book. Librarians and archivists at Northwestern University, the Center for the Study of the Korean War, the National Archives, and the Library of Congress patiently helped me identify many of the sources used. At Northwestern I benefited enormously from the criticisms, suggestions, and advice of Martha Biondi, Mark Bradley, Laura Hein, and Nancy MacLean. Michael Sherry, my adviser, provided unfailing encouragement, good cheer, and deep wisdom. He is, quite simply, the best. I am grateful to friends and colleagues who read numerous chapter drafts, offered invaluable feedback, and provided moral support and much-needed diversions as I wrote and revised the manuscript. They include, but are by no means limited to, Stefanie Bator, Tristan Cabello, Charlotte Cahill, Shawn Clybor, David Davidson, Sam Dorf, Erik Gellman, Ronnie Grinberg, Jason Johnson, David Keenan, Richard Lutjens, Stephen Mak, Victor Padilla, Jimmy Pieterse, Meghan Roberts, Strother Roberts, Thomas Rudczynski, Tobin Shearer, Nathaniel Small, David Sellers Smith, and Andrew Warne. At Cornell University Press, series editors Mark Bradley and Paul Kramer and the anonymous readers offered indispensable suggestions for improving the manuscript. Michael McGandy,

Emily Zoss, Kay Scheuer, and Candace Akins were enthusiastic about this project from the start and provided expert editorial guidance as the manuscript made its way through the publication process.

This book would not have been possible without the support of those closest to me. Lesley Perry demonstrated infinite patience during the hours I locked myself away to finish writing, distracted our cats when they demanded more attention as I worked, and persuaded me to get outside and enjoy life every once in a while. Finally, I wish to thank my parents, Dan and Andrea Green, for their warmth, inspiration, and love. This book is dedicated to them.

BLACK YANKS IN THE PACIFIC

Everyday Racial Politics in a Military Empire

In the late 1940s, Lemo Houston, a native of Alabama stationed in American-occupied Japan, began a sexual relationship with a woman named Setsuko Takechi. Such dalliances were common among his fellow black servicemen. However, unlike most of his peers, Houston then began a lengthy courtship. Takechi's family was appalled. Her father, distraught in part over his daughter's ongoing relationship with an African American, committed suicide. Takechi's remaining family disowned her. Nonetheless, Houston decided to seek rare military permission to marry his partner, who because of her race was otherwise ineligible for immigration and citizenship. Their homecoming, following months of paperwork and background checks, proved inauspicious. While visiting relatives in New York City, Houston was summoned to Washington, D.C., to receive his next military assignment, leaving his wife and their two daughters with his extended family. Houston returned to discover that relatives had locked them in an attic. As one daughter later remembered, those responsible did not want their black neighbors "to think they were harboring a 'Jap.'"[1]

African American Curtis Morrow of Chicago enlisted in the army in 1950 at the age of seventeen, volunteering for combat duty in Korea during his training. After being wounded and evacuated from frontline service, Morrow was given a temporary assignment in Pusan, the primary port of entry for Americans serving in the war. Following a visit to a Korean prostitute, Morrow joined a black companion for drinks in a local bar. "I never knew no Chinese before," his friend remarked at one point. "Sure, I used to see 'em around D.C. sometimes, but hell, I don't even remember ever speaking to any of 'em before. As for Korea, man, I never even heard of any Koreans before coming here." Morrow thought for a moment, took a sip from his glass, and replied, "The same thing goes for me. But if I live to get out of here, every time I see one, I'll be reminded of Korea." His memories, including a willingness to execute Korean and Chinese prisoners of war, featured a number of brutal encounters with Asian soldiers and civilians.[2]

Houston and Morrow were among the nearly two million black citizens who served in the military in the decade after World War II. To place this figure in perspective, the nation then contained fifteen million black men, women, and children. By the late 1950s, African Americans comprised a substantial portion of the approximately one million U.S. troops and their dependents stationed at foreign military bases, more than 250 of which were located in Asia and the Pacific.[3] Armed service at the dawn of the Cold War enabled tens of thousands of African Americans to interact daily with Asian peoples, Japanese and Koreans in particular—encounters on a scale impossible prior to 1945.

As the experiences of Houston and Morrow indicate, however, tension and conflict increasingly defined such interactions during the occupation of Japan (1945–1952), the Korean War (1950–1953), and beyond. How did these strained relations influence and reflect black engagement with a growing American military empire in East Asia? In the context of foreign occupation and war, Afro-Asian conflict and African American identification with the state and its military power reinforced each other. Black military service abroad encouraged African Americans to share many of the same racialized attitudes toward Asian peoples held by their white counterparts, to think of themselves first and foremost as Americans (and not as members of what some activists claimed was a global "colored" community), and to identify with their government's foreign policy objectives in Asia (if not its every strategic decision). By the time the Supreme Court declared *de jure* segregation unconstitutional in its landmark 1954 *Brown v. Board of Education* decision, African American investment in the state's overseas military expansion was largely secured. This book explores the incorporation of a class of disadvantaged citizens into the projection of American power and explains how its members came to support a growing military empire abroad.

The construction of permanent military installations in Japan and South Korea in the late 1940s and early 1950s established the foundation of this American sphere of influence. As it sought to coerce and defend these Cold War allies, to contain the Soviet Union and later the People's Republic of China, and to intimidate other potential adversaries under a regional Pax Americana, the United States created an expanding empire of bases. And yet, its enormous martial presence in East Asia cannot properly be labeled imperial, at least according to the classic definition of the term.[4] After all, the United States never exercised or sought direct, permanent authority over possessions there. The occupation of Japan came close—one historian has deemed it "the last immodest exercise in the colonial conceit known as 'the white man's burden' "—but American control was accepted by both conqueror and conquered as temporary.[5] Instead, a growing network of bases provided the sinews of a non-territorial military empire, enabling the United States to extend its coercive power over a vast swath of Asia.[6]

Combining histories of the occupation of Japan and the Korean War reveals the deeper contours and implications of this empire of bases. Both foreign policy endeavors involved many of the same historical actors and material resources. Occupation personnel in Japan were among the first sent to fight in Korea (the southern half of which the American military administered from 1945 to 1948). Most soldiers traveling to and from Korea passed through or served in Japan, which functioned as the military's main staging area for the war. Indeed, the occupation largely made American participation in the conflict possible. By the end of the war, America's construction of a military empire was in full swing, and Japan and South Korea continue to anchor a chain of bases along the Pacific Rim.[7]

To those serving on them or living in their shadows, these bases stood at the center of this empire in the making rather than defining its outer limits. As such, they provide a transnational lens through which to trace the building and maintenance of a military empire by its employees in uniform and the fervent opposition it often provoked in surrounding communities.[8] Everyday encounters on and around these bases could also generate new ways of thinking about race and citizenship among servicemen, which in turn challenged or altered prevailing opinions at home.[9] In this instance, most black soldiers were denied or chose not to pursue romantic and familial investments in East Asia, fostering their sense of insurmountable difference from Japanese and Korean civilians. At the same time, they came to value the obvious economic benefits and relative prestige that their postings provided. Although still subject to discrimination at home, these soldiers welcomed the indefinite deployment of American military power abroad. The thoughts on international affairs of these fathers, sons, brothers, and close friends (the number of black servicewomen overseas was minuscule at the time) usually carried more weight among African Americans stateside than the declarations of even the most revered public figure. The black press, which by mid-century had reached the height of its influence, provided continuous, celebratory coverage of these soldiers' military exploits.[10] Its reporting thus further ensured that their perspectives found a receptive audience at home.[11]

This postwar embrace of a military empire raises questions about prevailing understandings of African American engagement with Asia and U.S. foreign policy. One influential interpretation emphasizes African Americans' sense of kinship with Asian peoples in what has been called a twentieth-century "Black Pacific."[12] According to this view, circumstances in East Asia during the first half of the century, especially Japan's growing challenge to European colonialism, exerted considerable sway over African American debates on global affairs. Many historians have emphasized the ways that calls for Afro-Asian solidarity attracted black intellectuals, opinion makers, civil rights activists, and working-class radicals who believed that nonwhites around the world shared a common interest in forging a new international order founded on racial equality. While most black Americans who supported imperial Japan limited their activities to writing commentaries and giving speeches, a few, particularly among the working class and unemployed, sought to join what they considered a Japanese-led coalition intent on destroying white supremacy worldwide. In the aftermath of Pearl Harbor, however, war, defeat, and occupation allegedly erased Japan as a subject of concern for most African Americans.[13]

Cold War political repression, explains a related narrative, hastened the decline of a black internationalist ideology that fused opposition to Jim Crow with support for anticolonial struggles in Asia, Africa, and the Indian subcontinent. Up through World War II, this ideology steadily reshaped black political identities and understandings of the complex geopolitical roles played by race and racism. The onset of superpower rivalry sapped this burgeoning politics of much of its influence by side-lining its most outspoken proponents. State-sponsored persecution of black leftists such as W. E. B. Du Bois and Paul Robeson was abetted by black liberals' enthusiastic or grudging turn to anticommunism. These Cold War liberals, who came to dominate the leadership of most civil rights organizations, acceded to Washington's policy of subordinating decolonization to the requirements of containing communism. The striking turnaround in their beliefs (or at least public stances) was most evident in their responses to the Korean War and the sense of international crisis it triggered. In the past they had consistently viewed U.S. foreign policy, particularly in the nonwhite world, through the lens of domestic Jim Crow. These black spokespersons now portrayed American military intervention in Korea primarily as an exercise in the defense of freedom.[14]

This book takes a different approach to mid-century African American engagement with Asia, Asians, and foreign policy. It does not discount the relatively few but at times influential black elites and radicals who embraced a rhetoric of Afro-Asian solidarity. Nonetheless, it suggests that the prominence given their voices may overstate the reach of pro-Asian sentiment and its influence on black political thought. The sheer number of African Americans serving overseas also ensured that black interest in East Asia changed rather than dissipated after World War II. Few of these soldiers reached harmonious conclusions about Afro-Asian solidarity or enjoyed unproblematic relations with those they occupied, encountered in war, or remained stationed among. The domestic Cold War political environment, moreover, was rarely if ever the most important factor shaping the attitudes, interpretations, and goals of black servicemen. Nor did military propaganda play a significant role.[15] New personal experiences and opportunities in a military empire that expanded access to American consumer culture while discouraging intermarriage were often decisive. These soldiers, whom most historians would not call "activists" in the strictest sense of the term, used their sojourns in Asia to make sense of their places in a postwar world of often disorienting upheaval.

At its core this book integrates international relations into the racial politics of black servicemen's informal relationships and violent encounters with East Asian civilians and combatants.[16] Notions of Afro-Asian solidarity attracted few adherents in the postwar years in part because they conflicted with the interests and outlooks of thousands of black servicemen living on overseas bases, militarized enclaves central to the United States' strategy of maintaining its global military dominance and fighting the Cold War. Leftist black criticism of the American bid to establish an enduring hegemony in Asia experienced a similar fate. In this manner African American armed service fundamentally transformed Afro-Asian relations and helped forge a new black racial politics in an age of American military empire.

————

The following chapters, grouped in thematic pairs, trace in detail these striking historical developments. The opening two explore the appeal of military service in the immediate postwar years and the structural factors that regulated and influenced servicemen's activities abroad. African American men—mostly from agricultural or working-class backgrounds—enlisted primarily as a means to acquire economic security and material benefits unavailable in the civilian economy.[17] Despite the odious and well-documented discrimination endured in the wartime armed services, they quickly recognized the financial opportunities available in a burgeoning warfare-welfare state that combined an emphasis on national security and military preparedness with a relatively limited social safety net. The aspirations these men brought with them into the armed forces informed how they approached and interpreted their service abroad.

Government policy, based in part on white racial fears, increased African American assignments to Japan relative to Europe. More than ten thousand black soldiers served each year in an occupation that persisted for more than six. African American observers were at first ambivalent about the suitability of American rule over a nonwhite population. However, black occupationaires—and soon their dependents—enjoyed social services and creature comforts largely unavailable in their circumscribed communities at home. The American military government promoted personal consumption by soldiers and their families while demanding varying degrees of American-Japanese segregation, encouraging feelings of superiority toward an impoverished Japan and its people. Black servicemen's substantial remittances further swelled the number of African Americans materially invested in the occupation.

The middle two chapters explore sexual and romantic relationships between black soldiers and East Asian women and various barriers to Afro-Asian family formation. Japanese and Korean civilian leaders and American military commanders encouraged, condoned, or turned a blind eye to a thriving sex industry catering to American soldiers. Black servicemen who established relatively stable relationships overseas—despite increasing claims that their partners were motivated by a desire for financial gain—nonetheless remained acutely aware that their personal lives were subject to military necessity. The Korean War and sudden orders to redeploy permanently separated many couples. Those who sought to marry encountered a sea of red tape, beginning with the need for permission from generally uncooperative white officers. The few Asian wives of black servicemen who managed to enter the United States faced the widespread assumption that they were former prostitutes, and most found themselves isolated within or from often hostile black communities.

As Afro-Asian partnerships dissolved in Japan and Korea, African Americans expressed concern for the so-called brown babies left behind. However, those who felt a race-based responsibility to pursue adoption largely found the legal and economic requirements daunting. Most Japanese and Koreans shunned the children due to anti-black prejudice and deep-seated notions of ethnic purity, and because they stood for some as living reminders of an unwelcome American military presence. (In 1950, for example, only 30 percent of the Japanese supported the presence of American bases; eight years later that figure had plummeted to less than 10 percent.)[18] African Americans sharply criticized the mistreatment of Afro-Asian offspring, but the issue was soon eclipsed by a public campaign to address the pressing need for domestic black adoption. In time most came to regard the children as essentially Asian, and the exploitative conditions surrounding American bases and their enormous human toll largely faded from view.

The final chapter and epilogue examine black engagement with the Korean War and an integrating military and these events' enduring consequences. Some African Americans claimed Korea amounted to a race war, one that black soldiers and civilians should refuse to support. Many more, including servicemen on the ground and their advocates in the black press, argued for the necessity of military action against what seemed a clear-cut instance of communist aggression. Meanwhile, guerrilla warfare and American tactics, as well as the sense among many soldiers that they were fighting for an ungrateful and feckless population, encouraged contempt for Koreans. The appalling poverty and human misery black servicemen encountered reinforced their alienation from allies and enemies alike. African American journalists continually relayed and seconded these negative impressions of Korea, further disseminating them throughout the home front.

African American observers increasingly claimed that black and white GIs, by opposing an Asian enemy together in an integrating military, would recognize a common purpose. Black servicemen harbored few illusions about the durability of interracial bonds forged on the battlefield. However, by the war's conclusion they returned to a nation in which many Americans, black and white, celebrated the armed forces as an example for civilian life. Desegregation propelled the military into the vanguard of campaigns for equal opportunity for more than a decade. The Korean War also entrenched the American national security state and its commitment to a global military presence, sustaining African American economic dependence on armed service and the maintenance of bases overseas. Many black veterans of Korea decided that soldering was a promising lifetime career, and some stayed in uniform long enough to serve in Vietnam, in a war marked by similar varieties of Afro-Asian conflict.[19]

In remarks on the current role of African American servicemen abroad, a historian recently noted that after the Korean War a dwindling cluster of black spokespersons warned of the potential dangers posed by integration into Cold War American society. In the late 1950s, these individuals began to fear "that in finally achieving full citizenship, many black Americans would exchange their historical and cultural traditions for . . . an identification with dominant American nationalism and militarism." That trade-off would inevitably breed acceptance of "an American foreign policy hostile to democratic national liberation movements."[20] This book demonstrates that by the time those concerns were raised, the process was well underway. African American armed service in Japan and Korea had prompted a sizable contingent of black citizens to reassess their identities and priorities in a militarized global context. The following pages explore in detail what led them to distrust East Asian peoples and to accept the legitimacy of an expanding American military empire.

Wages of US empires
— similar to wages of whiteness

Chapter 1

Reconversion Blues and the Appeal of (Re)Enlistment

At the end of World War II the American military seemed an enemy of most black citizens. Amzie Moore, raised in the Mississippi Delta, had been drafted in 1942. After serving stateside and overseas, Moore claimed he "really didn't know what segregation was like" before entering the army.[1] The status of African American personnel worsened in the war's immediate aftermath: opportunities for training and advancement declined, and black servicemen encountered growing racial violence, especially in the South. By decade's end little had changed. The armed forces, and the army in particular, remained predominantly segregated and discriminatory. Notwithstanding President Harry Truman's 1948 executive order mandating "equality of opportunity" in the military, a conservative officers corps dragged its feet. The army's director of personnel and administration blithely predicted in early 1950 that martial segregation might continue "two years or fifty years."[2]

Nonetheless, African American men flocked to the military in record numbers during the half-decade of peace following Japan's surrender. Eleven months after the atomic bombing of Hiroshima, an officer in the Military Personnel Procurement division expressed delight with the army's recent recruitment efforts. Never before had so many volunteered in so short a period of time, he explained. Approximately 850,000 Americans had joined the army by the end of June 1946. Since the introduction of a recruitment drive the previous October, more than 16 percent of all volunteers—nearly 140,000 men—had been African American. This figure, he enthused, represented "the highest percentage of Negro enlistments in the history of the United States Army."[3]

Most military commanders, however, were horrified. Six days later, while President Truman finalized plans to resume the draft, the War Department announced the suspension of all voluntary black enlistments in the army except for those few qualifying for the "specialist classes." Its directive was the first of several attempts from mid-1946 through 1949 to curtail African American entry into the armed forces. To justify the measure, the Department pointed to the "overwhelming response" of black men to the recruitment initiative, for which military planners were thoroughly unprepared. Segregated units were overflowing with personnel; there simply was no more room.[4]

So began a cycle that ground on for nearly four years. Each spike in African American enlistments was followed by an official directive to limit the number of black servicemen, which was in turn rescinded once a proper balance, variously defined, had been obtained. Three months before the start of war in Korea, when military commanders finally abandoned racial quotas altogether, the number of black soldiers skyrocketed. African American enlistments accounted for 22 percent of the army total for April 1950. By July, *after* the outbreak of hostilities, that figure reached 25 percent.[5] If segregated military service was so odious during World War II, why did tens of thousands of black citizens attempt to enlist or reenlist soon thereafter? African American men understood voluntary service primarily as a means to secure stable employment during uncertain economic times. Coercion, direct or not (including the draft and family tradition), as well as fears of domestic persecution and violence, certainly played a role in the decisions of some black volunteers. But economic factors were of greatest importance, and they acquired more salience as the decade wore on. The American military offered what American civilian society would not: decent wages, low-cost housing, adequate health care, affordable commodities, and job security.

––––––––

On August 15, 1945, Claude A. Barnett, founder of the Associated Negro Press, sat alone in his Chicago office. Much of the city was in a

state of euphoria at news of Japan's formal surrender. However, the South
Side, like black enclaves across the country, was more conducive to quiet
contemplation. While white Americans "are celebrating the Peace," he
noted, the "joy seems very restrained in Negro neighborhoods." His fellow black Chicagoans, Barnett surmised, were looking beyond victory
to their postwar fortunes with apprehension: "Something of a pall seems
to hang over our folk." African American residents of New York City
registered similar anxieties. "Harlem was strangely quiet and almost tomb-
like in contrast with the wild jubilation in other parts of the city," reported
the African American *New York Amsterdam News*, since "the prospect of
peace seemed to open up a fearful vista." A black journalist observed that
many Harlem residents "interpreted the cessation of hostilities with the
Japs to be the automatic switch that would slide them back on relief, government dole jobs or even selling apples." African Americans were acutely
aware of the economic woes that threatened if, as another black newspaper put it, "the same color caste occupational system" continued. Their
fears would prove well founded.[6]

"50,000 Lose Jobs Here!" screamed a *Chicago Defender* banner headline. "The collapse of Japan this week," declared the accompanying article, "boomeranged on Negro workers here with the devastating effect
of an atomic bomb, blasting thousands from their well-paying wartime
jobs."[7] The *Pittsburgh Courier* warned of a looming "job famine" among
African Americans and declared universal employment "one of the last
casualties of the war."[8] Days later the National Urban League issued an
urgent call for full-employment and anti-discrimination legislation. The
exigencies of total war had led to full-time work for at least one million
African Americans, and twice as many black workers held skilled positions at war's end than had in the winter of 1941–42. The League estimated that cuts in industrial production would affect upwards of 800,000
black men and women, with between 500,000 and 600,000 losing their
jobs.[9] In a memorandum prepared for President Truman and subsequently
released to the public, the League emphasized the discriminatory practices of both employers and labor unions, the need to expand access to
housing, health services, and opportunities in the military, and the threat
of workplace competition posed by returning white veterans. Of all the
"racial aspects of the social and economic problems which the American
nation faces as it completes the transition from war to peace," it reported, the primary concern of black citizens was that postwar society
"find a way to use their skills properly."[10] Among African Americans

with access to unemployment compensation, many faced the loss of benefits unless they took part-time, unskilled work paying as little as fifty cents an hour. One black journalist penned a satirical job advertisement highlighting their predicament: "Help wanted—Low pay. Long hours. Little opportunity for advancement. . . . Negroes only need apply. Call [the] United States Employment Service."[11] The flush times had come to an end (see figure 1.1).

Black servicemen also found themselves disadvantaged in the postwar scramble for jobs. More than 95 percent of African American soldiers were employed in labor, quartermaster, and other service units, while discharges were furnished primarily on the basis of time spent in combat. With fewer eligibility points, black personnel were generally separated from the military much later than their white counterparts. The director of the National Negro Council sent an open telegram to President Truman decrying the "unbelievable violence" such policies visited upon the rights of black troops, since they "will be the last to return home and therefore have the least chance for any remaining jobs." Racial prejudice and military segregation also hindered the return of black veterans: officers routinely gave preference to their white brethren for inclusion on troop transports, leaving thousands of African Americans stranded overseas. When they finally reached American soil, few employment opportunities remained. A National Urban League investigation revealed that by 1946 veterans comprised half of all unemployed black workers registered with the United States Employment Service.[12]

Entwined with these concerns was the struggle to enact a permanent national Fair Employment Practices Committee (FEPC). The war had greatly increased the importance of the federal government to African American workers concentrated in defense industries and governmental agencies, sites monitored by an FEPC scheduled to expire after the cessation of hostilities. In the summer of 1945 civil rights advocates initiated a campaign to establish an enduring committee that would protect employees from racial discrimination in the private sector. If the state failed to defend African American economic interests at the local level, they asked, how could it possibly provide adequate employment opportunities amid widespread calls for a rapid postwar demobilization?[13]

As autumn turned to winter, the domestic outlook remained bleak. One quarter of all war workers had lost their jobs, real income for those still employed had fallen by an average of 15 percent in just three months,

Old Friends Meet Again.

1.1 The return of persistent mass unemployment looms menacingly in this editorial cartoon published two months after Japan's surrender. *Afro-American*, 13 October 1945. Courtesy of the Afro-American Newspapers Archives and Research Center.

and consumer prices had risen sharply. Black workers, of course, often bore the brunt of layoffs: unemployment among African Americans during the winter of 1945–46 increased at double the rate for whites.[14] Pianist Ivory Joe Hunter, in "Reconversion Blues" (1945), captured the economic distress suffered by many black citizens "since the Japs surrendered": "Hey,

I haven't got a lousy dime / So start your reconversion, let's go back to the smaller times."[15] By early February, moreover, a bill to create a permanent FEPC was in serious trouble. "The struggle for elimination of . . . discrimination in employment," declared the *Pittsburgh Courier*, "transcends the anti-lynching bill in importance."[16] Pro-business conservatives, who equated fair hiring practices with quotas, joined southern Democrats to kill the legislation. In the wake of a successful Senate filibuster, the FEPC bill was removed from consideration.[17] The following July the understaffed wartime FEPC officially closed its doors. The Committee, in its final report to the president, warned that minority workers faced an "unchecked revival" of discriminatory practices, while minority veterans continued to encounter far greater difficulties than their white counterparts in acquiring occupational training and stable employment.[18]

Such barriers to economic security and advancement persisted in the years to come. Ten months after the FEPC report, the Commerce Department released a survey indicating that more than one in four black veterans in the South was unemployed, while those working made considerably less than white veterans. The United States Employment Service reported that rising prices were crippling purchasing power, while a national housing crisis threatened black Americans already hemmed in by red-lining and restrictive covenants. The cost of living had reached an all-time high, 59 percent above the figure for 1939. In the spring of 1947 the executive secretary of the National Urban League announced that industrial education for African Americans presented "a more dismal picture today than it did at the close of the war." Turning to the plight of black veterans, he judged the situation "critical with no sign of improvement." Educational discrimination in the South and the ongoing migration of African Americans to the West and North, he concluded, called for a national rather than state-administered program of industrial training.[19] As of December 1948, less than 6 percent of African American veterans eligible for free, expense-paid vocational education courtesy of the GI Bill were enrolled.[20]

Working-class African Americans also faced declining economic assistance from organizations such as the National Association for the Advancement of Colored People (NAACP). During the tight wartime labor market, which increased the bargaining power of black labor, NAACP lawyers identified employment discrimination as one of the most pressing concerns of its economically diversifying constituency. Labor-related casework became so great a priority (offering opportunities for both legal success and institutional growth) that the Association assigned one in five of its attorneys to handle it. However, in the immediate postwar years the NAACP's attacks on inequalities in the private sector decreased; by 1950 such litigation had largely disappeared from its national agenda. This abrupt reversal was due in part to the organization's erratic approach to labor issues, one that involved little long-term planning. At the same time, growing attacks from the political right encouraged the Association to ally with organized labor, rendering legal assaults on unions for racial discrimination politically problematic. The NAACP opted instead to embed itself within a liberal, pro-labor but anticommunist Democratic coalition, one that counseled moderation and emphasized symbolic advances in the arena of civil rights. Black citizens had lost another major defender of their economic interests.[21]

African American living standards continued to deteriorate as the decade came to a close. By late 1947 unemployment rates among black industrial workers ran twice as high as those for whites, a difference greater than in 1940. The following spring the *Chicago Defender* spotlighted the recently enacted European Recovery Program (the Marshall Plan) and congressional calls for assistance to the continent's "displaced persons." It urged legislators instead to "get down to the business of passing public housing legislation" since, as the paper tartly observed, "we have displaced persons of our own." In early 1949 African American correspondents were reporting dramatic increases in black unemployment across the United States. As one glumly concluded, "little is seen to indicate that optimism should be the order of the day." The National Urban League reported days later that a "depression" was overtaking black workers, the unskilled in particular, with further layoffs expected. Moreover, in the summer of 1950 Congress once again failed to pass an FEPC bill. The outbreak of war in Korea, along with Truman's waning political capital, led to a shift in the administration's legislative priorities away from domestic initiatives. The FEPC was officially extinct, killed off by a new war (unsuccessful campaigns to revive the Committee arose sporadically throughout the 1950s). Military necessity, whose demands once constituted prime evidence for the FEPC's passage, ironically now served as its executioner.[22]

While African American civilians and returning veterans grappled with reconversion's economic fallout, the armed forces were bursting at the seams with black personnel. Shortly after Japan's surrender, a surge in interest strained to the breaking point the military's machinery for absorbing and segregating African Americans. The black reenlistment rate immediately exceeded expectations, particularly among those serving abroad. As 1945 turned to 1946, the ratio of blacks in the army climbed far above the wartime high of just under 10 percent: military planners feared reenlistments alone would push overall African American strength to 15 percent or more within a year. New recruits did their part as well. In the first six months of peace over 17 percent of volunteers were black, even though African Americans constituted less than 11 percent of male citizens of military age.[23]

The army initially responded to the challenge by organizing a committee. In late 1945 a board of officers was convened under the direction of Lieutenant General Alvan C. Gillem, Jr., to evaluate the future use of black troops. By the following April they were ready to submit their findings. Their report, *The Utilization of Negro Manpower in the Postwar Army*, called for increased occupational opportunities for African American servicemen, the elimination of all-black army divisions, equality in the commissioning of officers, and the assignment of black troops to communities where racial attitudes were supposedly benign (outside the American South and certain European locales, in other words). Most of their recommendations, notwithstanding sporadic attempts at implementation, remained operational on paper only. On the other hand, officials enthusiastically embraced the Gillem Board's proposal to set the proportion of African American personnel in the army at one in ten, roughly equal to the percentage of African Americans in the U.S. population.[24] The *New York Times*, following an announcement by the War Department, described the new policy as one that would prevent black men from again " 'greatly' over-subscribing" the number of positions intended for them. They were henceforth subject to a strict quota.[25]

The army's decision set off a lengthy battle between military officials on one side and African Americans seeking to enlist and their supporters on the other. In June 1946, there were approximately 175,000 black soldiers in the army; the Director of Personnel and Administration estimated that number could be reduced to 125,000 within a year. Time was of the essence: in the previous three months more than 20,000 black men had signed up. To thin the ranks and discourage applicants, the army established stringent entrance standards for African Americans and moved to discharge those abruptly judged inept. The War Department likewise barred

African American members of the Women's Army Corps from overseas duty.[26] In order to ensure familiarity with these new policies, officials distributed an "Army Talk" in April 1947, to be used as the foundation of a service-wide program of edification for officers and enlisted men. "Since the close of the war," it explained, "Negroes have been enlisting so far beyond the 10 percent estimated and allotted that the Army has temporarily restricted the further enlistment of Negroes to certain specialists" and to those scoring high enough on the army's entrance examination to indicate "that the man has the equivalent of a high school education." This restriction would be lifted only "when the 10 percent level has reestablished itself." The educational requirements, along with campaigns to purge black servicemen through sweeping discharges, proved highly effective. By mid-1947, African Americans constituted only 9 percent of the army's total strength.[27]

Black citizens were indignant. Horace Mann Bond, president of Lincoln University, pointed to the contradiction behind War Department pronouncements in late summer 1946 that a net decline in enlistments might require a resumption of draft calls. "It is a well known fact," he declared, "that in all other democratic countries, during peacetime, the ranks are filled with persons from the lower economic levels." The military could easily achieve its manpower requirements by retracting its "artificial limitation" on black personnel, Bond reasoned. The executive director of the Chicago Civil Liberty Committee deployed a novel argument against the quota, telegraphing President Truman to claim that army policy violated the Second Amendment to the Constitution. African Americans also lambasted the new entrance standards, noting that the educational requirements for black volunteers were now greater than those for whites. The military had, in effect, established a program of affirmative action for white men. Many interpreted the test-score requirement as a denial of both educational and employment opportunities. Asked if enlistments ought to be limited to high school graduates, one black veteran asserted that in the army young men could "learn and earn a living at the same time." The armed services, argued a middle-aged industrial worker, offered "an opportunity to get good training and yet make an adequate living. . . . I'd enlist myself if I were young enough."[28]

Others took a more direct approach. Nineteen-year-old Robert Kelly of Washington, D.C., brought suit to enlist in the army following a temporary ban on black volunteers. The War Department sought to have

Kelly enter through Selective Service rather than the recruiting office, but eventually capitulated under the advisement of Justice Department lawyers. The settlement of one lawsuit, however, merely sparked another. Pittsburgh resident Henry Stewart's first attempt to enlist ended when he was informed that only African Americans possessing highly technical skills were being accepted. Three months later he tried again. Permitted to take the general aptitude test, Stewart correctly answered fifty of fifty-four questions but was rejected on the grounds that he lacked adequate formal education. Stewart then filed an injunction in federal court seeking to prevent the army from accepting any new recruits until the educational requirements were equalized. Named as defendants were the commanding officer of the Pittsburgh recruiting district and the Secretary of War.[29]

As Stewart's lawsuit wound its way through the courts, the military partially relented. With recruiters falling short of their targets and Cold War tensions mounting, the Truman administration pressed Congress on two fronts: a temporary reinstatement of the draft and a permanent program of universal military training (UMT).[30] Meanwhile, in July 1947 the War Department dropped the educational restrictions on black enlistment as part of a program to bolster the army's peacetime strength (the 10 percent quota, however, remained in effect, at least in theory).[31] African Americans again responded enthusiastically. Within a year the number of black soldiers approached 64,000, or more than 11 percent of total army strength, in violation of the Gillem Board's recommendation. Military officials expressed predictable alarm.[32]

More notable is the skeptical eye some black observers had begun to cast on America's incipient national security state and its vocational appeal to so many African American men. A few feared creeping militarism. One columnist urged readers to "face facts" on the proposed UMT: "Let the army pamper and take care of a kid for a year during the 'depression' that's got to come, and then watch when he steps back out on the hard turf . . .'mid the pushing and shoving for a living. He's going to whine and say: 'Nobody cares about you in this country but the army.' Then, chum, you've got a generation of young war-mongers." The *Pittsburgh Courier* argued that growing military expenditures would necessitate either increased taxation or drastic reductions in federal social programs. It also counseled readers to oppose UMT in order to protect young black men from the psychological effects of segregation. "Colored citizens . . . must fight it," maintained a *Courier* editorial in early 1948, "because, as

"Look at the Small Print, Buddy!"

1.2 The military as a fast-talking carnival barker enticing black men to enlist. *Afro-American*, 17 January 1948. Courtesy of the Afro-American Newspapers Archives and Research Center.

currently conceived, it is a jim crow proposition which will humiliate and embitter our young men." One week later, the Baltimore *Afro-American* ran an editorial cartoon aimed directly at those considering a military career, suggesting that the "small print" of military blandishments allowed for little occupational mobility (see figure 1.2).[33]

Despite these warnings and the army's maintenance of racial segregation and other discriminatory practices, African American representation in the armed forces continued to climb. Military leaders, struggling to reach their manpower targets, were divided over how best to respond to the large pool of potential black volunteers. In the spring of 1949, Secretary of the Army Kenneth C. Royall transmitted to the Secretary of Defense a numerical justification for the racial quota. The estimated black reenlistment rate of an astonishing 75 percent, he explained, was a peacetime high. Royall's immediate successor, Gordon Gray, complained one month later that the higher educational standards of the navy and air force excluded most black Americans, thereby "throw[ing] that excess on the Army." President Truman's new Committee on Equality of Treatment and Opportunity in the Armed Services struggled through the rest of the year to reach an agreement with the army, its leader promising Secretary Gray at one point that even under a worst-case scenario the number of black enlisted men would reach no more than "33 percent of the total Army enrollment," but to no avail. The following spring, however, Gray finally capitulated. He agreed to discontinue the racial quota in April 1950, with the understanding that he retained the right to reinstate it if the expected increase in black servicemen proved unwieldy. The Committee for its part consented to compromise language that ensured any integration of the army would be gradual. After years of wrangling, African Americans had finally won the right for qualified applicants to volunteer for the military as they pleased.[34]

Black enlistments immediately jumped. African American commentators continued to take rhetorical jabs at the army for lagging behind the other services in desegregating its men, but to no appreciable effect.[35] In the months following announcement of the quota's demise, the number of black volunteers reached more than one quarter of the total. The *Pittsburgh Courier* reported in late July 1950 that despite war in Korea, young black men across the country "were swarming into recruiting offices." In Cleveland, a city with a population then about one eighth African American, many recruiting stations were forced to increase their staff after reportedly being "swamped" with applicants. The director of one local army center found dozens of men, a third of them black, waiting for the doors to open one morning. By year's end, the percentage of African American soldiers had risen one-and-a-half points, to nearly 12 percent, a substantial increase considering the number of whites drafted and veterans called back into the service. A shooting war had done nothing to stem the tide.[36]

—————

Coercion by the state, encouragement from one's family and friends, or some combination of the two persuaded some to enlist. Threats of a return to conscription were a constant in the tense postwar climate, especially following the February 1948 communist coup in Czechoslovakia. President Truman signed a Selective Service bill in June of that year, initiating a series of peacetime draft calls—not particularly difficult for the affluent to evade—that over the next two years ensnared roughly 300,000 Americans. The *Chicago Defender* reported that, although high school students under the age of twenty were exempt until graduation, more than 450,000 non-veteran African Americans were technically subject to the draft.[37] Dramatic increases in manpower requirements and accompanying changes to deferment policies also remained distinct possibilities. Preemptive enlistment in the face of conscription enabled many to secure advantageous terms of service.

Black men were subject to such pressure, as well as to family expectations. For Norvel West of Missouri, neighborhood wisdom dictated that "once you graduated from high school, [you went] into the service." An older brother had been drafted, buttressing West's sense of certainty, while many of his older acquaintances had already opted to volunteer.[38] Jessie Brown recalled he simply came "from an army family." Growing up outside St. Louis, he had listened to his father (a veteran of the First World War) and three brothers (veterans of the Second) describe the benefits of army life. At nineteen Brown decided that family tradition, in addition to the chance of being called to serve anyway, left little option but to enlist. Along with five teenage friends he traveled to St. Louis for processing. Following basic training at Fort Knox, Kentucky, Brown was inducted into an engineer combat battalion, quickly becoming a standout in his unit. After seven months in the army, he was up for promotion to sergeant. "I understood the military," he explained, "'cause I listened to my father and all my brothers and [the army] didn't hardly have to teach me anything." Brown then took the opportunity to transfer to the Far East Command, landing in Japan as a member of the American occupation. By this point in his life, "I knew I was going to do a total career" in the military.[39]

Fears of legal and extra-legal violence swayed others. Clentell Jackson, raised in relative comfort in north Minneapolis, had not given much thought to a military career. A run-in with the law in 1948 quickly changed his mind. One or more men in the neighborhood had been sexually involved with a white woman, who at some point went to the police and began naming names. Jackson hardly knew her, but his name came up, along with those of several friends. "We were scared," he later explained, "because the cops were picking up every-body . . . [and] our word wouldn't hold for anything." They spent the rest of the day hiding at an ice-skating arena in St. Paul, while the po-lice conducted house-to-house searches. Early the next morning, all seven sneaked down to the local recruiting station and promptly enlisted. "And once Uncle Sam had us," Jackson remarked with a laugh years af-terward, "the cops couldn't do anything, we were home free." A few months later Jackson found himself stationed in Japan, and, eventually, fighting in Korea.[40]

More than coercion or fear, economic necessity propelled the greatest number of African Americans into the military. Black citizens were among the first to recognize the range of benefits provided by a large standing army. In November 1945, the *Afro-American* published its second edito-rial in less than a year favoring universal military training. Only one of its rationales invoked national security. The others included "military, academic and vocational training at government expense" for a million black citizens and a "year away from home" for "500,000 Southern farm youths," which "would prove a godsend" to those otherwise "condemned by poverty and race prejudice to the status of peons." Even some of UMT's most vocal opponents found such arguments compelling. Although one black columnist remained "against military training and all . . . [the] Southern-bred, jim-crow generals," he shared with readers the "realist" arguments of his acquaintance Nicodemus McCallum. McCallum was well aware of the humiliations of military segregation. However, "for the ordinary Negro from Mississippi, Georgia, or for that matter from Harlem," he noted, "housing facilities were better in the Army than they were on the outside." Then there was the matter of health. Many African Americans had never seen a doctor, while the army subjected soldiers to a battery of medical and psychiatric tests. Such examinations not only constituted free, government-financed health care, McCallum reasoned, they also "made Negroes at least conscious that those types of services were available for human consumption." Finally, in his estimation, ma-terial comfort and basic economics were key. In addition to acquiring decent food and clean, warm clothing, black citizens in the military could expect to receive equal pay for equal work. "If you are a black sergeant you get the same money as you would if you are a white sergeant," he concluded, "and that's more than happens in most places, especially in the South."[41]

Black periodicals from across an ideological spectrum highlighted enlistment's tangible rewards with striking regularity. Even those outlets editorially hostile to American Cold War foreign policy, such as the staunchly leftist *California Eagle*, joined the pro-enlistment bandwagon in their news pages. In fact, the *Eagle* published some of the first positive stories on peacetime military life. Readers learned in January 1946 of Tassie Desaux, recently signed up for another two-year tour, who found "Army life good after South Carolina," his former home. The following month, two soldiers from Los Angeles spent a portion of their time on furlough assisting a once-disabled veteran to reenter the service. All three were reportedly "sold on the regular army," since it provided "security beyond that of the average job in civilian life." The *Eagle* later featured thirty-four-year-old veteran Frank French, who responded enthusiastically to a direct mailing from his previous employer. "The army was just about the best boss I've had," he explained. Other periodicals followed suit. The *Afro-American* weighed in with an editorial calling for a "Fifth Freedom" beyond Franklin Roosevelt's celebrated four: the unfettered freedom to enlist. The paper recognized that, given ongoing military segregation, some readers might balk at the idea. It countered with an appeal to "enlightened selfishness." The army, it explained, "offers guaranteed wages, insurance, pension[s], hospitalization and education far beyond anything disadvantaged workers can secure."[42]

Black servicemen put forward similar reasoning and vigorously protested claims to the contrary. NAACP executive secretary Walter White found himself in a heated confrontation with several veterans over the question of black attitudes toward the military. Following a May 1946 speech to the Palmetto State Teachers Association in South Carolina, he attended a reception at the local USO. There he was accosted by a group of veterans who, according to White, "at times almost belligerently" challenged his claim that black soldiers overwhelmingly despised the army and hoped to escape as soon as possible. One young man, employing "a rolled newspaper to emphasize his point," insisted that most wished to stay in uniform, especially if it enabled foreign occupation duty. He was joined by a chorus of his fellow veterans. A rather nonplussed White wrote that the encounter indicated "a regrettable development among Negro youth," criticizing the men for "indulging in . . . escapism" since "one, two, five or ten years spent overseas will throw them just that much further behind in the struggle for jobs, advancement in their professions or trades, . . . and the building of places for themselves in society." White, not alone among black spokespersons, could not yet envision military service as a profession with significant growth potential.[43]

Indirect rebuttals to White's claims emerge from the recollections of those who enlisted. A soldier from Missouri remembered one salient advantage to volunteering: "It offered—I don't want to say a way out of the ghetto, but it offered a way to do something more constructive with your life." According to Beverly Scott, born and raised in North Carolina, "There was no better institution in American life . . . than the army for the black man in the forties and fifties. Things weren't perfect, but they were better than any civilian institution." "From the first day I went in the army," he continued, "I had no thought of getting out." For many, the immediate economic returns outweighed any drawbacks, and improved material circumstances encouraged reenlistment. Isaac Gardner, Jr., grew up in Harlan County, Kentucky, coal-mining country. A self-described "mountain boy," Gardner volunteered because he dreaded the thought of working in the mines. After basic training the army flew him to Japan, with a stopover in Hawaii. As the plane was being refueled, the soldiers were treated to a complimentary meal in one of the island's best restaurants. Gardner remembered being astonished by the experience, never having been "exposed to such finery."[44]

A group of black servicemen interviewed overseas in mid-1948 echoed these sentiments. The men asked a visiting journalist to remind mothers and wives back home of the American GI's proper diet, adequate clothing, and access to medical care. One third voiced their desire to acquire twenty years of service in order to retire on a military pension while still young. "A large number re-enlist because they like the life," the interviewer explained, while others "get out, stay at home a few months, and decide to come back in." With consumer prices on the rise and decent housing in short supply, the men agreed, civilian life could rarely compete with the army.[45]

Nor, it seemed, could higher education. One black Floridian enlisted in 1949 after being "kicked out" of college because he could no longer afford the monthly tuition of $56. "Tired of begging" his family for college money, and unwilling to take a menial position at the local sawmill, he "just joined the service."[46] In a reflection of the African American press's growing awareness, if not complete acceptance, of such opportunities for personal advancement offered by the military, editorial items

Unfair (?) Competition!

1.3 College life seemed unable to compete with a military offering an array of goods and services. *Chicago Defender*, 11 September 1948. Courtesy of the *Chicago Defender*.

began to contradict earlier warnings against enlistment. One *Chicago Defender* cartoon captured the mood among many black men contemplating their career options (see figure 1.3).

The wages of armed service gradually extended into ever-larger segments of the civilian population, increasing the number of black citizens economically invested in American militarization. Some soldiers pooled their resources to support civil rights organizations. Over fifteen hundred men of the all-black 24th Infantry Regiment, stationed in Japan, together contributed nearly four thousand dollars to the NAACP's national office.[47] Many more sent funds directly home. Indeed, the prospect of remittances was a powerful enticement for black men with families to support, enabling them to assume the role of breadwinner. Charles Berry had grown up in Chattanooga, Tennessee, where "the only employment that you really had was working in a hotel, or some type of menial work." At seventeen, hoping to marry his high school sweetheart and begin a family with "a nice home and car, and maybe a couple dollars in the bank," he dropped out of school and convinced his mother to sign his enlistment papers. At first concerned for his safety and future prospects, Berry's mother experienced a change of heart once "she started getting the allotment checks." Berry eventually served in both Japan and Korea.[48]

Ivory Perry, raised by a sharecropping family in rural Arkansas, was frustrated by his limited job prospects. Particularly distressing to him was an inability to provide financial support to his younger siblings. Although enlisting in the military meant leaving family, Perry knew his room and board would be taken care of, and he intended to save enough money to send a portion of his income home each month. At the swearing-in ceremony he noticed that many of his fellow black inductees were veterans of World War II, and while on board a train to basic training he met a number of young black men who had also volunteered in the hopes of providing for their families. One year later Perry's cousin, unable to afford college and facing the prospect of earning poverty wages picking cotton, enlisted and joined him in East Asia.[49]

Ira Neal, a high school dropout from Tennessee, first attempted to join the air force. He traveled to Biloxi, Mississippi, only to be informed that the quota for African Americans had been filled. Neal then signed with the army at Fort Dix, New Jersey. "There wasn't a lot for a black kid to do [at] that day and time in the South," he recalled, "no jobs." Only sixteen years old, he convinced his mother to sign the consent forms and to lie about his age. "I think my mother was glad in a sense," he explained, "because I was able to help provide support for the family." Many of Neal's friends and acquaintances were also moving directly into the service after graduating or dropping out of school. In addition to the all-important "three hots and a cot," they earned a starting salary of $75 a month (an income that, after free food, shelter, and clothing were taken into account, leapt to the equivalent of more than $200, according to one estimate). Neal regularly sent home at least half his earnings while stationed on the other side of the Pacific.[50]

For many black soldiers, assignments to postwar Europe or Asia were especially prized. In addition to the absence of Jim Crow laws, the advantages of occupation duty included a 25 percent "hardship" bonus (until 1949), greatly reduced living expenses, and the possibility of sending for family, which could improve an entire household's economic standing. However, although military commanders gradually, if grudgingly, agreed to drop barriers to black enlistments in the late 1940s, they remained determined to assign African Americans to the Far East rather than to Europe, Germany in particular. As World War II drew to a close, sensational accounts of wholesale black sexual assaults against European women circulated in the mainstream media. The *Chicago Daily Tribune* quoted a former intelligence officer who called the alleged misdeeds of African American troops in Germany "one of the most disgraceful episodes in American history."[51] Court-martial records reveal that between July 1942 and November 1946, 256 black soldiers (and 202 whites) were convicted of rape in the European theater (the Army Judge Advocate General's office dropped racial labels from its crime records soon thereafter).[52] African American observers argued that such figures were undoubtedly distorted. One, who investigated several of the criminal cases, noted that some white officers, "resentful of the publicly displayed favorable attitudes of German women toward Negro soldiers," had instigated trumped-up charges against black servicemen under their command. Another pointed to the fact that not a single black member of the military police was stationed in Germany. Anecdotal evidence from German civilians, collected in a series of reports from the American zone of occupation, indicates that no serious disturbances occurred in areas housing black troops.[53]

Most of the accusations leveled against African American servicemen were instead rooted in concerns over sexual contact of any sort between black men and white women. A report prepared by the Senate War Investigating Committee's legal counsel in 1946 publicly damned black soldiers in Germany with allegations of widespread misconduct, chief among them sexual relations with German women. "A large portion of the Negro troops are being used as service troops, principally as truck drivers," it complained. "This has resulted in . . . their ready access to Army supplies, which they have used for the purpose of gaining favor with frauleins." That June, General Dwight Eisenhower, former military governor of the U.S. occupation zone, received a missive from an outraged white American who demanded, "Why are [black servicemen] not moved elsewhere, say to Japan where there are no white people for them to exploit their negro blood upon[?]" Two-and-a-half years later an internal memorandum described a letter sent by Congressman Carl T. Curtis of Nebraska to the Secretary of Defense: "Advises that [a] constituent has in recent months made [an] extended trip to Europe. Greatly distressed over the problems being created by the maintenance of colored troops in Bavaria. Pointed out [the] large number of colored babies being born to white girls living there."[54]

Military officials, bowing to enormous pressure from white civilians, as well as to their own prejudices, set out to slash the number of African American personnel in the theater. The War Department ordered the army in mid-1946 to "discontinue shipment" of black soldiers to Europe (the Pacific, according to one directive, was the "only overseas theatre currently in need of such personnel").[55] The army in turn secured authorization to initiate a program, aimed primarily at African American troops, to order dishonorable (or "blue") discharges for any individual in the European Command deemed "a detriment to the good reputation of the United States Army." (The same tactic had been used against homosexuals during the war.) Others were to be dismissed with honorable ("white") discharges for being "inefficient" or otherwise "unable to adjust themselves" to military life. At year's end the civilian aide to the Secretary of War returned from a tour of American military installations to report that black servicemen would constitute half of all those so removed from Europe. The *Pittsburgh Courier* later discovered, however, that the records of those sent home "were carefully checked by the War Department. As a result, only one out of every ten men . . . was given such a discharge when they reached the States. The rest have been retained honorably in the service." The program's principal effect, in other words, was to remove experienced black troops from Europe without jeopardizing their future utilization elsewhere.[56]

Thus at the same time that African Americans were clamoring for opportunities to serve in the military, the number of black soldiers in Europe plummeted. The 18,000 stationed there in January 1947—as opposed to the 35,000 then assigned to the Pacific—fell to 10,000 by April 1948 and to less than 4,000 by the start of 1949.[57] The Far East Command (FEC), on the other hand, witnessed a much less dramatic decline in black personnel during these years, and it remained a theater of choice for military commanders responding to domestic pressures and to their own distaste at the prospect of black-white intimacy. America's enormous military presence in Asia also provided officers with the convenient explanation that they were merely following the

Gillem Board's recommendation to avoid stationing African Americans among hostile populations.[58] Indeed, the call to confine black servicemen to "localities where community attitudes are most favorable," FEC headquarters repeatedly insisted, "does not present a problem in this theater."[59]

Chapter 2

The American Dream in a Prostrate Japan

Shortly after the start of war in Korea, a black columnist posed a question: "Have you ever seriously considered what might happen here in America if we should enter an all-out war and lose it?" In response to his query, the author contemplated American practices in East Asia. "I have just had a look at Japan," he cautioned, "and if [it] can be used as a yardstick . . . here are some of the things we might expect." There followed an extensive catalog of socioeconomic ills. Loss of purchasing power "would be only the beginning. . . . If the Russians followed the pattern we have set in Japan," the largest retailers "would probably end up as Russian post exchanges where Americans could work but not where they could be customers." Discrimination would extend to toilets and drinking fountains, "with the better facilities being plainly marked 'For Russians only.'" In general, "there would be two standards observed. . . . Russians must be served first at all times. Then would come the serving of American needs." The author concluded his illustration of "the U.S. pattern in Japan now" with a warning: "Once one sees [Japan] and does not remain in it long enough to become calloused," the occupation foretold what might occur if the United States were conquered.[1]

The column was remarkable not only for its oblique allusions to Jim Crow but also because it offered a comprehensive attack on American occupation policies. Did it reflect mainstream black sentiment in 1950, among those presumably more sympathetic than whites to the plight of the Japanese?[2] What of African Americans by then allegedly "calloused" by occupation duty? Most black servicemen stationed in Japan had enlisted to enhance their socioeconomic status, while their remittances encouraged family members to identify with peacetime armed service. Conditions for Americans and Japanese under the occupation strongly reinforced these personal investments among black soldiers and their kin.

A distinction must be made, however, between the overall American enterprise and the experiences of black personnel. African Americans were at once integral to the white-dominated occupation force and apart from it. They served under most of the same rules and regulations and enjoyed many of the same privileges as their white counterparts, yet segregation persisted. Black personnel generally worked and lived in their own enclaves, interacting with the Japanese on their own terms. These servicemen, and often their wives and children, acquired goods and services largely unavailable in their circumscribed communities stateside. The Japanese, struggling to survive and dependent for their meager livelihoods upon the American-led Supreme Command for the Allied Powers (SCAP), worked to sell the nation and its culture for their occupiers' consumption.[3] An international African American audience at first debated the suitability of benefiting economically from American rule over a nonwhite people. As the occupation wore on, however, such qualms grew infrequent: black citizens on both sides of the Pacific reconciled themselves to American hegemony in Japan. Military policies and black economic interests, working in tandem, led to an acceptance and even an embrace of the personal opportunities provided by the occupation. These circumstances together did much to set the tenor of social relations between black occupationaires and Japanese civilians.

A strikingly festive mood pervaded the dockside ritual of departure for servicemen traveling to Japan. During the war troop transports had left under cover of darkness. Now, in the light of day, exuberant crowds of civilians and soldiers mingled under balloons, banners, and ubiquitous American flags, while brass bands struck up popular tunes. Enlisted men held signs reading "Tokyo Here We Come" or "Gotta See a Geisha

Girl." Despite the excitement and cheerful farewells, however, the troops had a long and tedious journey ahead of them. In the years before large-scale air transport to Asia became economically practical, the military relied almost exclusively on sea travel. The voyage from Seattle took two weeks, from San Francisco almost three. Transports sailing directly from the East Coast passed through the Panama Canal, a route requiring nearly two months. Aside from occasional rough seas, there was little to engage the men's attention—recreational facilities were few and brief-ings on Japanese conditions almost nonexistent. They read, played cards, spoke with fellow passengers and speculated about what the occupation held in store for them. Most would disembark at Yokohama, described by one contemporary as being "to Tokyo rather as Newark or Jersey City is to New York." Initial greetings came from the first contingent of occupationaires: the outer jetty sported outsized black and red letters reading "KILROY," a nod to the graffiti produced by GIs during the war.

Once docked, the ships unloaded troops on a wharf that seemed an exercise in controlled confusion. American and Japanese workers struggled to move cargo alongside army buses and trucks waiting to transfer new arrivals to their assignments. At the local replacement de-pot, servicemen attended a mandatory orientation covering such basics as SCAP fraternization policies, currency exchange, black market regula-tions, and venereal disease prevention, capped by a cursory overview of Japan and its people. They typically received no substantive information on postwar life for the Japanese. Rushed through the depot in a few days or even hours, the men were then scattered across the American com-mand. Occupationaires frequently knew little more than they had upon departing the United States. What they discovered for themselves de-pended in large measure on when they arrived, where they served, and how long they stayed.[4]

The first American forces landed in a nation approaching social and economic collapse. In a land numbering approximately seventy-four mil-lion in 1941, nearly three million (roughly 4 percent of the population) had perished in war, with countless more injured, ill, or malnourished. More than 60 percent of urban housing had been destroyed, and some nine million Japanese were homeless. During eight years of fighting in Asia and the Pacific, Japan had witnessed steadily declining food produc-tion; most ominous was a shortage of rice. Lack of fertilizer, poor weather, manpower shortages, and insufficient machinery conspired to reduce the 1945 yield by nearly 40 percent from the previous year. Japan also could no longer depend on appropriated rice from Korea and other former colonies. By the winter of 1945–46, official rations for adults provided a mere 1,233 calories per day, little more than half the estimated nutritional requirements. Shortages of already scarce resources were exacerbated by the gradual return of six-and-a-half million repatriated soldiers and civilian settlers, combined with a soaring postwar birth rate.

The war had been as much an economic as a military defeat. Japan lost up to a third of its national wealth, a fifth of all household goods, and perhaps half of its total income potential. An American presidential envoy reported in October 1945 that "the entire economic structure of Japan's greatest cities has been wrecked." Japanese citizens, facing a 70 percent drop in real wages, triple-digit inflation, and potential famine, were reduced to foraging in the countryside and trading whatever possessions remained for food and clothing. In late 1945 they relied on the black market for half their daily needs (by comparison, the black market in Germany then amounted to less than 10 percent of all economic transactions). Among Japanese men, women, and children it was known as a " 'bamboo shoot lifestyle' (*takenoko seikatsu*), a metaphor for life below the subsistence line." Just as bamboo shoots are prepared by removing the outer husks one by one, so the Japanese stripped themselves of one layer of possessions after another. Luxurious silk kimonos were bartered for handfuls of rancid food.[5]

Yet despite physical and emotional exhaustion, idleness was virtually unknown. As one historian of the Japanese consumer economy observes, "a curious vitality pervaded the early postwar period." Since inertia in a shattered Japan meant likely starvation, street markets sprang up in nearly every urban center, offering astonishing varieties of goods. Resourceful hustlers sold makeshift products to their fellow citizens, while observing varying degrees of occupational integrity. Footwear provides a case in point. Recycled duralumin—salvaged from aircraft bodies—was used for the production of sturdy *geta*-style clogs. At the same time, a shortage of leather led dishonest cobblers to mend shoes with dried squid, which disintegrated in the rain.[6] Many Japanese pinned their hopes on providing souvenirs, entertainment, and other services to foreign occupation personnel. American servicemen appeared especially eager to acquire any type of memento, at nearly any price. An Associated Press correspondent wrote that among the curb-side stalls offering ersatz Japanese wares, "the prices are high, and the quality pathetically low, but the GIs buy readily. 'What the hell,' they say. 'It ain't money. It's only yen.' "[7] It was in this environment, in the late summer and fall of 1945, that occupationaires established a new American presence.

As the invasion of the home islands unfolded, African American observers were torn over black participation in the enterprise. One reporter lauded the service troops stationed in the Philippines—relatively few black soldiers had seen combat against the Japanese—who stood "poised by the thousands" to enter "the enemy's homeland to clinch the peace." "Just as during the war," he enthused, "the service troops are among the first going in and the last coming out." (Indeed, eight all-black service companies, made up of more than 1,500 soldiers, disembarked at Yokohama minutes after Japan formally surrendered aboard the USS *Missouri*.) Some months later, the poet and journalist Langston Hughes's fictional everyman complained in the pages of the *Chicago Defender* that white Americans "do not want to be bothered with no occupation at no GI salary. . . . So they are going to make the Negroes do the occupation for them, and the white GIs are coming home and making some of this Reconversion money." To which Hughes replied, "It might not be so bad for the Negroes. I had rather be a soldier in . . . Asia than in Camp Claiborne, Louisiana, any day." Some downplayed enthusiasm for occupation duty, reflecting a belief that black servicemen wished to return home as soon as possible. A bemused dispatch from Manila began by noting, "Strange as it may seem, Negro GIs here are anxiously awaiting orders which will land them in Japan." The author attributed their eagerness to "natural curiosity" and warned that "unusual enthusiasm for the Japan assignment must not be interpreted as a wish to stay overseas any longer than necessary." None of the men interviewed for the piece exhibited hatred for the Japanese people. "All of them looked upon this assignment as just one more military job in another strange country," for they issued "no threats of personal violence against the Japanese, only interest in them as a strange people."[8]

Others were less charitable toward the Japanese and those who appeared to sympathize with them. A reporter for the *Afro-American* complained of thousands of "mere soldiers" who "by innate human instinct are feeling compassion for the Japs that, by this correspondent's studied evaluation, is not deserved." He excoriated American occupationaires who, by drinking, carousing, and fraternizing with Japanese women of dubious repute, were "making a laughing stock of themselves in the eyes of the Japanese." Some in the black press also criticized the occupied for failing to display proper deference toward their conquerors. One editorial noted that the Japanese government had offered American reporters an opportunity to attend a session of the Diet. The invitation contained a formal request that none arrive intoxicated. "This sneering insinuation and innuendo is typical of white supremacy in America," protested the author, who cast Japan as an unrepentant champion of its own ethnoracial superiority. "The little yellow fellows have discovered that there are a half dozen ways of calling their enemy"—in this instance, all Americans, regardless of race—"no good without saying it directly." According to this interpretation, African American benevolence toward the Japanese was inexplicable.[9]

Another line of reasoning positioned the Japanese as victims of white supremacy. An editorial cartoon juxtaposed two striking images (see figure 2.1). The first depicted an American general, presumably Douglas MacArthur, imperiously extending "American Dictates" before a bowing "Japan," the second, an uncouth white man delivering "Southern Dictates on the Race 'Problem'" to a bowing Uncle Sam. Although directed primarily at a federal government accused of cowardice in the realm of civil rights, the illustration conflated domestic racism and an arrogance of power overseas. A September 1945 editorial, published alongside a photograph of a Japanese man bowing before a white occupationaire, exhibited a similar attitude. "This," it declared, "is what you would call a picture of a Jap 'Uncle Tom.'" The piece went on to link the destinies of the Japanese under the occupation, worldwide victims of colonialism, and racial minorities in the United States, while simultaneously betraying lingering anti-Japanese sentiment: "Don't get the idea that Uncle Toms over here or abroad represent people who can be . . . *perpetually* oppressed by a master race. We learned better than that when Japan declared war on us . . . and we discovered that some extra polite Japs who had been valets and gardeners on the Pacific Coast were officers in the Japanese Army and Navy."[10] (The accusation about "valets and gardeners" presumably referred to Toraichi Kono, a former personal assistant to Charlie Chaplin arrested on suspicion of espionage in June 1941.)[11] Contradictory as these sentiments were, the coming years witnessed the emergence of a consensus (although never uncontested) regarding African Americans' proper role in the U.S.-dominated Far East.

The black media trained its most vociferous attacks on evidence of segregation in off-duty pursuits. On the one hand, correspondents celebrated the work performed by African American soldiers. A report from Yokohama claimed that most black personnel stationed in the city were

Yes Sir, Yes Sir!

2.1 Racism at home was analogous to American arrogance in Japan, according to this editorial cartoon published three months after the war. *Chicago Defender*, 10 November 1945. Courtesy of the *Chicago Defender*.

"not laid into the hard, dreary work they have known so long in the Pacific." Instead, "Tan Yanks . . . [who] draw expressions of awe from diminutive Japs are, for the first time, enjoying their jobs of strawbossing Japanese labor around the docks of this shattered city."[12] The author of another piece similarly found high morale among black soldiers assigned to guard duty in Tokyo, despite the length of their deployments. Recreation was a different story, however. Segregation reportedly first arose in the field of prostitution. What once had been a color-blind red light district fifteen miles north of Tokyo was, by October 1945, unofficially off-limits to African American troops. Military police (MPs) directed the men to visit brothels set aside for black personnel. The situation, complained one reporter, represented a "flagrant insult to colored soldiers" in "one of the most fertile fields of racial discrimination." Segregation was discovered in more wholesome pursuits as well. The *Pittsburgh Courier* denounced various recreation centers, provided by SCAP for all enlisted men, for turning black occupationaires away. White troops used "Nazi methods" to introduce "a segregated setup wherever possible," accused the *Afro-American*, pointing to a newly erected post exchange (PX). "Now barred from the new one which is fully equipped with useful and luxury items," black servicemen were limited to a local PX of relatively inferior quality. African American coverage of the early occupation generally emphasized the transplantation of American-style Jim Crow to Japanese soil.[13]

In fact, the first six months were more fluid and chaotic than these accounts suggest. White officers and enlisted men discriminated against black soldiers, but by no means uniformly. Interracial groups of Americans occasionally ventured out to explore their new environment. The policies of General Robert L. Eichelberger, commander of the multiracial but segregated Eighth Army (which would assume sole responsibility for the occupation's army needs the following year), facilitated these expeditions. Eichelberger's directives provided enlisted men with substantial free time, the ability to explore Japan without escort, and complimentary transportation on Japanese trains. "I want every soldier given the opportunity to see as much of Japan as possible while he is stationed here," he explained.[14] Most of his men welcomed the chance to do so. Fresh from austere wartime service and stationed in an unfamiliar environment, they also found countless ways to cause trouble. In early November the Central Liaison Office in Tokyo submitted to SCAP headquarters a series of Japanese reports on "remarkable incidents in which American soldiers were involved, as well as information that may be of use in finding the offenders." "About 8 p.m. September 22," began one, "several U.S. men (including two negroes) came to the cabaret of Shige Sato . . . for recreation, and hired five waitresses." Asked at the end of the evening to settle their bill, the occupationaires claimed a lack of funds but promised to return in the near future. They departed after scrawling an IOU signed with fake names, and more than a month later their debt remained unpaid. As this episode suggests, black and white soldiers together took advantage of the early occupation's social disorder and Japanese vulnerability.[15]

Some officials feared law and order was disintegrating. One study exaggerated, but not by much, the impact of the war on Japanese social mores when it concluded that the "confusion which followed the defeat was catastrophic to the old morality."[16] In a land where theft had been a rarity, petty crime flourished, often at the expense of American personnel. Although active resistance to the occupation was neither organized nor prevalent, isolated incidents occurred, including minor assaults and armed robbery. Any Japanese physical challenge to the American presence met swift and severe punishment. Occupationaires fueled these attacks or retaliated by engaging in a range of misbehavior. During the occupation's first months, U.S. troops committed criminal acts ranging from disorderly conduct and larceny to rape and murder.[17] African Americans were no exception, and SCAP officials dutifully recorded Japanese allegations of misconduct. In late 1945, for example, "The People" of one Tokyo district requested the removal of black troops on the grounds that "the women and children are very roughly treated." A similar complaint arrived from Yokohama one year later. (Because military authorities apparently never investigated the allegations, they are impossible to verify.)[18] SCAP censorship codes, which outlawed the publication of any material deemed "inimical to the objectives of the Occupation," kept most incidents out of the Japanese press.[19]

State-sponsored brothels posed the greatest practical challenge to occupation authorities. At the moment of surrender the Japanese government provided local businessmen with instructions and funds to create Recreation and Amusement Associations (RAAs), an extension of its military's wartime use of coerced prostitution. Officials intended for the RAAs to act as a "shock-absorber," protecting daughters of the upper and middle classes from unwanted sexual advances while maintaining pure Japanese blood-lines.[20] "With a kitty of well over two million dollars," according to a contemporary account, "the geisha entrepreneurs went to Japan's small villages and towns . . . and bought up girls. It was an easy matter, for thousands of girls had lost their jobs with the ending of hostilities."[21] By the end of 1945 an estimated 20,000 impoverished women were working in RAA districts across the country. A large number of establishments, which typically housed dance halls and even beer gardens, were concentrated in the Tokyo-Yokohama metropolitan area. One brothel serviced so many occupationaires it earned the moniker "Willow Run," after the Ford Motor Company's massive bomber factory. Predictably, rates of venereal disease among Japanese prostitutes and American personnel soared, reaching a peak in the Eighth Army of 27 percent by January 1946. SCAP responded by declaring all RAA establishments off-limits. Venereal disease rates gradually declined, but prostitution remained common. Private entertainment venues, large and small, and informal prostitution replaced the RAAs for the remainder of the occupation.[22]

American commanders simultaneously railed against lax discipline among troops jaded by wartime service. In September 1945 an officer with the military police compiled recommendations to "establish a system of preserving order and . . . regulating the conduct of allied personnel on visitors' status in the City of Tokyo." Since occupationaires did not yet understand the "rules of the game," MPs needed to redouble their efforts "to keep visitors out of trouble in this strange land with strange customs." The officer encouraged them to monitor rampant "derelictions in the wearing of the uniform." Upon receiving the report, his superior agreed that the "present situation in downtown Tokyo resembles the Mardi Gras." "Sailors, soldiers and Air Corps personnel," he complained, "are wondering [sic] about in the weirdest possible uniforms."[23] Black personnel certainly committed these and other minor infractions, for tens of thousands arrived as members of service units with the first waves of Americans. Their numbers peaked at approximately 40,000 in late 1945, out of a total American occupying force of 430,000. Just over 30,000 were evenly divided between the main islands of Honshu and Kyushu, with 15,000 assigned to the Tokyo-Yokohama sector. The remainder were scattered across the sparsely inhabited islands of Hokkaido and Shikoku. Black troops were relatively free at that point to explore the same urban areas as their white counterparts. Mostly veterans of the lengthy Pacific campaigns, they too were weary of rigid military discipline.[24]

During the occupation's anarchic early phase they also participated in a spree of remittances. With Japanese income restricted by law and the level of rationed goods inadequate to sustain life, civilians relied on the black market, where American goods sold at a premium. Servicemen, initially paid in local currency, immediately began speculating in illicit transactions. "The new arrival learns . . . that Japanese yen, if handled properly, will multiply like rabbits," observed a visiting reporter. She added, with a touch of hyperbole, that a "conscientious trader could, by starting with a bar of soap and using cigarettes and Japanese whiskey as intermediate currency," convert pocket change into a small fortune in mere days. Occupied Japan was "a carpetbagger's dream," another American visitor wrote in his diary, particularly for the "businessman with . . . an American uniform." Occupationaires sent money home by purchasing a postal order or military check for which yen were converted to dollars. The only requirement was a list of prior financial transactions, completed by the remitter. The military seldom investigated the veracity of these declared business dealings, and it allowed servicemen to remit up to 125 percent of their base income, even though any surplus likely came from black-market schemes or currency speculation. Occupationaires' low cost of living further swelled the flow of cash stateside.[25]

These remittances reached astonishing proportions. General MacArthur's chief fiscal officer discovered that occupationaires were sending home eight million dollars more than their total earnings each month. American officials, however, were disinclined to prevent servicemen from remitting unearned income. It took almost a year for SCAP to tackle black-market transactions by paying occupationaires in military scrip, illegal for the Japanese to possess and the only currency accepted by those responsible for transmitting funds. By then, occupationaires had mailed home $35 million more than their entire combined pay for the theater. The losers in this financial game were both Japanese and American, or at least those Americans not occupationaires or their kin: the former because of the imbalance of power and resources, and the latter since the United States Treasury was obligated to back up all currency sent by citizens overseas. Millions of dollars were monthly charged to the federal government and distributed among soldiers' families and friends. African Americans relegated to service battalions were particularly well positioned to profit from the system. Sales of military goods kick-started most of the illicit revenue, and service units were in charge of their storage, transportation, and distribution. Remarked one black correspondent, "as long as colored troops are the guardians of goods and clothing, they will not only be the best fed and best dressed, but will always have many friends among the civilians." Their routine access to these items outlasted the introduction of military scrip, and thus too did their ability to barter for supplementary Japanese goods and services.[26]

The occupation's first months also brought confirmation that Japan would be primarily responsible for financing the American presence. SCAP authorities were more concerned with punishing the Japanese and boosting their soldiers' morale than with reining in expenses. The costs to Japan during the first ninety days of occupation were greater than its entire armed forces budget for 1930, and they amounted to one-third of the nation's federal allocations. Although occupation expenses later declined as a percentage the government's operating costs, they remained its largest expenditure. The Japanese also learned they were expected to provide more than basic services. SCAP charged Japan for items such as flowers for officers' quarters and personal telegrams and telephone calls to the United States. Expenses often approached the absurd: in one year the government spent 820 million yen (nearly $55 million) in indemnities to Japanese injured by occupationaires in traffic accidents.[27] It was by then abundantly clear that American needs and desires were to come first, and Japan was to foot the bill.

––––––––

With American control firmly established, the occupation assumed a more regulated and enduring ambiance. Throughout 1946 combat veterans (mostly white) departed, replaced by "high-school commandos," as one observer labeled them, callow teenagers who sought to prove their toughness by harassing Japanese civilians. African American occupationaires, many of whom elected to reenlist rather than grapple with economic uncertainty stateside, were perhaps more evenly divided between mature veterans and fresh recruits. However, their newly minted white officers arrived determined to advance their careers through the maintenance of strict discipline and exemplary personnel administration. Of greatest consequence were new SCAP directives that required or encouraged the construction of physical and emotional barriers between occupier and occupied.[28]

One manifestation of this development was the hardening of American-Japanese segregation. During the occupation's hectic early months, simple pragmatism dictated most restrictions on the activities of American personnel. A combination of security concerns and Japan's acute food shortage had led SCAP to place all buses, streetcars, restaurants, bars, and hotels off-limits to American forces. Special rail cars, clean, uncrowded, and marked "occupying forces" (*Shinchū-gun*) were set aside for allied personnel regardless of race, while the Japanese were confined to dilapidated, often windowless cars. SCAP and the Joint Chiefs of Staff had been reluctant to ban American-Japanese socializing outright. A policy of strict non-fraternization in occupied Germany had lasted less than five months and proven a public relations disaster. General MacArthur further believed such measures were both unenforceable and insulting to American troops. "They keep trying to get me to stop all this Madame Butterflying around," he privately complained, "[but] I wouldn't issue a non-fraternization order for all the tea in China."[29] However, local commanders in Japan unaware of his sentiments placed additional venues off-limits, producing a crazy quilt system of social restrictions.[30]

The occupational command erected a more uniform and rigid system in 1946. Recreational facilities reserved for occupationaires now featured prominent notices reading "For Allied Personnel Only" or "Japanese Keep Out." SCAP, which employed considerable indigenous labor, insisted on separate entrances for Americans and Japanese in many of its office buildings. The army systematically declared one social space after another off-limits either to its forces or to the Japanese (or mandated that only one group frequent a venue at a given time). In March, General Eichelberger announced that "public displays of affection by men in uniform towards the women of any nation are in poor taste. Particularly is this so in Japan among those who were so recently our enemies and where the people have never been accustomed to such demonstrations." "The sight of our soldiers walking along the streets with their arms around Japanese girls," he continued, "is equally repugnant to Americans at home and to those in the occupation areas as well as to most Japanese." Eichelberger informed his men that such activity was now considered disorderly conduct, punishable by a ten dollar fine, a night in the stockade, and an appearance before one's commanding officer the following day. The army thereafter prohibited Japanese women from riding in military vehicles or visiting single men's quarters. It moved with similar dispatch to bar occupationaires from various theaters, waterways, beaches, and entire neighborhoods, with varying degrees of success. In the words of one astute observer, "Fraternization was not exactly illegal; there was just no legal place to fraternize." Of course, many occupationaires continued to engage in social and sexual relations with Japanese women, albeit more discreetly. The *Afro-American*, contemplating the imposition of " 'after dark' social equality" in Japan, sardonically quipped that "the Deep South must be chuckling to itself over this forthright adoption of its unwritten code."[31]

Stringent American-Japanese segregation altered relations between occupier and occupied in two immediate ways. First, the amount of informal, platonic socializing rapidly declined. According to one American visitor, restrictions "geared to the level of the most irresponsible eighteen-year-old GI" lent the occupation a distinctly "colonial atmosphere." In the words of another, "most of the ordinary day-to-day contact between Americans and the native population is on a master-servant basis." Black occupationaires thus straddled two inequitable social environments. Segregated from white Americans at work and subject to racial discrimination, they could simultaneously enjoy the psychological wages of Japan's heightened colonial ambience. One black observer, taking note of Japanese-only drinking fountains, remarked that "Tokyo today looks like Mississippi," yet with African Americans among the privileged classes. Second, most occupation personnel became increasingly blind to the plight of indigent Japanese. One second-generation Japanese American (or Nisei), who worked for military intelligence, donned her most ragged clothes in order to inspect conditions for homeless refugees living in the Tokyo subway. There she found countless men, women, and children struggling to survive alongside rotting garbage and open latrines. Only by disguising herself as a local, however, was this occupationaire able to visit the subway; MPs now stood at the doors to prevent American entry.[32]

An overhauled troop information program did little to increase awareness of Japanese distress. In an effort to promote understanding and reduce interpersonal friction, the army in 1946 mandated coursework on local customs. In theory, every soldier received at least one hour of instruction per week on esoteric topics including "Japanese flower arrangements, incense burning, marriage, dress, tea ceremonies, and fishing with cormorants" (a species of diving bird). The head of SCAP's Information Section explained that if the occupationaire "knows why the Japanese act and think the way they do, he is likely to be more amiable and polite. . . . He won't be so quick to push a Japanese off the sidewalk." One text utilized for the Troop Information Hour contained several banalities, including: "Like most other people the Japanese eat three meals a day."[33] (That such was perhaps not the case for many Japanese in the midst of widespread food shortages evidently did not occur to the author.) Military authorities, however benign their intentions, once again failed to provide servicemen with an accurate picture of Japanese living conditions. Furthermore, many unit commanders considered information programs a low priority if not a complete waste of resources, and few devoted much time or energy to them (some simply ignored instructions to provide weekly lectures).[34] Individual soldiers would, or would not, continue to discover on their own how most Japanese survived, only now from a position of greater social distance.

While SCAP tinkered with its program for troop edification, the chief of administrative affairs at the Yokohama replacement depot was asked his opinion of newly arriving occupationaires. Explaining that he found the men quite satisfactory, he added, almost as an afterthought, that approximately half the replacements were black. This startling figure was in part the result of African Americans' growing enthusiasm for armed service and their exclusion from much of postwar Europe. However, it was also the product of agreements by an international group of military and civilian policymakers in Asia and the United States to restrict black personnel to a handful of areas. Just as African American troops were diverted from postwar Europe to the Pacific theater, they now found themselves funneled into Japan.[35]

Such policies originated in China during World War II. A story then circulating among African Americans held that Generalissimo Chiang Kai-shek specifically requested that no black troops be sent to his aid. The rumor was accurate. At Chiang's urging, African American truck battalions working on the Burma Road were prohibited from moving east of its Chinese terminus. Following the war, and with only a few black troops remaining, the commanding general of American forces solicited Chiang's views on the prospect of their future service in Nationalist China. He reported to the War Department that the Generalissimo remained adamantly opposed. Chiang insisted the Chinese Communists would "exploit" the presence of black servicemen by arguing that "the Americans were withdrawing their white troops and supplanting them with their Negro troops to accomplish their materialistic designs in China." More to the point, "the introduction of Negro troops would . . . add to his problems for the Chinese do not accept them readily." The American commander recommended that "Negro troops not be considered for employment" in China for the foreseeable future, and the War Department agreed.[36]

The inclination to exclude black personnel from entire regions in Asia and the Pacific and to deploy them instead on the Japanese main islands remained strong in the years that followed. It first resurfaced as a major policy initiative on the island of Okinawa. General Eichelberger announced in January 1947 that the all-black 24th Infantry Regiment, 5,000 strong and stationed on Okinawa guarding Japanese prisoners since the end of the war, would be transferred to Camp Gifu in central Japan. Members of the regiment began departing little more than a week later, replaced by Filipino scouts.[37] The War Department provided the rationale, much accepted by members of the black press, that the move represented an effort to equalize opportunities in the army, improve military race relations, and initiate a gradual integration of occupation forces.[38]

In fact, the move was part of a larger racial rearrangement of American troops, one that involved the combined Philippine-Ryukyu command (Okinawa is the largest island in the Ryukyu archipelago). Racial strife had been brewing in the Philippines since its recapture by American forces, and black personnel faced hostility from both Filipino men and white soldiers. One black private wrote to the *Chicago Defender* to complain that "even the people . . . here in Manila are prejudiced against us" (he placed most of the blame on the influence of bigoted white troops). The paper subsequently reported the beating of two black soldiers by an "armed Filipino gang" and the appearance in Manila of "crudely drawn posters, signed 'ex-guerrillas,'" that read, "We want to abolish Negroes in this town." Tensions reached a peak in the winter of 1945–46, with the outbreak of black-Filipino race riots and a three-hour gun battle between black and white soldiers.[39] The American command complained in late 1947 that the ratio of black servicemen and Filipino scouts to white troops was "excessive" and "increasing." Notwithstanding the transfer of the 24th Infantry Regiment from Okinawa to Japan, it predicted that African Americans would make up nearly a quarter of its authorized strength by 1948, a percentage "considerably in excess of the Army overall ratio."[40] The Philippine government for its part repeatedly objected to the presence of black servicemen and the violence it generated. Before long, President Manuel Roxas reached an informal agreement with American generals, implemented in early 1948, that black personnel would no longer be stationed in his country.[41] In the wake of these negotiations, white soldiers were redeployed to the Philippines, Filipino scouts replaced African Americans on the Ryukyus, and black troops stationed in the Philippines were either returned to the United States or sent to Yokohama for assignment to the Eighth Army. (The Far East Command likewise came to oppose assigning black soldiers to the shrinking American force stationed in southern Korea.)[42] Thus despite significant reductions in the number of the American troops assigned to Japan beginning in 1946, the number of black occupationaires remained relatively constant, generally fluctuating between ten and fifteen thousand. By the start of the Korean War, the 24th Infantry Regiment not only possessed a full contingent of three battalions (as opposed to every white regiment in Japan) but was approximately 10 percent over-strength.[43]

At roughly the same time that the number of African American replacements in Japan began to rise sharply, the occupation began celebrating its first anniversary. In August 1946, General Eichelberger delivered the opening salvo in a propaganda battle for best-American-military-assignment honors. "When I saw General Eisenhower in Washington last December," he wrote in a letter to *Time* magazine, "he wondered why I would want to come back to this 'terrible place.'" And yet, when Eisenhower "came out here two months ago, he admitted that this was the best place in the world for a soldier to serve." "It is true that when we came in here we had nothing," Eichelberger continued, but "now we have 25 fine hotels in operation, golf courses, stadia, hundreds of movies, [and] some of the finest clubs I have ever seen." He closed by quoting a sign posted in front of one enlisted men's club: "You never had it so good!" Eichelberger then issued a public report on the occupation's first year, stating that his goal was to make duty in Japan "the most pleasant, most interesting and most prized assignment for United States soldiers."[44] The *Pacific Stars and Stripes*—a newspaper produced by and for enlisted men—joined the celebrations with a special magazine supplement devoted entirely to the one-year anniversary. Following an excerpt from Irving Berlin's "This Is the Army" ("This is the Army, Mr. Jones / No private rooms or telephones / You've had your breakfast in bed before / But you won't have it there, anymore"), the author observed that "the Army has done its best to make Mr. Berlin eat his lyrics—and they've succeeded to a somewhat spectacular point."[45] The increased emphasis on accommodations, facilities, and diversions was no longer aimed solely at servicemen, however. As the occupation assumed greater permanence, American wives and children began relocating to Japan, first in the hundreds, eventually by the thousands.

Plans for dependent accommodations on American bases commenced soon after Japan's surrender. The *Pacific Stars and Stripes'* first article on the topic appeared in November 1945.[46] The following February the War Department announced that, with necessary housing, food, and medical care now available, men of all ranks could request transfer of their dependents if they agreed to remain overseas at least one additional year.[47] Days later General MacArthur publicly affirmed his unconditional support of the plan. He nonetheless warned that living conditions would be "those of the occupied areas and . . . not comparable in many ways with those of continental America." MacArthur then explicitly linked occupation duty to American expansionist mythology. "It will represent a type of pioneering reminiscent of the pioneer days of our own West during the nineteenth century," he declared in his inimitable style, "but just as those days developed the best of American womanhood, so it is believed the wives of our officers and soldiers will welcome the opportunity of sharing the hardship with their husbands."[48] With the first groups of dependents preparing to depart in the spring and summer

of 1946, military officials continued to warn of "rugged" life in the occupied territories.[49] As it developed, however, those bound for Japan
need not have worried much.

Construction of permanent accommodations began in earnest in the
second half of 1946, with an eye toward attracting military wives.[50]
SCAP ordered the Japanese government to provide indigenous labor and
building materials for housing projects on American bases, despite the
fact that 180,000 residents of Tokyo alone were living in tin shacks and
other temporary shelters.[51] Having broken ground, the army established
a goal of accommodating 6,000 households within a year; by 1948 the
number of American military families living in Japan was 10,000 and
growing.[52] SCAP assured its soldiers there would be no discrimination by
rank. The Yokohama military-community plan called for "an equal number of officers' and enlisted men's homes," albeit "separated by a park."
Housing dimensions were determined by family size rather than military
status. The chief of dependent housing for the Eighth Army Engineers
added that accommodations would be comfortable but not "luxurious."
Luxury, however, lay in the eye of the beholder. Below an artist's rendi-
tion of a four-family unit (figure 2.2), a reporter with the *Pacific Stars and
Stripes* informed occupationaires that the "typical home . . . will be a
modern, Western-style two-story duplex, completely furnished" with
"rugs, draperies, furniture, and heating facilities." Floor plans came in
two standard models: three-bedroom, one-and-a-half bath; or two-
bedroom, one bath. "Although standardization is necessary for economic
and technical reasons," the author continued, "there will be local variations on the design to prevent the appearance of a 'workman's row.'" In
this vein, the chief engineering officer announced an effort "to get some
kind of architectural treatment without any material change in design,"
principally through differently colored roofs and variations in building
arrangement.[53] Levittown had crossed the Pacific. Joked diplomat George
Kennan, "I know many of the Japs deserve a worse fate than to have the
tastes and habits of American suburbia imposed on them."[54]

American residential enclaves gradually achieved near total self-
sufficiency. SCAP originally envisioned "complete communities"—"built
by Japanese workmen to American specifications"—"including shopping
centers, recreation halls, barber shops and playgrounds." Indeed, occu-
pants of these housing developments soon acquired their own bakeries,
dry cleaners, bus systems, newspapers, gas stations, and radio networks.
Along with homes and small businesses came military sponsorship of

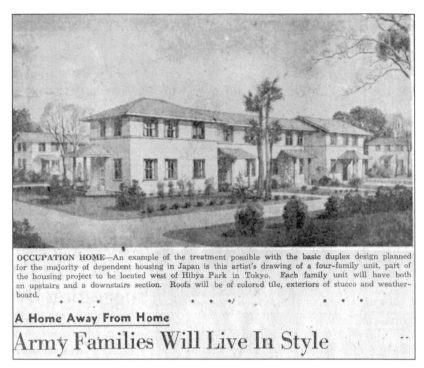

OCCUPATION HOME—An example of the treatment possible with the basic duplex design planned for the majority of dependent housing in Japan is this artist's drawing of a four-family unit, part of the housing project to be located west of Hibya Park in Tokyo. Each family unit will have both an upstairs and a downstairs section. Roofs will be of colored tile, exteriors of stucco and weatherboard.

A Home Away From Home
Army Families Will Live In Style

2.2 Levittown follows the flag: plans for dependent housing in Japan. *Pacific Stars and Stripes*, 31 March 1946. Courtesy of the MacArthur Memorial Archives, Norfolk, Va.

social services. Free medical and dental care was available to all. Dependents, protected by standard GI inoculations, were provided access to hospital facilities. The Army Quartermaster Corps prepared for the needs of infants and children by securing an initial shipment of 17,600 four-ounce cans of strained vegetables, in addition to its extant stocks of "powdered whole milk, powdered skim milk, condensed, evaporated and malted milk and similar preparations of milk products." Food for dependents, even jars of caviar, began arriving by refrigerator ship from the United States, all for sale at bargain prices.[55]

For help around their new homes, occupationaires began hiring Japanese maids, with the military once again providing invaluable assistance. According to one dispatch, "the Army, anticipating the need American families will have for trained servants," went so far as to establish "a 'Domestic Science' school" in the city of Sendai. Instructors provided young Japanese women with a four-week course in "maidcraft," a discipline that included such topics as "courtesy, tact, cleaning, washing, mending, setting tables, serving, making beds, and doing dishes." Lessons in traditional American cooking were also included. Although newly certified and self-taught domestics were in great demand, postwar Japanese poverty and unemployment kept wages remarkably low. A maid could be retained for ten dollars a month, perhaps fifteen if she spoke English well. Single men living in barracks or quonset-hut communities hired Japanese workers to clean their living quarters, launder their clothes, and handle routine kitchen duties. At the height of the occupation, some 15,000 U.S. military families employed more than 25,000 servants. Awe-struck Japanese asked one American if all housewives had maids in the United States. In response to this and similar queries, he endeavored "to portray an America of more modest means, explaining that most citizens lived more Spartan lives than did occupationaires in Japan." SCAP authorities had succeeded quite spectacularly in their efforts to make accommodations for officers, enlisted men, and their dependents as comfortable as possible.[56]

All modern militaries supply their personnel with food, shelter, and basic services to one degree or another; what made the American occupation exceptional was its commitment to personal consumption, epitomized by the PX system. SCAP in October 1946 replaced the temporary Tokyo PX with a new facility, the "largest Army store in the world." According to the *Pacific Stars and Stripes*, it "rival[ed] any American department store for variety and decoration." A correspondent for the *Afro-American* gushed that "the PX in Tokyo would put Macy's to shame both in prices and in materials offered." Besides five floors of merchandise, the exchange included a children's nursery, a barber and beauty shop, and dry-cleaning service. An on-site English language school provided instruction to every Japanese salesclerk. With more than $5 million worth of merchandise in stock on opening day, officials estimated sales of $15 million over the ensuing year. Seven months later, the Eighth Army Exchange was operating three main department stores—in Tokyo, Yokohama, and Osaka—while supervising and supplying an additional ninety-two branches scattered across Japan. Anticipated annual gross sales reached $50 million. Servicemen were also entitled to ship merchandise home at little or no cost. In September 1947, Congress reauthorized the mailing of gift packages, duty-free up to the first $50 in value, to anyone in the United States. Occupation officials therefore announced plans to provide complimentary gift-wrapping and shipping services to customers at the larger exchanges.[57]

SCAP even took its PX show on the road. The Eighth Army early recognized that the arrival of dependents at the more isolated military installations, far removed from metropolitan shopping centers, generated a logistical challenge. In the words of one observer, "there was only one solution—take the merchandise to the outposts." The army appropriated a Japanese train of ten cars (soon expanded to eleven) and converted it into a mobile department store, complete with living quarters for the staff. A workforce of twenty-four Japanese salesgirls and stock boys labored under the supervision of American personnel. These Japanese, like their counterparts in the stationary exchanges, were clearly relegated to the service sector. They maintained an extensive line of merchandise ranging from women's and children's clothing to floor lamps and household appliances. Once stocked, the train departed a Yokohama warehouse for the hinterlands, traversing the island chain's larger waterways by ferry. "The entire circuit," explained the *Pacific Stars and Stripes*, "would be comparable to a trip in the United States starting in New York and ending in Kansas City, fanning off to small towns for one-day stands." The P-X-Train, as it was known, arrived every six to eight weeks at station platforms across Japan. Doors opened at 10 a.m. to overflowing crowds of occupationaires encouraged to purchase tax-free American goods at discount.[58]

Black servicemen and their families were both able and eager to take advantage of these consumption opportunities, which resonated among African Americans at home. One member of an all-black engineering unit explained that he and his peers "were concerned with buying furniture and dishes . . . and having our wives and children accompany us to Japan [to] enjoy that good life."[59] Exact figures for African American dependents in Japan are unavailable, but evidence suggests many black occupationaires successfully sent for their immediate kin. (See figure 2.3 for examples of the photographs of reunited families that appeared with regularity in the black press starting in late 1946.) The introduction of new dependent-request procedures in mid-1947, which gave priority to those with at least eight months service in Japan, increased the number of eligible black personnel.[60] Press coverage of life in Japan, in addition to personal letters home, kept black communities abreast of ever-improving circumstances for African American occupationaires. Virtually all of these dispatches celebrated the socioeconomic benefits available through the occupation. For instance, a columnist with the *Chicago Defender*, who previously had criticized the armed services for their treatment of black

Americans Make Themselves at Home in Japan

2.3 Black families from Pennsylvania, Florida, and California enjoy the occupation's comfortable lifestyle while "at home in Japan." According to the original caption, the family at center gathers for a meal "in comfortable quarters," while the couple at right "examines their collection of Japanese dolls at their home in Yokohama." *Afro-American*, 17 April 1948. Courtesy of the Afro-American Newspapers Archives and Research Center.

enlisted men, titled his spring 1947 update, "Well Shut My Mouth." Reporting on life in Yokohama and Japan in general, the author affirmed that wives and children found "paradise when they hit Nippon." Black occupationaires enjoyed "bulging commissaries, western style homes with electric refrigerators, . . . [and] good transportation"—that is, some of the amenities most lacking in black communities stateside. Especially noteworthy was the role reversal for African American military wives, many of whom had worked long hours as domestics in the United States (in addition to their unpaid labor in the home). These women's "dish washing, suds busting, and scrubbing days are over for a while," explained the author, since the servants they now supervised "are a dime a dozen and excellent."[61]

Similar accounts appeared in the black press for years, even beyond the occupation's formal conclusion. With the signing of a peace treaty looming in the fall of 1951, one correspondent described "the saddest people in the world": black occupation families who feared the prospect of "return to America and civilian life." "All of the basic necessities of life—food, clothing and shelter—are provided," he wrote, "and to this many have added . . . frills which they could ill afford at home." Local PXs offered goods at prices less than half of those stateside, the "difference com[ing] out of the American taxpayers' pockets." As for occupationaires' children, they attended schools that, "in many respects, are an improvement over public schools in the States," with smaller classes, more individual attention, and better-prepared teachers. The occupation offered African American servicemen and their families an unprecedented "gravy train," "making life one grand holiday." Eighteen months later, *Ebony* magazine published an admiring article on the "easy, plush life" and "lordly living" enjoyed by black personnel and their families stationed on the bases maintained by the United States following the peace treaty. "Luxuriously quartered in private rent-free rooms equivalent to a first class hotel or located with their families in big near-free homes in government housing areas," enthused the author, they retained "gracious Japanese servants to look after their every need." Indeed, the piece featured a private from North Carolina who, in addition to "working an eight-hour day, with plenty of leisure time," was "relieved by his maid of even the most menial soldierly chores." Black servicemen in Japan, the article concluded, "can and do live like kings."[62]

———

As the occupation wore on in years, American-Japanese interactions betrayed growing friction. The Japanese people were gradually escaping absolute destitution and acquiring more independence, while the construction of bases with fully functioning dependent communities provided the American enterprise with an unmistakable, and unwelcome, aura of permanence. A journalist stationed in Japan since the end of the war accused SCAP officials of possessing "a Philippine complex," of "expect[ing] to be here for 40 years." A member of the State Department reported that occupationaires "now approach being regarded as perhaps benevolent oppressors with the benevolence wearing rather thin."[63] Inter-Asian conflict and rising Cold War tensions, which by 1948 had prompted the American government to adopt a "reverse course" policy in Japan that emphasized economic stability over democratization, sparked serious public disturbances, some of which involved African American troops. A revision of fraternization policies, designed to encourage more equitable social relations between occupier and occupied, failed to reverse these trends.

In April 1948 serious rioting broke out in the port city of Kobe, driven not by the Japanese but by local Koreans. Few in SCAP were sympathetic to Japan's significant Korean population, a disadvantaged minority confined to overcrowded ghettos. Many occupationaires considered them a thoroughly intransigent group, "the Irish of the Far East."[64] During a Japanese Red Scare that spring and summer, SCAP condoned a crackdown on left-wing labor activity and Korean popular movements. An association of Korean schools was one target, for SCAP feared that separate educational systems were intensifying ethnic antagonisms and suspected that the schools were sources of communist propaganda. Occupation authorities ordered the Japanese government to close them by force. One hundred and fifty Korean protestors stormed Kobe's prefectural office and held the Japanese governor captive.[65] Proclaimed the Eighth Army's intelligence chief, "Communists are behind these disorders, just as they are in southern Korea." "The Japanese police are not physically able to arrest them," he continued, "so we are doing it. We are using our Kobe troops—Negro troops."[66]

Black soldiers promptly arrested the protestors. The following day, in response to renewed demonstrations by some 30,000 Koreans, General Eichelberger issued a shoot-to-kill order. Subsequent clashes injured hundreds, many seriously, and a sixteen-year-old boy was killed. Local police, imitating American crowd-control practices, turned fire hoses on Korean demonstrators. One black occupationaire later recalled that his unit was trained in similar methods for use against Japanese labor activists. To black servicemen involved in quelling these disturbances, it was a striking inversion of their fortunes at home. Two months after the Kobe riots, for example, African American protesters in Los Angeles were fire-hosed during a failed attempt to desegregate a swimming pool. The subsequent use of African American troops, many from states in which they could not vote, to monitor Japanese elections compounded the ironies.[67]

The American command, seeking to generate goodwill and to encourage among servicemen "an attitude of friendly interest and guidance toward the Japanese people," began in September 1949 to rescind most anti-fraternization edicts. SCAP was, in essence, attempting to return to its initial, much-celebrated policy. MacArthur issued orders, crafted in impeccable military dialect, "to establish . . . as far as practicable the same relationship between Occupation personnel and the indigenous population of Japan as exists between United States troops . . . and the indigenous population of the United States." (He conveniently ignored the fact that the presence of black soldiers on military bases in the American South had long incited anger and violence among indigenous whites.) SCAP swiftly reduced off-limit areas to a minimum, abolishing most restrictions on the movement and activities of occupationaires. Approved hotels, inns, theaters, and other public accommodations were thereafter in bounds for American soldiers, the ban on overnight stays in Japanese homes ended, and Japanese citizens were permitted to visit service clubs and to participate in American social activities more generally. SCAP hoped to improve morale and to encourage wholesome social relations with the Japanese, reducing the number of illicit encounters. Yet the damage already done was largely irreversible. "Army installations had come to be considered as centers of vice," reported one observer. Most Japanese and many occupationaires believed that, aside from those areas inhabited by dependents, "prostitution, gambling, drunkenness, and crime" ran "unchecked" in and around American bases. Unsavory activities were indeed common enough to elicit Japanese protest. Such perceptions continued to fuel reality, and vice versa, for years to come.[68]

As previously noted, black personnel were both integral to the American occupying force and excluded, formally and informally, from many of its centers of power. They labored and lived under the occupation's regulations and privileges, but remained consigned to segregated enclaves. Interactions between African American occupationaires and Japanese civilians were shaped not only by the attitudes, beliefs, and material needs both sides brought to the table, but also by the immediate demands of the occupation and a segregated military. In essence, these were young black men of modest or impoverished backgrounds who found themselves privileged occupiers of a people most had previously known only through caricatured portrayals in the media, working out in their own minds their relationship to the Japanese as they implemented U.S. policy.

Black occupationaires were engaged first and foremost in a martial enterprise. Many worked long hours each day at physically demanding jobs. African American troops relegated to service battalions often labored on the docks of Yokohama and other Japanese ports. One soldier, who served in a rare African American combat team, noticed that virtually every other black serviceman outside his post worked on the waterfront, moving cargo and loading and driving trucks. "I call[ed] them 'sweat battalions,'" he later explained, "'cause that's what you did, you *worked*."[69] These soldiers benefited from the help of locals, however, for hundreds of Japanese stevedores sweated on the docks themselves under the supervision of black noncommissioned officers.[70] In the racial hierarchy of the occupation workplace, white personnel, particularly those in administrative positions, rarely interacted with Japanese on the job. Black occupationaires, on the other hand, because they toiled chiefly in service units, were much more likely to work alongside, or rather immediately above, large numbers of Japanese. They were often the first Americans the Japanese encountered in a sustained manner. Particularly at the more isolated military installations, such as the 24th Infantry

Regiment's Camp Gifu (located 250 miles west of Tokyo), black-Japanese working relationships were virtually unmediated by the presence of white personnel. (One soldier wrote anonymously from the camp that, "for all practical purposes," it was a "solid colored community.")[71] However, power relations on the job remained unmistakable (see figure 2.4). African American infantrymen stationed at these remote bases trained incessantly for lack of other occupation duties, while Japanese from surrounding communities labored in camp-maintenance squads. The latter were overseen by armed African American MPs (see figure 2.5).[72]

The other principal duty of black occupationaires—guarding military goods—likewise entailed substantial contact with Japanese civilians, occasionally devolving into violence. African American service personnel's access to precious food and clothing made them popular among some Japanese, particularly during the occupation's bleak early years. Distributing small gifts of pilfered military supplies went far in winning appreciation from locals, but it also reinforced the dominant position of black servicemen since the Japanese rarely had anything to offer in return. Moreover, outright theft, at least by the occupied, was punished severely. Investigations by two African American soldiers attached to a supply depot, for example, led to the recovery of a large cache of stolen military goods and PX merchandise. Half a dozen Japanese members of a black market ring were subsequently arrested and sentenced to lengthy prison terms. On another occasion, a black serviceman assigned to a salvage yard was approached by a group of Japanese men and women hoping to acquire some surplus military tarps. The GI, believing they intended to sell the items illegally, arranged a sting and arrested seven of them. Other incidents were more troubling. One black service battalion in Kobe routinely clashed with thieves. An African American correspondent touted the unit's prowess, claiming that "these boys make others look like pansies." "Their sentries shoot down Japanese or anybody else swiping army goods," he added with appreciation.[73]

The occupation involved more than workday responsibilities, of course; leisure and entertainment were as important to black servicemen in Japan as they were to American soldiers elsewhere in the world. SCAP provided its black personnel with varying opportunities for diversion, yet on the whole they remained inferior to those offered white troops. Regarding on-base recreation, black occupationaires later remembered their facilities with either resigned acceptance or great fondness, depending on location. As one said of his camp on the outskirts of Osaka: "We

2.4 Japanese tailors tend to a member of the 24th Infantry Regiment at Camp Gifu, "where every soldier's uniform is fitted free of charge." The sergeant at right was identified as the "officer in charge" of overseeing the Japanese workers. *Afro-American*, 1 January 1949. Courtesy of the Afro-American Newspapers Archives and Research Center.

2.5 A black MP from California keeps a close eye on Japanese employees at Camp Gifu. "Frequently," explained the *California Eagle*, "the first contact the Japanese have with Americans comes through association with our [black] soldiers." *California Eagle*, 5 August 1948.

didn't have the best of facilities, but we did have roofs over our heads."
Another, who arrived at Camp Gifu in early 1949, remembered that after
strenuous military exercises, "life was good" back in camp. The *California Eagle* reported that African American MPs stationed in Yokohama
enjoyed access to "theatres, clubs, libraries, evening classes, a gymna-
sium, bowling alleys, volley ball and tennis courts, [and] a golf course."[74]
Other descriptions of the services available at all-black installations reflect
this spectrum of amenities. The most significant—and unintended—
consequence of SCAP's relative neglect of recreational facilities for African American troops was that black servicemen were more likely to seek
entertainment and adventure among the Japanese.[75] The arrival of dependents increased the social isolation of many occupationaires, regardless of
race, but as one observer noted of white military communities, "there
was every diversion you could ask for. . . . You could live on one of these
bases for three years, never sticking your nose outside the gates, and
scarcely realize you'd ever left home. Many did exactly that."[76] The majority of African American troops, on the other hand, necessarily looked
off-base in search of entertainment.

Black and white occupationaires still enjoyed Japanese nightlife jointly
on occasion. In the spring of 1950 a black corporal returned from what
the *Afro-American* described as three years of "pleasure" in "exotic Japan."
The twenty-one-year-old from Mount Vernon, New York, describing
life in the Tokyo-Yokohama area, explained that "colored and white soldiers are working, eating, sleeping, drinking and 'balling' together, and
it works out just fine." Yet despite his claim, interracial American socializing was by then extremely rare, in contrast to the occupation's early
months. American troops vigorously defended their racialized Japanese
turf, and street clashes were frequent. On Saturday nights in cities such as
Tokyo and Kobe it was common for black and white soldiers, fueled by
copiously available alcohol, to pummel each other before crowds of curious Japanese onlookers. General Eichelberger placed the blame for these
disturbances squarely on the shoulders of black personnel, who he insisted were uniquely inclined "to get out at night in the Mohammedan
heaven furnished by some millions of Japanese girls." New arrivals
quickly learned that certain neighborhoods were marked in occupationaires' minds as either "white" or "black," and that racial encroachment
invariably provoked a violent response. One African American unit complained of repeated physical attacks by white soldiers on those of its members who ventured into the "Lily-White Town" of Tokorozawa. A black

serviceman stationed in Yokohama reported that a dance held in a neigh-
boring city turned into a "shooting gallery" when heavily armed white
MPs cleared the hall and then fired warning shots as the black soldiers
fled to a nearby train station.[77]

In fact, most African American personnel were disinclined to spend
their free time among potentially hostile white servicemen and the substantial number of Japanese they influenced. These soldiers quickly established autonomous recreational zones, welcoming environments in which
black occupationaires could enjoy themselves and the company of Japanese women free from harassment. An African American Red Cross
worker compared Yokohama, where she encountered "the greatest concentration of colored Americans" in Japan, to Harlem. Occupationaire
Ira Neal realized soon after his arrival in the spring of 1948 that being
stationed in Yokohama "was just like being here in the United States. By
that I mean most of the black troops . . . were located [in the] inner-city,
most of the white troops in the suburbs." When Neal visited Tokyo he
received "just the exact opposite in terms of reception—because Tokyo
was mostly white troops. . . . So I was never comfortable."[78] Prejudicial
behavior by the Japanese aroused particular resentment. In 1950, one of
the few black soldiers stationed in Tokyo penned a letter, which attracted
considerable attention after being cited in a widely distributed NAACP
report, protesting Japanese discrimination. In "many places such as the P.X.
and commissary," he wrote, "one can notice how the Japanese clerks . . .
turn without question to wait on a white face first. . . . [I]t galls me to the
inner fibers of my very being." The Japanese in white-dominated neighborhoods, he complained, practiced a form of racial discrimination "as
flagrant as . . . in Georgia."[79]

Within African American enclaves, social relations were generally
more agreeable, albeit unequal. Discussing the fact that some black soldiers never openly visited Japanese in their homes, one serviceman explained that he and his peers "were just [of] a different class level." Yet
out on the town, the troops would gather together with their Japanese
dates, treating the women to drinks and enjoying live entertainment
provided by local entrepreneurs or produced by the troops themselves.[80]
Ira Neal recalled that a "lot of guys reenlisted because they wanted to go
back. In fact, when I reenlisted I said, 'send me back to Japan!'" These
men clearly relished their standing in the occupation's black entertainment districts. Neal candidly summarized the experience: "In Yokohama, [a] black man was king. Down there in the city we had all the

clubs, all the women, all the whatever we wanted."[81] Indeed, as his remarks suggest, the enormous American military presence in Japan, and
soon war-torn South Korea, gave rise to countless sexual relationships
between black men and Asian women. These intimate encounters, influenced by such factors as military policy and black economic interests,
played a significant role in shaping African American engagement with
U.S. power in the region.

Chapter 3

The Public Politics of Intimate Affairs

One month after the surrender of Japan, an influential black newspaper published an informal poll on Afro-Asian intimacy. It asked five black residents of Baltimore, "When our forces occupy Japan, do you think our soldiers should fraternize with Japanese women?" Only one answered negatively, arguing on pragmatic grounds that "under ordinary circumstances such fraternization might be wholesome for all concerned, but business and pleasure do not mix, and this occupation is definitely business. Our men are under military orders." The remaining four, evenly divided between women and men, offered variations on a theme that African American soldiers were entitled to such relationships, which would also alleviate current and future hostilities. One argued that black servicemen should seek out opportunities for fraternization "because our boys have a right to as much as any other group." "I think it would be in keeping with what any humans do when thrown together," responded another. "When races begin to intermingle we realize that there is only one human race."[1] A week later, an article in the paper with the headline "WHY AMERICAN SOLDIERS WILL GET ALONG WITH JAPANESE GIRLS" kept the focus of speculation on heterosexual relations with Asian women. "Fraternization is a natural outcome of close association," the author declared, "no matter whether we think of it in terms of romance or whether we think of it in terms of realism. If we don't want our soldiers to fraternize with the Japanese women, we'll have to change our plans for occupation!"[2]

These remarks suggest the initial ambivalence, even enthusiasm, with which many black Americans speculated on the prospect of sexual relations in East Asia. The focus on heterosexual romance was also part of a larger pattern of envisioning postwar Afro-Asian social relations: observers deployed the trope of interracial intimacy to express hopes for black-Japanese cooperation within the United States as well. In July 1946, *Ebony* announced—prematurely, it would turn out—the successful integration of African Americans and returning Japanese Americans in Los Angeles. During the war, "Little Tokyo" had been rechristened "Bronzeville," as black workers and their families settled in one of the few neighborhoods available to them. Following the end of Japanese American internment, many white onlookers—the Hearst press in particular—almost gleefully predicted violence. According to *Ebony*, "fearful" Japanese American returnees encountered not hostility but a warm embrace, as "two minorities, both victims of race hate," experienced "a miracle in race relations." "It is the wedding of Little Tokyo and Bronzeville," the magazine declared. "It is the mating of two communities of different race, different language, different habits and customs." Sustaining the metaphor, the author confidently proclaimed that "in this blending of common interests, Bronzeville and Little Tokyo have been betrothed. Out of a marriage of convenience has come a genuine attachment and affection between the two peoples." Intimate and gendered rhetoric suffused such predictions of Afro-Asian amity, whether abroad or at home, while largely casting Asian peoples as subordinate partners.[3]

These optimistic expectations were sorely tested in the years that followed. At the conclusion of World War II, African American ambivalence toward the Japanese stood in stark contrast to white racial hostility. Over the next decade, black and white attitudes, heavily influenced by representations of and encounters with Japanese women, moved primarily in opposite directions. Much white antipathy toward the Japanese was replaced by a variety of benevolent paternalism. A postwar cultural offensive, which ignored black Americans, soothed anti-Japanese prejudice by disseminating "fables of romantic love between white U.S. servicemen and Asian women," in the words of one historian. According to another, for many white filmmakers, authors, and soldiers, "Japanese women symbolized humility over arrogance, consideration over cruelty, and loyal service over treachery."[4] By contrast, the optimism with which many African Americans initially viewed Afro-Asian romance gave way to growing antagonism. Heterosexual relations in Japan and South Korea fed a suspicion of Asian women's motives and morals, while barriers to relatively stable Afro-Asian partnerships hindered servicemen's familial investments overseas and sustained a focus instead on the financial rewards of their service. Prostitution, dating, and marriage in East Asia, explored here in the order that black GIs generally encountered them, directly involved only those African Americans serving abroad, but as topics of concern they engaged many more in an international public conversation about the meaning of Afro-Asian intimacy and the proper role of black soldiers overseas.[5]

————————

Recent studies have shed considerable light on the complex histories of Japanese and Korean thoughts on race and interracial sex. The Japanese, for example, have long prized light over dark skin, which they have associated with barbarism.[6] Many Koreans have shared with their regional neighbors increasingly "racialized senses of belonging" that discouraged intimate association with those from outside "political territories [that] have been conflated with imaginary biological entities."[7] And yet, only following encounters with African enslavement among Europeans, and especially from the mid-nineteenth century onward, did some Japanese and other East Asians begin to adopt a more familiar scientific racism. As a result, according to one anthropologist, "the position blacks have come to occupy in the Japanese hierarchy of races not only echoes Western racial paradigms but borrows from them."[8] By the early twentieth century, many East Asians referred to Africans and their descendants as members of the "black slave race," notwithstanding their own vigorous protests against white supremacy.[9]

The arrival of American occupationaires tended to reinforce anti-black prejudice in Japan. White GIs were notorious for spreading horror stories among civilian populations about their African American counterparts. Japanese who had previously been warned by their government of the American inclination for rape, pillage, and murder were now informed by white servicemen that these were the exclusive hobbies of black troops.[10] Some Japanese issued racist warnings of their own. Less than two weeks after Japan's surrender, a group identified as the National Salvation Party littered Tokyo with flyers that read, "The women of our imperial nation must not have intercourse with the black race. Those who violate this order deserve the death sentence. Therefore make absolutely sure to keep the purity of the Yamato race!" Notably, the warning identified only African American men as a threat to Japanese purity. In a slightly less threatening vein, contemporary folk wisdom held that impregnation by, and perhaps merely intercourse with, a black man could "stain" the womb. To wit, if a Japanese woman gave birth to a mixed-race child, her next (and sometimes even her third) with a Japanese father would exhibit an unwelcome tinge to the body, betraying the woman's previous interracial indiscretion.[11] Notions of black men's potentially dangerous sexuality persisted throughout the occupation and beyond. African American soldiers held a special fascination for Japanese purveyors of fiction, despite the fact that white GIs tend to predominate in the nation's social memory of the era. " 'Blood' is . . . commonly invoked to explain the behavior of black GIs in occupation literature, especially when this behavior transgresses Japanese social norms," explains a student of the subject. "The postwar Japanese discourse on blacks devotes more attention to physiological, or 'racial,' elements (with an overwhelming emphasis on sexuality) than it does when depicting whites, who are primarily viewed as cultural beings."[12] Unsurprisingly, the African American as occupying-soldier-qua-rapist became a cliché of postwar Japanese popular culture.[13]

Given the range and extent of anti-black propaganda in Japan, why were any Japanese women willing to associate, sexually or otherwise, with African American occupationaires? The simplest answer is that reality intruded upon preconception: some found black servicemen especially kind and generous.[14] Coinciding with this discovery was the desperate need to acquire sustenance for oneself or one's family by any available means. An employee at a dance club in Osaka explained in the spring of 1946 that she had "recently become a special dancer for Negroes and do not dance with Whites." (The job of "dancer" was one that at the time often involved informal prostitution.) Her private description of this new life, in the stilted English of a secret SCAP translation, reveals both her economic motives and her understanding of racial differences among Americans: "Whites are stingy and are not profitable for us. As I come to the dance hall for money making, I am compelled to dance with black people. Negroes are far more skillful in dancing than white men and I feel quite happy." Clearly, being at first "compelled" to associate with black men had not prevented this woman from admiring what she understood to be their unique, if stereotyped, abilities. African American generosity toward such women also led to friction with Japanese men. At the same time that the Osakan dancer was extolling the virtues of black GIs, a male resident of Yokohama complained privately of the roots of their "mischief": "They take away food from us and give it to their women to please them."[15] His account was undoubtedly a fabrication, given the generous rations provided occupationaires and their easy access to the ubiquitous PXs. Much more likely is that the author was chagrined at his loss of provider status and envious of black GIs for their ability to shower small gifts upon informal sexual partners.[16] Such resentments did not, however, prevent a growing number of Japanese entrepreneurs from catering to the sexual desires of American troops.

SCAP's outlawing of state-sponsored (often coercive) prostitution and the promulgation of formal anti-fraternization edicts accelerated the growth of a more freewheeling sex trade.[17] Neither American military commanders nor the Japanese government had an interest in banning commercialized sex altogether. The former were concerned primarily with controlling rates of venereal disease among occupationaires (through the compulsory physical examination and treatment of suspected prostitutes) and maintaining the outward appearance of respectability, particularly after the arrival of American dependents.[18] Japanese officials too sought to curb the spread of venereal disease but placed greater emphasis on protecting daughters of the upper and middle classes from unwanted sexual advances and sequestering prostitution from polite society. They also recognized the potentially vital contributions of the sex trade to postwar reconstruction. As one historian observes, "It is no exaggeration to say that it was not the textile, chemical or other industries that were rehabilitating the immediate postwar Japanese economy but the sex industry." Indeed, by the occupation's close, prostitutes' earnings brought in the equivalent of $200 million in foreign exchange annually, an enormous boost to the struggling economy.[19] In December 1946 the Japanese Home Ministry announced that because women had an inherent right to become prostitutes, the government would establish "red-line" districts, named for the ink color used to delineate them on police maps, where redesignated "entertainers"—a significant minority of whom were Korean—were to be employed in privately owned "special bars and restaurants." This policy, with American military officials' tacit approval, remained in force for more than a decade, and estimates of the number of women so employed range from forty-five to seventy thousand per year.[20]

As state-sponsored brothels shut their doors and state-regulated ones opened theirs, Japanese and American officials expressed alarm at the appearance of tens of thousands of overt sex workers—"pan-pan" in GI parlance—who refused to be confined to the red-line districts. Some openly solicited clients near American bases and in city centers popular with occupationaires. A civilian occupation employee wrote that any serviceman who "went to Yurakucho Station, directly behind" SCAP headquarters, had "his pick of all that was parading there." Since such "voluntary prostitution" was not, technically speaking, illegal, the women were routinely harassed by Japanese police and American MPs but seldom arrested. Off-limits and anti-fraternization directives, in effect until late 1949, were of little consequence, except, of course, to encourage prostitution. In the words of one occupationaire, "GIs seeking sex just went deeper into the vast off-limits areas, which MPs never visited at all."[21] These casual, commercialized sexual encounters inevitably produced children, despite servicemen's access to prophylactics (the American military's principal concern was the prevention of disease, not pregnancy) and the Japanese legalization of abortion in 1948.[22] Japan's militarized sex industry outlasted the repeal of anti-fraternization regulations and achieved remarkable proportions by the early 1950s, peaking in 1952.[23] The reason why may be summed up in a word: Korea.

Surprisingly, African American observers paid Japanese prostitution little attention before the Korean War, despite its prevalence. Cohabitation with and potential marriage to Japanese women captured the bulk of their attention. Extensive African American scrutiny of prostitution catering to U.S. troops began instead on the Korean peninsula and only later turned to Japan. Given the black press's overarching role as an advocate for African Americans and their endeavors, in neither case did its members rebuke black servicemen for participating in these all-American activities. Black correspondents instead conveyed a new understanding of commercialized sex as both acceptable and necessary for the effective deployment of American military power, at least in Asia.

Within weeks of landing in Korea, African American soldiers and journalists routinely complained that local women were sexually unobtainable. At first blush this seems odd, since the arrival of American troops (predominantly white) in 1945 spawned numerous camptowns catering to the sexual desires of servicemen.[24] Moreover, sexualized power relations have remained a fundamental element of American-Korean interactions through the present. One historian has described "the continuous subordination of one female generation after another to the sexual servicing of American males, to the requirements of a trade in female flesh that simply cannot be exaggerated. It's the most common form of Korean-American interaction."[25] The temporary removal of American forces in 1948–49 and the social chaos of war momentarily disrupted this state of affairs. The *Pittsburgh Courier* reported a month into the conflict that "fighting in Korea will be no fun. Word comes back that . . . the women [are] taboo as far as men from the outside world are concerned." According to one correspondent, black soldiers discovered that most young women fled from "liberated" cities, where one might find "many men and old women—but few girls." Besides, guerrilla warfare made city streets dangerous at night, rendering "the mechanics of girl hunting a bit difficult." On-limits recreational facilities appeared at first glance especially tame.[26]

Some black observers went so far as to blame the lack of sexual access to Korean women for the American military's poor initial showing in the conflict. One journalist declared that there was "less fraternization between Korean girls and GIs than in any country where our forces are spread around the globe. [Soldiers] will dare you to turn up any brown babies . . . and they will swear that prostitution is almost nil in Korea. They will be absolutely right, and therein lies the Korean-American sex problem." The author portrayed both a lack of sexual outlets and "overindulgence" as demoralizing to military personnel. He and his sources in uniform debated "whether the girls themselves were responsible or whether they were afraid of reprisals," while allowing that the widespread use of racial epithets—"gook" in particular—produced "bitter resentment and hatred . . . for the American soldiers" and led young Korean men to "set up rigid vigils over their women." The author also took the opportunity to contrast the lot of combat personnel in Korea with the lives many of them had enjoyed as occupationaires. Although "Japan, too, has a strict code of behavior, GIs still have more latitude, due to the highly developed westernization of Nippon. A fast-moving, modern city, Tokyo is well supplied with brothels . . . where a lonesome soldier can enjoy female companionship."[27]

Open and organized prostitution quickly reestablished itself in Korea. Two months into the war a group of black soldiers reported the creation of a cryptically named "Special Service Center" for American military personnel. Curious, the men paid a visit, and inside "found the most attractive girls, called 'comforters' here." However, African American GIs, like their white counterparts, usually remarked upon the alleged unattractiveness of Korea and its people. Many objected to the peninsula's widespread poverty, lack of sanitation, and unfamiliar odors. Korean women, in the words of one black serviceman, "don't wash often enough for me[,] and I would not wash either if I had only cold water, no towel and an unheated outside privy."[28] Fear of venereal disease deterred others. A *Chicago Defender* correspondent noted that "because of the new germ killing anti-biotics and other safeguards a few GIs are straying," but assured his readers that "no permanent relationships are built up." The ubiquity of Korean sex workers (combined with the scarcity of local girl-friends) disturbed some black soldiers. A serviceman from Washington, D.C., explained that "it isn't the VD that bothers me, it's the fact that these girls are street walkers." Although conceding that not all Korean women were prostitutes, he remarked that "the only ones I meet are."[29]

American combat personnel soon learned they might, with luck, earn a vacation in Japan. "Without a sexualized 'rest and recreation' (R&R) period," one historian has asked, "would the U.S. military command be able to send young men off" on long tours of duty? Those in charge of directing the Korean campaign evidently believed they could not. Combat troops became entitled, at least theoretically, to a five-day leave in Japan for every six weeks of frontline service. Particularly as the war settled into a stalemate, this form of R&R acquired an array of alternative, sexually explicit definitions: "Rock and Ruin," "Rape and Run," "Rape and Restitution," and so on. ("For drawing room talk," advised the compilers of an unofficial 1951 *Dictionary of Rice Paddy Lingo*, "use 'seeing the shrines or playing golf.'") Most popular among enlisted men was the term "I&I"—"Intercourse and Intoxication." According to one observer, "Perhaps no where in the world in the early Fifties were those two states easier to achieve for a man of limited means [than] they were in Japan."[30] In 1951 a "concerned" FEC General Headquarters assembled a voluminous classified report on "conduct prejudicial to good order and military discipline" by those on R&R in Japan, ranging from uniform violations and drunk and disorderly conduct to robbery, assault, and rape, but otherwise took no direct action. Recognizing R&R's boost to morale, however unruly in practice, it never contemplated canceling the program.[31]

As hundreds of thousands of servicemen passed through Japan, to and from the war or on short-term leave, African American combat troops, occupationaires, and journalists took note of the dramatically expanding sex industry.[32] Speaking euphemistically in terms of "commodity prices," one black correspondent reported that "the biggest gripe that soldiers in

Japan have about inflation concerns the high cost of love. The biggest complainers are old Far East men." The author first noticed the change when he "came upon a soldier exchanging heated words with a comely Nipponese lass. . . . 'Can you image that dame,' snapped the soldier, . . . 'asking me for three thousand yen (approximately $10)? Why, before the Korean War broke out, you could get the best of them for two bucks.'" "I've been around here since 1947," groused another, "and things were good until all these young squirts, who have never been away from home before, started . . . shelling out yen by the fistful." Readers of the *Afro-American* encountered reports of "streetwalkers in abundance trying to pick up a lonesome soldier" in Tokyo, a development "so acute since the outbreak of the Korean War that no girl from a respectable Japanese family would be caught on the Ginza [the city's main shopping avenue] after dark." The streets surrounding the Yokohama Service Club were "the favorite cruising beaches" of local prostitutes, the entire area "infested with Geisha houses, speakeasies and beer halls." One black GI provided readers with an apt summary of the perspective of many American servicemen: "A guy on short-term leave hasn't got a lot of time to waste jockeying for position. With the native girls you . . . make a fast play and you are all set. No calling up begging for dates, no long courtships and promising to marry and all that sort of thing." Another black soldier explained that even those Japanese women involved in ostensibly noncommercial relationships with GIs were "becoming mercenary," out to "get all they can while the getting is good." African Americans stateside could easily have envisioned Japan as one large brothel, its young women all potential prostitutes.[33]

The formal end to the occupation reinforced these developments. The San Francisco Peace Treaty and the Japan–United States Security Treaty, both signed in September 1951, took effect the following April. Although the peace treaty officially brought the occupation to a close, the security agreement granted the United States control over Okinawa, the right to maintain "security forces" throughout the home islands (two years later there were 34 army camps, 38 air bases, two naval bases and a number of smaller installations), and the right to help quell internal disturbances at the Japanese government's request, all while prohibiting Japan from leasing military facilities to any other country without the United States' prior consent. For the next fifteen months the ongoing war in Korea ensured that countless soldiers would be granted leave in Japan or stationed there to await orders to deploy. At the same time, the peace treaty transferred to the American government one half the cost of maintaining its armed forces in Japan. As free public transportation and sightseeing ended and the largest American recreational facilities shut their doors due to belt-tightening by the military, Japanese entrepreneurs picked up the slack.[34]

American critics thereafter shifted their focus to the "rough conditions" of the "enormous red-light districts . . . organized, staffed and run by the Japanese." One journalist decried the fact that servicemen were "increasingly turning to recreation offered by profit-seeking Japanese who operate beer halls, bars, red-light resorts and strip-tease shows." By the conclusion of the Korean War, the small Japanese community of Chitose served as a prominent symbol of the perceived vice pandemic. One account described the newly assigned commander of a nearby American base as "shocked to find 564 houses of prostitution, 66 beer halls, and 'hundreds of lesser sucker traps and deadfalls.'" These disreputable establishments operated so flagrantly that to the Japanese Chitose was known as "the world's most evil town," to Americans as "the sex circus." African American observers consequently accused the Japanese, and Japanese women in particular, of taking moral and economic advantage of black servicemen. Less than a month after the peace treaty went into effect, *Jet* magazine reported on a global "prostitution menace" and Japan's uniquely "monstrous" variant: "An international army of prostitutes has leeched itself onto U.S. GIs. . . . They are the legion of female sex merchants, who, as camp followers, manage to turn up in vast numbers wherever large groups of GIs with American dollars in their pockets are stationed."[35] Every black soldier in Asia, it seemed, was a target of this "army" of immoral women and its members' materialist designs.

———

Barriers to the formation of more stable and romantic Afro-Asian partnerships included American immigration law and the military's active discouragement of serious relationships with, let alone marriage to, Asian women. From the start of the occupation, SCAP routinely called soldiers' attention to the fact that the United States prohibited the immigration of "persons not having a preponderance of White, African, or Chinese blood."[36] Servicemen were constantly reminded of the practical and personal effects of the 1921 and 1924 Immigration Acts. Their seeming inability to bring Asian partners home convinced many to approach their relations with local women casually and with little thought

Returns With Japanese Bride

3.1 One of fifteen black-Japanese couples married in the summer of 1947 departs for the United States aboard an army transport. Their smiles suggest the initial optimism for Afro-Asian romance. *Afro-American*, 19 June 1948. Courtesy of the Afro-American Newspapers Archives and Research Center.

toward eventual marriage. In late summer 1947, however, a fleeting moment of opportunity arose. President Truman signed an amendment to the 1945 Soldier Brides Act, enabling racially ineligible alien wives to immigrate. There was, of course, a catch: couples had only thirty days in which to navigate the SCAP bureaucracy and then to marry. A total of 823 American-Japanese weddings were performed, including fifteen (1.8 percent) involving black servicemen (see figure 3.1).[37] Once this brief window closed, it would not be reopened until August 1950, after the Korean War separated many couples.[38]

Legal bans on Asian immigration provided military authorities with one rationale to oppose permanent relationships. The Department of the Army, having granted theater commanders ultimate authority over marriage requests, did not intend to keep servicemen married to foreigners in their posts. In January 1947 the Assistant Secretary of War explained that overseas marriages were normally authorized only if the soldier was already scheduled for rotation home, in order "to keep from placing in jeopardy the judgment and loyalty of persons representing this Government in occupied territory." A subsequent SCAP memorandum bluntly informed occupationaires that "no one will be reenlisted if married to a Japanese national." Obviously, this policy would have appeared economically threatening to many black servicemen. Two years later, a SCAP spokesman explained that since "experience in occupied countries has proven that it is not feasible to retain service personnel" married to foreigners, "were approval granted . . . [a] family would immediately be separated by reason of the soldier's transfer" to the United States. The author self-righteously added that "to grant permission to marry when the wife cannot enter the United States would be to flaunt the sanctity of the marriage ceremony." Accordingly, General MacArthur continued to deny all marriage applications in the absence of "very unusual circumstances," a category that did not include the presence of a child.[39]

Military commanders were also motivated by concern for the maintenance of SCAP's perceived legitimacy and by racism. The Assistant Secretary of War claimed that any study of the marriage "problem" in Japan "must necessarily include a consideration of . . . [the] prestige of our occupation forces." Furthermore, a liberalization of marriage policy "would not necessarily result in the enhancement of prestige of Japanese women. Japanese women associating in marital relations would inevitably be ostracized by many of their people. It is also believed that such marriages, if contracted, would have a high rate of divorce, separation, and desertion."[40] A pronouncement by the army's Legislative and Liaison Division resorted to essentialism. "The Japanese are a very gregarious people who need and require companionship in order to be happy," it explained in a letter to Senator Claude Pepper of Florida. The author, speaking of a serviceman pursuing the possibility of marriage, "visualize[d] much unhappiness for him. Because of the fact that his wife would not be accepted, she then would lack the social contacts which, as I have stated before, Japanese people need." The overall effect of such official bias was, in the words of one study, "to prevent intermarriage wherever possible and encourage GIs to opt for informal, unstable relationships," a state of affairs that has endured as the "consistent policy of the U.S. Army throughout its activities in Asia."[41]

These military regulations could have tragic consequences for African American servicemen and their Asian partners. Shortly after American officials instituted and announced the severe restrictions on marriage, Private Charles Kinchelow and his Japanese lover committed suicide. Distraught over Kinchelow's impending rotation to the United States, the two poisoned themselves in a roadside Shinto shrine. The incident became a brief *cause célèbre* in the black press. "Undoubtedly he would have liked to marry her and bring her back to the United States," the *Pittsburgh Courier* declared indignantly, "but apparently that was forbidden by the all-wise and undoubtedly prejudice-free American high officials. So, rather than be separated forever, the two young brown people chose death." Not merely SCAP policy but the entire history of white male behavior in Asia became a target of censure. "How different this is from the traditional attitude of the white men in the Orient," the author continued, "as set forth in Puccini's 'Madam Butterfly' and Pierre Loti's 'Madame

Chrysanthemum,'" tales of abandonment of young Japanese women by American and European men. "This has been the white custom in the Orient. . . . It is an attitude which has contributed much to the effectiveness of the slogan 'Asia for the Asiatics' and to the downfall of white imperialism." The young couple's suicide, in this view, was symbolic of Afro-Asian solidarity in contrast to global white arrogance. "Had the whites in the Orient showed the respect and affection for womanhood that Private Kinchelow so dramatically displayed," the editorial concluded, "the whole history of the Pacific might have been different, and for that matter so might the history of the rest of the world."[42] Black correspondents suggested the personal tragedy was so poignant that it inspired others, even white occupationaires, to do likewise. Within weeks a *Chicago Defender* columnist claimed that "investigators probing the suicide deaths of a Japanese girl and her white GI lover in Japan learned from the girl's friends that she had become deeply impressed" by the actions of the doomed couple.[43]

Over the following years, however, as the extent of militarized prostitution in East Asia became more evident and marriage remained a near impossibility, this narrative of mutual Afro-Asian empathy dissipated. Partly taking its place was a celebration of the undemanding adulation supposedly enjoyed by African American servicemen. Ten months after the Kinchelow incident, the same *Defender* columnist spoke of black soldiers "feathering their nests . . . with pretty Japanese 'coibitoes'"—i.e., *koibito* (roughly "lover"), a term common among occupationaires. These women, he later explained, were simply a manifestation of the "Oriental custom" of concubinage. The author described "10,000 Negro soldiers" besotted by "native heartthrobs who look pretty, wait on them hand and foot, are faithful and demand little." Such relationships were no longer predicated on lifelong commitment, for "GI Joe . . . says the Negro gals will be right there on Central Ave., and South Parkway, and Lenox, when his tour in heaven is over and he returns to the States."[44]

In fact, some black soldiers continued to agonize over threats to their romantic interests and struggled to gain legal recognition of their relationships. Corporal George Brown, stationed in Kyoto, wrote to the NAACP Legal Committee for assistance after several years as an occupationaire. In his unit of fewer than one hundred men, at least eight, including Brown, had children with Japanese girlfriends. Because "the laws of the Army and of the country make it almost entirely impossible for GIs to marry women of Japanese blood," he and others were "left helpless when they inquire[d] for advice or consideration from authorities." There remains no record of a reply from the NAACP, a failure to act that probably came as no surprise to Brown, for many servicemen believed the Association reluctant to intervene in such matters. The men of the all-black 77th Engineer Combat Company submitted a similar complaint to Charles Bussey, their African American commander. As Bussey later recalled, several of those stationed at Camp Gifu "had 'hooches,' rooms in the village they shared with their girlfriends or their wives," the latter being partners in locally approved Shinto marriages "unregistered and unsanctioned by the U.S. Army and by the Department of State." At an impromptu company meeting in the spring of 1950, he was addressed by his first sergeant: "Several of the men have applied to marry Japanese girls, some as long as two years ago. . . . There's no reason for these delays except for the standard prejudice of the State Department." The men contemplated notifying the NAACP, even though "it's not the kind of issue they'd like to fight [for], . . . 'cause every Negro soldier that marries a foreign woman means some Negro woman doesn't get married." Bussey exerted what pressure he could, but to no avail. "Meanwhile the Korean War came along," he explained, "and swooped up some of the men who had so long ago petitioned for marriage. They were gobbled up in that war."[45]

That war, which the United States actively joined a few weeks after Bussey learned of his men's difficulties, permanently severed numerous Afro-Asian relationships, even among servicemen neither killed nor captured. During the first three months of hostilities, four divisions and dozens of smaller service and combat units, including the all-black 24th Infantry Regiment, were shipped to the fighting. More than 50,000 members of the armed forces, or roughly half of all American occupationaires, had left Japan. Death, surrender, rotation stateside for the seriously wounded, and the near impossibility of obtaining leave during the war's desperate first months kept most soldiers from seeing their Japanese girlfriends again. The opening of a second immigration window for Asian military brides came too late for many. Those men subsequently transferred directly to the United States from Korea and of limited means were often helpless in their desire to rejoin Japanese partners.[46]

Nonetheless, when the prospect of utter defeat in Korea transformed into the illusion of a quick, decisive victory in the fall of 1950, African American speculation quickly turned to an anticipated deluge of weddings. An *Afro-American* correspondent toured the Camp Gifu area and reported that he "found an amazing number of 'Brown Babies' fathered by men now fighting in Korea." Recent financial hardships had led some mothers to abandon their children, but "highly informed persons" predicted the "wholesale marriage of colored GIs to Japanese women when the 24th Infantry Regiment returns to Japan." A soldier with the 24th revealed that of the regiment's 388 men in the process of applying for permission to marry, sixty already had children with their Japanese partners, and perhaps another fifty babies were on the way. More than a dozen women, however, had already lost boyfriends to the war. A week later the *New York Amsterdam News* announced that "one of the Gifu 'brides,' whose tan GI husband was killed in action, has committed suicide, taking her infant daughter with her." The *Chicago Defender* suggested "it would not be surprising" if widowed Japanese mothers "destroyed the children to prevent further suffering and to save face." One reporter closed an otherwise upbeat dispatch on an ominous note: "Some claim that the Army will sidestep the matter by keeping the regiment out of Japan until after the marriage deadline passes." (The 24th would, in fact, remain in Korea for almost another year due to the military's desperate need for manpower.)[47]

Expectations for the reunion and marriage of many black-Japanese couples triggered a heated public debate over the exact nature of these relationships and the motives of Japanese women. Its proximate cause was a lone article tucked away in the *Afro-American*'s magazine section, focusing ostensibly on conflicts between black servicemen and the small number of black servicewomen and civilian employees recently assigned to the theater. The piece set ablaze long-smoldering concerns over the meaning of Afro-Asian intimacy and its consequences for African American employment with the military. As the author later noted with surprise, "No other stories which this reporter wrote during four months in the Far East . . . provoked such widespread comment both in America and abroad." Indeed, "many persons both military and civilian . . . jumped into the controversy," while black newspapers across the country joined the fray.[48]

What began as verbal sparring over questions of courtesy and romantic availability quickly metastasized into an interrogation of Japanese morals and material ambitions. At first glance little of the article's content seems particularly inflammatory. It began with typical battle-of-the-sexes fare: "Colored women on civilian duty . . . are being ignored by colored soldiers . . . to the point that many of the women swear . . . they will never speak to a colored soldier who has been stationed in

Japan." The root of this inattention was the *musume* (literally "daughter"), or "moose" in standard American slang. The black soldier "out on the loose in Japan," the author reported, "found that the morals of the Japanese girls, coupled with the fact that he is here as a conqueror of the Japanese people, make it far more easy for him to have a 'good time' by dating Japanese girls than going around with his own." Even the lowest ranked serviceman, because of his salary, benefits, and status as an American occupationaire, could afford to "maintain a 'Moose' and still take care of his other obligations." The article painted a vivid portrait of "lavishly dressed Japanese girls who are wearing the very latest clothes from the States"—"purchase[d] from the Army PX"—"at the expense" of their African American boyfriends. With these words the author inadvertently sparked a very public controversy.[49]

Unsurprisingly, some soldiers defended their actions and, to a lesser degree, the Japanese. A "deeply incensed" Lieutenant L. Clinton Moorman, stationed in Korea and engaged to a Japanese citizen, called the story "degrading" to those "sincerely interested in Japanese women." Despite the presence of a few bad apples, the typical Japanese he and his men dated seriously was "loyal, devoted, thrifty, and a good home-maker. Always you come first in her life."[50] (Implied in his remarks was a backlash against the postwar black feminism then sharply critiquing African American gender relations and the demands placed on black women, many of whom worked outside the home.)[51] Moorman, the public information officer for the 24th Infantry Regiment, also protested directly to the piece's author. "Any number of the fellows would be married to Japanese girls if it were not for the present law," he noted in an open letter. "But yet many have married by Shinto fashion," while others "have what many states in America honor—common law marriages." He closed with a prescient lament: "The United States has finally permitted the fellows to marry. Do you think [your] article places their future wives in a decent light?"[52] Sergeant Sidney Joulon, also on duty in Korea, attempted to clarify the role of black servicemen in East Asia, insisting they were "not here as conquerors but as ambassadors of democracy and good will" (a common assertion at mid-century).[53] As for the "lavishly dressed" girlfriends of popular belief, Joulon maintained that the gift of a "10 cent handkerchief" was enough to win the appreciation of a young Japanese woman.[54]

By year's end, and especially as the war threatened to separate most black-Japanese couples permanently, more and more servicemen disavowed these seemingly unworkable relationships. Frederick J. Bryant wrote to the *Afro-American* to describe his prior experiences in occupied Japan. Having arrived in late 1945, he "doubt[ed] seriously that conditions [had] changed" since his return to the United States. "Love," Bryant explained, "does not enter into the picture, except in a very few instances." Nor would lesser affection, if it existed to any great extent, survive the war in Korea. "The boys who come back home (the fortunate ones)," he predicted, "will release forever their feelings for foreign companionship" and "marry good American girls."[55] While Bryant's words provided gentle reassurance to those concerned about the conduct and welfare of servicemen abroad, others were more pointed. Private Elmer Neely wrote to the *Pittsburgh Courier* from Yokohama, after having "read numerous articles on the relations between the American Negro soldier and Japanese women. They seem to be to the effect that Negro GIs are falling heels over head in love with every other Japanese girl they run across." To the contrary, Neely, engaged to an African American woman, doubted "if 2 per cent of the soldiers in this country are that much concerned over any Japanese girl." His stance was not, he claimed, due to any personal animus, but rather to the fact that "their personal standards are just far off from those of our better women. Those Japanese women who take advantage of what they see in the GI do it at a fluctuating price that has nothing to do with genuine affection."[56]

The debate over Asian women's motives engaged black civilians as well. Ethel Payne, later to become a celebrated journalist, introduced herself to the public by contributing to the outcry.[57] Payne had arrived in Japan in 1948 to begin work as a hostess at an army service club. Thirty months later, as director of the occupation's Club Seaview in Yokohama, she was approached by a *Chicago Defender* correspondent. What "technique" employed by Japanese women, he mused, "so inspires American GIs and have won so many of their hearts?" Payne, by then a strong opponent of black-Japanese relationships, framed her response in terms of Asian mendacity (postwar black feminist arguments were again left implicit). "By tradition," she claimed, "the Japanese woman is submissive. To the man of her choice . . . she presents a convincing [but] superficial respectfulness and affection." "Musume," she added, "has played it cool. . . . Her very helplessness has been a powerful weapon and an asset to her and she is using it fully." Payne was seconded by a coworker, who added, "There is no comparison between the deceit of the Japanese woman and that of the American."[58]

One week later an article in the *Defender*, adapted from Payne's diary, appeared under the front-page headline "JAPANESE GIRLS PLAYING GIS FOR SUCKERS: 'CHOCOLATE JOE' USED, AMUSED, CONFUSED."[59] Occupation duty, it explained, had been an "idyllic [p]aradise" until the Korean War intervened, "an escape from the irking confinement of the social caste system and segregation" of the United States, where "the lowliest private with his base pay of $80 could live like a king." The Japanese, once recovered from the "shock" of seeing a black man in uniform, "found him a good deal more 'soft to the touch,' kinder and [more] generous" than his white peers. Moreover, "already disciplined by a thousand years of Emperor worship and iron military control," the Japanese "recognized authority and bowed to it." Nonetheless, Payne insisted, it was all a ruse, one that enabled Japanese women to exploit black servicemen and, by extension, those dependent on military salaries and remittances. "Suziko San" used her "helplessness . . . to the hilt. . . . From then on, it was open dikes. One had to have a woman's ration card at the PX, but this could be arranged. . . . Gradually, [she] took over completely." Japan's flourishing black market in goods and currency further abetted these financial schemes: military scrip could be illegally converted into yen, then resold for precious American dollars. Because "Suziko San was a clever operator, she soon handled Joe's pay envelope." The line separating rapacious prostitution from genuine affection was nearly indiscernible.[60]

Similar allegations continued to appear in the black media, before dying down once the anticipated flood of Afro-Asian marriages failed to materialize. The majority of Atlanta residents interviewed by the *Pittsburgh Courier* in late 1950 thought Afro-Asian partnerships "terrible" and "awful." Several, in the author's words, "said that it was all right for the boys to leave 'brown babies' over there, but they should not marry."[61] In response to a September 1951 article on the growing plight of illegitimate Afro-Asian children, which noted the role played by military policies that discouraged marriage, a black soldier stationed in Germany argued that the source of the problem was rather the upbringing and behavior of Japanese women. "If you will check on the birth and sex rate in Japan," he insisted, employing a popular stereotype of the Japanese woman as geisha, "you will find that most of the girls . . . are very sexually over-trained."[62] By the end of the occupation, notions of the immorality of Japanese women involved with servicemen had become conventional wisdom among most African Americans. Even an otherwise sympathetic *Ebony* article, published in mid-1954, cast these women in a less-than-flattering

light. Some were "simple farm girls excited by the kindness and generosity of foreigners," or "restless women . . . who left their homes and sought
honest jobs. Finding none, they easily slipped into the comfortable, free
roles of 'occupation wives.'" Many more, however, were "hardened prostitutes, driven into alliances with GIs through hunger or greed."[63] Black
servicemen and stateside observers generally believed by that point that
their economic interests were largely incompatible with Afro-Asian
romance.

The experiences of two black soldiers in the occupation's immediate
aftermath provide insights into the personal struggles of those attempting to reconcile their romantic and financial investments overseas. Curtis
Morrow, a veteran of the Korean War, began serving on an airbase on
the Japanese island of Kyushu in mid-1952. For three months he enjoyed
the diversions of military life in post-occupation Japan. "I was simply
fascinated by the Japanese women and they with me," Morrow later remembered. "Of course, much of their fascination could've had to do
with economics. . . . [M]y monthly pay was $115 or twice the salary of a
laborer; plus I had no other expenses. At my request the army automatically deducted money from my salary for allotment checks, which they
sent to my family on a monthly basis. All I didn't give to [Japanese]
women, I partied away." However, one night he met a young woman
named Kaeko, with whom he began a relationship that lasted nearly two
years. "She was what we GIs call[ed] a kept girl," he explained, "which
means she'd just wait until she met someone . . . to take care of her."
Both he and Kaeko recognized the precariousness of their circumstances:
"We were well aware that our being together depended on world politics. My life as a soldier . . . wasn't mine to call the shots. I could be ordered to pack up and ship out on a moment's notice." Although their life
together "was like being married," Morrow hesitated to apply for permission to wed, in part because of reports from the United States on the
difficulties encountered by Afro-Asian couples.

In time, however, they grew closer, and Morrow reluctantly investigated what red tape stood in the way. His initial findings were discouraging. Morrow's white commanding officer persuaded him to rethink
the matter. "Hell, when you return to America and lay eyes on your own
women again," he advised, "you'll be glad as hell you remained single. I
suggest you return to the States, then decide what you want to do." The
interview, which unfolded much as Morrow suspected it would, left him
"with a strange sense of relief." Back at work he discussed the matter

with a fellow black soldier, who seconded the white officer's reasoning. "You know the way I look at it," he counseled, "every place supplies its own. So why get hung up here in gook-land." Morrow agreed, although he sought to extend his tour in order to continue the relationship. His request denied, the couple was permanently separated.[64]

Jessie Brown, after a tour of duty along the Korean front, was reassigned to Yokohama, processing replacements for the ongoing conflict. "At that time," he later explained, a few black soldiers were "marrying the girls, bringing them home. I had known this girl before [the war], and she joined me where I was stationed . . . , and we stayed together until it was time to leave. But we decided . . . to get married." Brown, however, began to have second thoughts. "Why bring someone from that far away, of another race, all the way back to America," he asked himself, "and what's going to happen when she wants to go back to see her people? I'm not financially able." He nonetheless chose to make an inquiry with his sergeant major, "a white guy from Atlanta." "He listened to everything . . . and said, 'You want to get married.' I said, 'Yeah.' He went and got my records. He pulled them out and looked at them. He said to me, 'You're on your way home. And if you don't catch that plane you're going to pay $600 for the seat.'" After experiencing firsthand one of the military's less subtle methods for derailing a relationship, Brown bade his girlfriend a hasty farewell with promises to return. "But on the way from there," he recalled of the flight home, "I was glad the sergeant did that for me, 'cause in a way I got back and grew up." And yet, fifty years later a tone of uncertainty, and perhaps regret, crept into Brown's voice: "I wouldn't have wanted to bring her from over there to here. I don't think I would have."[65]

Relatively few Asian wives of black servicemen entered the United States in these years, although precise figures are elusive. The Immigration and Naturalization Service, while it recorded the number of foreign military brides admitted to the United States until 1951, chose not to identify their husbands by race. Reliable figures do exist for the windows for Asian immigration opened before the December 1952 passage of the McCarran-Walter Act, which equalized the legal status of all military brides. In addition to the fifteen black-Japanese marriages conducted in the summer of 1947, just over 1,000 were approved during the eighteen months of opportunity following the start of war in Korea (see figure 3.2).[66] In the

3.2 An African American serviceman, accompanied by his Japanese partner and their child, fills out the last of the marriage paperwork. *Pittsburgh Courier*, 17 March 1951. Courtesy of the Pittsburgh Courier Archives.

decade-and-a-half after World War II, the total number of black-Japanese marriages likely fell somewhere between three and five thousand.[67] Considerably fewer black-Korean marriages occurred during these years (although again precise figures are largely unavailable). In 1951, for instance, a mere eleven Korean women entered the United States as wives of American citizens, mostly servicemen. Only one had married an African American.[68]

Military approval of a marriage before McCarran-Walter, however, did not automatically confer U.S. citizenship—and therefore the right to permanent residence—on an Asian bride. The saga of African American Sergeant Alexis Porche and Miyo Matsumoto is illustrative. Following a wedding conducted under Shinto rites, the couple struggled for years to secure formal recognition by the American military government. As the process dragged on month after month, Matsumoto became pregnant, adding still greater urgency to the negotiations. Two months after the birth of a daughter, occupation authorities relented and declared the couple legally married. Under long-standing military practice, Porche was promptly transferred back to the United States, although he managed to secure American citizenship for his daughter. His wife, on the other hand, obtained only temporary visitation rights—a six-month visa—to live with her husband and child.[69]

Servicemen returning with Asian wives often faced a dramatic decline in living standards, which could put considerable strains on their marriages. An editor for the San Francisco *Nichi-Bei Times* explained that financial woes were contributing to larger adjustment problems: "Many of these 'unhappy brides' shared the popular mistaken impression . . . that all people in the United States live as sumptuously" as soldiers on American bases in Asia. Most had enjoyed relatively comfortable circumstances due to their partners' overseas pay and PX access. Relocation stateside usually entailed a reduction in household income and an increase in daily expenses. Those servicemen who reentered civilian life seldom acquired well-paying jobs at first, a problem especially acute among African American veterans. A nationwide housing shortage forced many couples to join relatives in cramped quarters. Recognizing the potential for marital discord, the Red Cross in 1951 began sponsoring courses for Asian brides on the economic realities of American life at mid-century. Because "most of these girls will go to the farming and poorer sections of the United States," instructors sought to prepare them for the "Sears, Roebuck form of existence rather than the Vogue pattern."[70]

Differing state intermarriage laws bewildered military officials assigning soldiers married to Asian women to domestic posts. Officers considered the laws of a serviceman's home state when first weighing a marriage application, on the assumption that he would stay put once mustered out of service: a soldier from Idaho was much less likely to obtain permission than one from Illinois.[71] All local statutes came into play when a married serviceman was up for rotation to a base stateside. A memorandum circulated within the army's Career Management Division attempted to tackle the intricate structure of the nation's various state marriage laws. "In order to prevent embarrassment to [the] personnel involved," it cautioned, officials were to give out assignments consistent with each state's legislation governing interracial unions. In order to assist personnel directors in adhering to the rules, the memorandum included a list of twenty-eight states and their specific injunctions against intermarriage. None of them, however, directly addressed Afro-Asian couples.[72]

The unanticipated questions that arose from these unions proved especially confounding. A 1953 study of American–Japanese couples considered the predicament of two black husbands. Both had remained in the military and were thus "to a certain degree, protected from some of the problems that Negroes with Japanese wives might encounter in civilian life." Although the couples had faced few problems in Ohio, they puzzled over what might occur if they traveled to Georgia or Mississippi.[73] That same year a black journalist accused the army of failing to anticipate the unique difficulties that Afro-Asian couples confronted. Operating in an American racial climate "already complex enough," "officials frequently were at a loss as to what to do with a Negro married to a Japanese girl in a state where interracial (meaning white and Negro) marriages are prohibited by law." The inhabitants of one southern community, he reported, complained repeatedly about a black-Japanese couple living off-base. The local post commander, unsure of standard operating procedure in such a case, ironically provided the enlisted man and his wife with luxurious on-base accommodations traditionally reserved for high-ranking officers.[74]

The fluid nature of American racial classifications abetted the confusion. In April 1952 the NAACP journal *The Crisis* described "an extraordinary racial transformation, one reminiscent of Hitler's generosity when he made the Nipponese 'honorary Aryans.'" "In Oklahoma," it announced, "a Japanese is white." The state government reached that conclusion while pondering the case of a Japanese citizen applying to all-black Langston University. Because Japanese Americans were then attending the state's white public schools, the governor requested a decision from his attorney general, who ruled that Japanese people were "white" for the purposes of Oklahoma's segregation laws. Admission to Langston was denied. "This irrationality," complained *The Crisis*, "opens up all sorts of complications. . . . Oklahoma, for instance, has a law forbidding Negroes and whites to marry each other. What happens then to a Negro GI who returns to Tulsa with his Japanese bride? How do you classify the offspring of a Negro-Japanese union? . . . It is all very sad—or funny." Ludicrous though it may have seemed, the Langston case was emblematic of profound shifts in the American racial landscape that contributed to an often chilly reception for Afro-Asian couples and their segregation within and from African American and Asian American communities.[75]

These couples began arriving in significant numbers at precisely the moment a new domestic racial order emerged, in which the socioeconomic trajectories of black and Asian citizens sharply diverged. Prior to World War II, African Americans, Asian Americans, and other racial minorities on the West Coast typically lived in the same neighborhoods and encountered similar varieties of prejudice, although they rarely joined forces politically. During the wartime internment of Japanese Americans, black families took advantage of opportunities to move into the newly vacated homes. The poet and novelist Maya Angelou, whose family migrated to San Francisco shortly after Pearl Harbor, explained that "no member of my family and none of the family friends ever mentioned the absent Japanese. It was if they had never owned or lived in the houses we inhabited." As internees were released and began returning to their former neighborhoods, Afro-Asian tensions rose, although open hostility remained rare. However, Japanese Americans' postwar rehabilitation in the minds of many whites proceeded hand-in-hand with their socioeconomic advancement. One historian notes that "Little Tokyo's white landlords openly favored Japanese Americans who wished to 'reclaim' the district from black residents." Meanwhile, the Nisei's rising public image facilitated the gradual assimilation of Japanese Americans into white neighborhoods.[76]

These developments irked many black citizens, particularly in light of the power relations then in operation overseas. The relative deference and status African American servicemen and their families enjoyed in Asia contrasted sharply with the ground African Americans seemed to be losing at home. Immigration policy became one of the first battlegrounds. A black columnist complained in March 1949 of an early version of what eventually became the McCarran-Walter Act. The bill tied the removal of barriers to Asian immigration—"a good move" in his estimation—to severe restrictions on immigration from the Caribbean. "Are we to take it that the degree of color prejudice in this country must be kept at its present height," he asked, "so that what is lifted off the Oriental be saddled on the Negro?" Racial advancement, it seemed, was a zero-sum game. The author also noted the global politics at play: "Of course, the lightening of the prejudice against the Oriental is to win his favor against communism in the East but as for Negroes they don't count." The Cold War struggle for hearts and minds appeared to favor Asians, but not as of yet the interests of black people.[77]

Closer to home, black observers could not help but notice the differing fortunes of African Americans and Asian Americans. "Now, eight years after Pearl Harbor," protested one, "Japanese people in the United States are held in higher esteem than those of a darker hue." Higher esteem was intertwined with economic advancement. "The Japanese . . . go where they please, live as they will, and hold higher type jobs than do other colored Americans." Even their kin overseas seemed to benefit: "silks, crockery and other oriental [*sic*] commodities are now on our shelves and counters and the so-called dastardly sneak blow delivered by the 'yellow-bellied devils' has been all but forgiven, if not forgotten." Meanwhile, the black American remained a second-class citizen. "The Japs," the author declared, "are accorded more freedom and liberty than he." A few years later, Claude Barnett of the influential Associated Negro Press voiced similar complaints regarding the behavior and upward mobility of Asian Americans. In response to a light-skinned acquaintance's claims of personal friendliness on the part of the Nisei, Barnett asked, "Is there any possibility that your color looks so much like theirs that they do not identify you with [the] black race?" "When the Japanese were driven out of California and put in concentration camps," he insisted, "the only people who succored them . . . were colored folk." And yet, "no one could have been more coolly indifferent to colored people than those same Japanese when they were permitted to return to Little Tokyo in Los Angeles and other areas to reclaim their possessions." It was into this tense atmosphere that Afro-Asian couples disembarked in the early 1950s.[78]

The African American press consequently, and rather accurately, emphasized the physical and emotional isolation of Asian women married to black servicemen, in contrast to a growing tendency in the white media and mainstream popular culture to cast the Asian military bride as a model minority housewife.[79] Voluntary seclusion, according to black press accounts, began early. One correspondent deemed those yet to leave Japan "a clannish lot [who] spend much of their spare time visiting with each other."[80] Once in the United States, the women were routinely shunned by other Japanese Americans. "The Nisei seem to prefer to identify themselves with whites," complained one, "and shy away from associations with Negroes." Many were unable to maintain longtime friendships with women married to white military personnel. "It seems that the Japanese girls who married white soldiers got very high hat when they came to America," grumbled another, "and drew a color line on us and our husbands." Black-Japanese couples encountered hostility in African American communities as well. *Ebony* in early 1953 described Japanese brides as "exceedingly unsophisticated young women . . . writing seemingly childish letters to their relatives back home." While they found "the gadgets wonderfully baffling," their in-laws and husbands' acquaintances "turned out to be the most aloof people they ever met. The wives have received half-hearted welcomes . . . and been unable to make new friends." Newly arrived families were therefore inclined to "live in a tiny Japanese–Negro world of their own," collectively forming "one of the strangest social cliques in Negro communities."[81]

Black–Korean couples were too few in number in the 1950s to attract an equivalent degree of public scrutiny (or to produce much in the way of a historical record). However, one recent study, focusing primarily on a later period, reveals striking similarities. Its author discovered that women married to African Americans typically "suffer[ed] greater and more blatant ostracism from other Koreans" than did those with white husbands. "The general view [was] that women married to blacks . . . married into the dregs of foreign society and . . . must therefore also have come from the dregs of Korean society." Most of the women were assumed by both Korean Americans and African Americans to have been former prostitutes, and black–Korean couples socialized almost exclusively with one another.[82]

Word of the difficulties Afro–Asian couples encountered in the United States reached East Asia with growing frequency, discouraging many from pursuing marriage in the first place. In early 1952 *Jet* magazine reported that some wives, "unable to adjust to America," had left of their own accord. Others refused to join their partners stateside while fruitlessly attempting to arrange passage for their children. Curtis Morrow, whose hesitant inquiries into marriage came to naught, recalled encountering black servicemen who returned to Japan with their spouses "because of the opposition they were forced to deal with in the States; some even took their discharges in Japan rather than return to America." The popular Japanese newsmagazine *Woman's Asahi* featured a report on military wives living in the United States, claiming that those married to black men were "the most unhappy brides in the world." A 1953 *Ebony* article, "The Loneliest Brides in America," echoed these observations: "By marrying Negroes, these Japanese girls have cast their lot with the Negro people and are hurt to find that they do not readily fit into the Negro world." For black sailor Edward Coble, who had been stationed in Japan for two-and-a-half years and hoped to marry his Japanese partner before returning home, the article confirmed a distressing trend. He wrote to the magazine to protest the "highly un-American treatment" afforded these couples: "Until recently, it was thought by many in Japan that Negroes would be the last to discriminate against Japanese warbrides, [but] we find the effect of this manifest unfriendliness . . . becoming more and more apparent. . . . Knowledge of the cool reception that most of them can expect . . . is driving more and more Japanese girls to refuse the marriage proposals" of African American servicemen. A few couples might avoid the problem by staying in Japan, he granted, but for "those of us who have ambitions and responsibilities that make eventual return to the U.S. mandatory, it is a sorely perplexing state of affairs."[83]

Perplexing as the larger transformation from ambivalence and cautious hope to hostility and widespread disdain may have appeared at the time, in hindsight its multiple roots are evident. Generally speaking, foreign occupation and war proved less than conducive to Afro-Asian family formation and goodwill. More to the point, state aversion to intermarriage, Asian anti-black prejudice, and African Americans' growing financial stake in an empire of bases together undermined black soldiers' romantic interests abroad, which in turn reinforced an emphasis on the material benefits of their service in Asia. These soldiers' intimate affairs, which commanded so much public scrutiny, had another significant outcome: a generation of biracial children.

Chapter 4

A Brown Baby Crisis

A few weeks after the landing of American occupationaires, a white intelligence officer attended an impromptu Japanese social gathering in Tokyo. Following several rounds of sake, the off-duty officer felt the increasing gaiety posed an opportune moment to ask a "delicate question": How did the Japanese feel about interracial fraternization? His relatively prosperous Japanese host assumed the role of spokesperson and, according to a letter the officer wrote to a colleague stationed in China, "did not hesitate to denounce it emphatically." Due to language barriers, racial differences, and lingering wartime hatreds, his host argued, American soldiers were uninterested in pursuing serious relationships. Their indifference, he predicted, would become self-evident the following summer, when "a prodigious crop" of fatherless American-Japanese children arrived. For years, perhaps decades, these children "would be a constant reminder of American excess and Japanese folly." The room fell silent as the Japanese guests solemnly nodded in agreement.[1]

This repudiation of biracial children was not confined to Japan's miniscule upper crust; the issue engaged many Japanese eking out a living. During the occupation's first year, for example, SCAP censors intercepted a private letter passing along exaggerated rumors about the anticipated number of mixed-race offspring. Not only were "twenty thousand women in Yokohama intimately related with Allied soldiers," but word had arrived of "thirteen thousand hybrids" expected in the central region of Kansai. The author found the birth of Afro-Asian children particularly distressing: "It is enough to make one shudder when one hears that there are three thousand Japanese women with Negro children in Yokohama."[2]

Although Japanese citizens early pondered the fate of Afro-Asian children, African Americans at home only gradually became apprised of their existence and the difficulties they faced. The first account in the black press appeared in early 1947. Ensconced in a column summarizing items of interest in the field of domestic race relations was a brief report from a meeting of the Anthropological Society of Washington. Dr. Gordon Bowles, considered a leading authority on Japan, claimed that of the growing number of biracial occupation children, "a large proportion were American Negro-Japanese."[3] His remarks inaugurated a lengthy public discussion about an East Asian "brown baby crisis," the latest in a series that followed in the wake of mid-century black military service abroad. One arose in Britain during and immediately after World War II, and a second in occupied Germany. By the early 1950s, East Asia was attracting growing black attention as the site of a new generation of biracial children, individuals of ambiguous racial identity, national belonging, and citizenship. The number of such children in each of these countries was remarkably similar. Black sociologist St. Clair Drake found approximately 1,200 biracial offspring in Britain, out of 70,000 GI children.[4] Of the 94,000 German occupation babies, at least two thousand were *Mischlingskinder*, children fathered by African American soldiers.[5] By the mid-1950s, the number in both Japan and South Korea stood somewhere between one and two thousand.

However, a wide gulf separated African American impressions of the treatment afforded these children in Europe and Asia. Ironically, given prewar and wartime black denunciations of German racism and British colonialism and debates over the uncertain appeal of Japanese calls for nonwhite solidarity, in the postwar years the roles were reversed. While African American observers generally lauded Germany and Britain for their treatment of brown babies—positive coverage of developments in Europe could also double as criticism of domestic racial segregation—they sharply attacked Japan and, to a lesser extent, South Korea.[6] Their impressions were largely correct. Although European attitudes toward mixed-race offspring were by no means universally benign, Afro-Asian children suffered extreme hardship. Most Japanese and Koreans shunned or attacked them due to racial prejudice and monoethnic notions of national identity and out of frustration over an unwelcome American military presence.

Some black citizens initially felt a race-based sense of responsibility for the children. In contrast to African American endeavors to assist European brown babies, however, no sustained campaigns arose for the support of biracial children in Asia.[7] This imbalance was due in part to American immigration law, but also because Afro-Asians, unlike Afro-Europeans, had little historical precedent in African American communities. Moreover, the Cold War imperatives that encouraged cultural celebrations of the adoption of Asian orphans and abandoned white-Asian children—the latter in light of communist charges of Euro-American imperialism and irresponsibility in the Third World—did not extend to Afro-Asians.[8] Most black soldiers and civilians also found the legal and economic requirements for international adoption prohibitive. At the same time, the mistreatment of these children angered many African Americans, enhancing their sense of insurmountable difference from Asian peoples. Japanese and Koreans, through their widespread rejection of Afro-Asian offspring, appeared neither committed to racial equality nor likely partners in struggles against white racism. And when African American interest in the fate of these children eventually faded, so too did recognition of one of the human costs of a military empire.

———

Like their Japanese hosts, occupationaires received conflicting reports on the number of GI babies. In March 1946 the *Pacific Stars and Stripes* published the initial findings of the Tokyo-Yokohama Metropolitan Police Board. Officials there estimated that at least 14,000 illegitimate American-Japanese children would reside in their bailiwick alone by mid-June. The Japanese head of the Criminal Investigation Section placed the figure at 15,000, and explained that the total for all of Japan would undoubtedly be several times that.[9] Less than a week later, occupationaires were told to disregard both estimates. An American sergeant, writing in the serviceman's newspaper of record, maintained that "extensive news investigation" revealed "the figure of 14,000 misses the mark of truth by a wide margin. In fact, there are no actual figures available whatsoever."[10] It seemed no one knew anything for sure about the extent of problem, although they were certain it existed.

Two years later, in the pages of the *Saturday Evening Post,* journalist Darrell Berrigan sought to rectify the situation. He included estimates of the number of occupation children—between one and four thousand—but complained, "there are no official figures. There never will be so long as the Allied authorities have anything to say about it." To admit that a problem existed, or to allow others to conduct their own tallies, would have tarnished SCAP's carefully crafted image of a perfect occupation. The GI father, moreover, was free from any official responsibilities for his child: "He can, if he feels like it, admit paternity and make an allotment to the child or its mother. Apparently he does not wish to do this, for GHQ, Tokyo, has never had such a request." Berrigan concluded his exposé with an attempt to shame both irresponsible occupationaires and white readers by highlighting the sole known instance of a father sending packages of food and clothing to a Japanese mother: "This faithful American, by the way, is a Southern Negro." ("Unfortunately," he added, "the girl turned the baby over to an orphanage long ago and has been profiting handsomely from the black-market sale of the food and clothing.")[11] Infuriated SCAP officials immediately revoked Berrigan's press credentials and expelled him from the country. Making his way to Thailand, he died soon thereafter.[12]

Berrigan touched on two subjects—paternity and citizenship—that would define the lives of a generation of American-Asian children. The United States, beginning with its turn-of-the-century acquisition of the Philippines, had long refused to provide social welfare benefits or citizenship to illegitimate biracial children in Asia, in contrast to the British, French, and Dutch. The policies that encouraged servicemen to abandon their offspring in Japan were also in keeping with American military practice in other occupied nations. In Germany, for example, the occupation government proclaimed that "no individual in the military service will be required or requested to admit paternity."[13] The chief of SCAP's Legal Section announced that a February 1946 decree denying local civil courts jurisdiction over Allied personnel prohibited Japanese women from filing paternity suits. An occupationaire could establish paternity and thus the American citizenship of his child only through a state court after returning home (of course, he would then need to provide for his dependent's transportation across the Pacific).[14] The legal, economic, and logistical difficulties involved in such a convoluted process were substantial. Moreover, the pre-1952 ban on immigration for individuals lacking "a preponderance of White, African, or Chinese blood" enabled functionaries with the Immigration and Naturalization Service to bar entry for many American-Asian children.[15]

Japanese and Korean law and culture rendered some of these children legal non-entities and most permanent outsiders. Japan's patriarchal nationality laws meant that GI babies acquired citizenship only if their American fathers failed or refused to acknowledge paternity, which then saddled them with a lifetime stigma of illegitimacy. Because of the enduring myth of Japanese ethnic purity, these citizens' legal status conflicted with popular attitudes that deemed them foreigners. In South Korea circumstances conspired to enhance such virtual statelessness. Until 1968 birth registration was entered only under the surname of the father, and in most cases the American GI parent had long since departed (regardless, it was nearly impossible to force him to admit paternity). Unlisted in a local census, an American-Korean child lacked any official record of existence.[16] These individuals' obvious illegitimacy further contributed to their social marginalization. Among people of a self-described "single race" (*tanil minjok*) nation, such children were clearly outsiders.[17] The postwar terms for mixed-race offspring in Japan—"illegitimate children of the U.S.A." (*Amerika no otoshigo*), "children sent by the war" (*senso no moshigo*), and "international orphans" (*kokusai koji*)—and South Korea—"the twisted" (*t'wigi*) and "Yankee bastard" (*yangk'i sekki*)—testify to the lack of a sense of responsibility for them within their host countries.[18] Those fathered by African Americans were subject to harsher epithets. Their physical characteristics identified them as "black" and even more foreign to Japanese and Korean societies, while in the eyes of American officials they remained "Asian" and essentially alien to the United States.

By the time Darrell Berrigan's article appeared, a handful of institutions were caring for white- and black-Japanese children. In a letter to the NAACP, a Japanese nun solicited financial assistance for a private Christian orphanage intended to shelter at least one hundred American-Japanese children. The author lamented that of the "3,490 half-breeds throughout Japan" (84 percent of their fathers allegedly American, 83 percent soldiers), half were being raised by single mothers. Less than five hundred were housed in institutions designated for their care.[19] One orphanage established solely for GI babies, the Our Lady of Lourdes Home in Yokohama, had by the spring of 1948 reached a capacity of 130 children. Two-and-a-half years later it housed 165, nearly one-third of whom a *Pittsburgh Courier* correspondent estimated were Afro-Asian.[20]

Among African Americans abroad and at home, former socialite Miki Sawada quickly became the public face of Japanese efforts to find a place for Afro-Asian offspring. Granddaughter of the founder of the Mitsubishi firm and married to a Japanese ambassador, Sawada learned of the dangers faced by American-Japanese offspring through various media accounts in the summer of 1946: the body of an Afro-Asian infant found floating in a river; a Eurasian child discovered dead in the street. These reports acquired a sense of immediacy four months later, when a thin bundle fell from an overhead luggage rack and landed in Sawada's lap. Inside she discovered the corpse of an Afro-Asian child. Determined to provide for the welfare of abandoned biracial children, Sawada founded the Elizabeth Saunders Home—named for a British governess who remained in Japan during the war—thirty miles north of Yokohama in early 1948. Although originally entrusted with only three children, five years later the Home housed 118, of whom 103 had been fathered by Americans. At least thirty-four were black-Japanese. Like her counterparts at the Lourdes Home, Sawada insisted that the children be segregated from Japanese society, educated in English-language schools if possible, and eventually sent to the United States. (The chief of SCAP's Public Health and Welfare Section politely disagreed: "The kindest thing that we can do is not to segregate them. They have to stay here after we've left.") Despite Sawada's good intentions and tireless promotion of aid to the GI babies of Japan, she was convinced that most of the children's mothers were prostitutes who had passed along their moral failings. She was also no stranger to Japanese anti-black prejudice, as would become evident in the years ahead.[21]

Nonetheless, Sawada initially enjoyed support from black servicemen and journalists grateful that something was being done to care for Afro-Asian children. Following a positive mention of her efforts in *Ebony* in 1951, one sailor wrote to the magazine from Europe with "orchids to Miki Sawada" and encouragement "to keep up the good work that she and her helpers are doing." Another serviceman, a former occupationaire stationed in Korea, informed *Ebony*'s readers that he had encountered "many Japanese girls [with] Negro children, filled with hopes of their GI fathers returning," and "was wondering what was happening to the babies not already murdered by their mothers." Relieved that an institution had been established to care for "those innocent infants," he extended "many thanks" to Sawada "for her thoughtfulness." Black servicemen in Japan offered more tangible assistance. One reporter, noting that "the city of

Yokohama abounds with brown babies," described the difficulties in acquiring food, medical care, clothing, and school supplies. Because the cash-strapped Japanese government provided meager funds—no contributions from SCAP or the U.S. government were mentioned—black occupationaires stepped in to help. Patrons of the all-black Golden Dragon Club were the largest and most consistent benefactors: servicemen donated cash monthly to the club's director, who in turn delivered the funds to the Saunders Home. According to the same account, the Home was "practically . . . adopted" by members of the 24th Infantry Regiment. When stationed nearby the men traveled to play with the children, and after redeployment to Korea several continued to send monthly donations.[22] However, some servicemen recognized the deficiencies inherent in such ad hoc relief efforts. In the spring of 1951, Thomas Pettigrew wrote to the NAACP from Korea to suggest an international "Brown Babies Fund," supported by contributions from black personnel stationed around the world. The men in his unit had already expressed a willingness to make regular donations. Pettigrew explained that as "a member of the Armed Forces, there are limitations to what I can do," and proposed that the NAACP take charge of the endeavor. It appears he never received a reply, and his proposal came to nothing.[23]

In the case of a father rushed to the Korean front, the results could be particularly distressing. African American Sergeant Robert Dickerson married Mieko Oishi in a Japanese ceremony (unrecognized by military authorities) while serving with the occupation. Their first child, Juanita, was born in early 1949; Tanya, their second, several weeks after her father was deployed to Korea. By then Dickerson was reported missing in action and presumed dead. His wife, ill and traumatized, wrote to her mother-in-law explaining that she had been cut off from her family for marrying an African American and wished to bring the children to the United States. Latonia Dickerson replied from Buffalo that "you and the children are the only ties I have left with my son" and began inquiries into obtaining visas. The results were dispiriting. A reporter for the *Chicago Defender* referred her to the Buffalo Veterans Administration, whose chief attorney noted his lack of jurisdiction and directed her to the American Red Cross, where a liaison worker pointed her in the direction of the local International Institute, which then began the arduous process of attempting to cut through State Department red tape. The historical record ends there, but given the impossibility of establishing paternity following Dickerson's death, and thus his daughters' lack of any claim to

American citizenship, it is doubtful the two ever joined their extended family in the United States.[24]

During and immediately after the war, a pair of international black celebrities briefly offered their assistance to the brown babies of Japan, drawing additional attention their plight. Boxer Joe Louis departed for a widely publicized goodwill tour of Asia in late 1951. He presented the Lourdes Home with a check for 34,000 yen (about $95 at the contemporary exchange rate), part of his proceeds from exhibition bouts at American military bases and Japanese arenas. Louis continued on to Taiwan, where he dined with nationalist Chinese political and military leaders. On his return journey he stopped again in Japan, visiting hospitalized Korean War veterans and delivering Christmas gifts to the Lourdes Home and a second check for 54,000 yen ($150), donated by the Tokyo branch of the VFW. Louis also staged a benefit fight for the Saunders Home, raising enough money for an additional cottage—to be named in his honor—on the orphanage grounds. Two years later expatriate entertainer Josephine Baker, an acquaintance of Sawada, flew to Japan for a series of concerts to benefit the Saunders Home. She gave twenty-two performances during her three-week stay, visiting often with the children.[25] These tours generated considerable stateside publicity for the efforts of Sawada and her colleagues. Nonetheless, many African American observers had already begun to harshly criticize the Japanese for their conduct toward Afro-Asian offspring.

Several months before Louis's tour, for example, the *Chicago Defender* ran an exposé on Japan's "crop of sloe-eyed curly topped brown babies." By then, it seemed increasingly unlikely that those of their fathers fighting in Korea would return to Japan after the war. Noting the absurdity of a situation in which the one-drop rule traditionally used to define Americans as legally black could not be used to circumvent U.S. immigration law, the author declared the Afro-Asians "children without a country." As for their mothers, many had "displayed [an] eagerness to have babies as this meant a stronger hold upon the soldier and increased financial support." (Ironically, this accusation mirrored mid-century stereotypes of African American single mothers). With financial assistance no longer forthcoming, the author predicted, most would abandon their children or put them up for adoption, violations of traditional African American codes of moral conduct that emphasized maternal responsibility. The article then turned to Japanese racial attitudes and their implications for the children's future. "Under the occupation," it explained, "the Japanese have no choice but to give to all of the representatives of the Supreme Commander the respect and obedience which their presence demand[s]." Nonetheless, the military's flagrant segregation of African American personnel had made a strong impression, while a "thousand years of [a] rigid caste system . . . has not made for tolerance and understanding by the Japanese people." The author then highlighted an investigation of an orphanage for mixed-race children that revealed that gifts of food and clothing had been distributed solely to the offspring of white GIs. (Responding to the piece, one black occupationaire acknowledged "the 'brown baby' problem" but asked the *Defender*'s readers, "What do you expect to happen in a land where the problem of food is more important than morals?")[26]

The following months witnessed several more articles in this vein. One suggested that the Japanese mothers of Afro-Asian offspring were of questionable morality by describing an infant who refused to fall asleep unless loud music was played, since it had been "weaned in a rough night club." The *Afro-American* bemoaned the licentiousness of the occupation while reporting that the mother of black-Japanese half sisters "had a succession of GI lovers" and had since become "a street girl."[27] In January 1951 it printed photographs of Afro-Asian children discovered in the Saunders Home under a headline stating that they had been "STARVED, MISTREATED AND ABANDONED" (see figure 4.1). The accompanying text indicated that one was the Home's lone brown baby adopted by an American couple in Japan, while another had survived attempted infanticide.[28] A correspondent for the paper reported that in addition to the "spindly legged, diseased babies that have been picked up in fields, in the Imperial Palace Moat, [and] in public toilets," "many have died from starvation, murder and neglect." (Miki Sawada later disclosed that at least two dozen infants in her care quickly succumbed to prior malnourishment or pneumonia.) Those who survived faced harassment from an early age. *Jet* magazine published a photograph of two distraught black-Japanese children who had been taunted and physically attacked by local youngsters, explaining that "full blooded Japanese . . . dislike racially-mixed children."[29]

Customarily optimistic *Ebony* magazine carried one of the most widely read accounts of the black-Japanese. Its September 1951 article described the "plight of more than 2,000 illegitimate children of Japanese mothers and American GI fathers, a large percentage of them Negro soldiers." Ten months after the first black occupationaires landed, a "curly-haired,

Starved, Mistreated and Abandoned, These Unwanted Babies Found Home in Japan

4.1 According to the original caption, the first child's mother "killed herself," the second's "tried to kill him," and the third's had "completely disappeared." *Afro-American*, 13 January 1951. Courtesy of the Afro-American Newspapers Archives and Research Center.

brown-skinned Japanese citizen was born. With his birth the 'race problem' began in Japan." Not only did SCAP ignore the children of its personnel, but legal restrictions had prevented black military families stationed in Japan from adopting more than a handful of Afro-Asian orphans. No Japanese family, the author pointedly added, had ever adopted such a child. Aside from the "many" GI fathers thwarted in their attempts to marry, few escaped censure: "It is a story of the wholesale abandonment of children not only by their mothers but by an entire nation [i.e., Japan] as well as by the occupying army which created the problem." Most ominously, because "the Japanese people are as race-minded as Georgia whites, the children of the conquerors are already feeling the cruelty of race prejudice." Reader reaction was vehement. A black serviceman stationed in Europe lamented the inexplicable Japanese lack of compassion. Perhaps some day, he indignantly concluded, they "will realize that the kids are human . . . and should be treated as such." One woman wrote from Miami to express her sympathy for the children and to suggest they be removed from Japan, "whereby they may grow up with the feeling that they 'belong.' "[30]

GI babies could be brought to the United States most expeditiously—and often only—by means of a private bill, specific legislation intended for an individual or small group of related foreigners.[31] However, in the decade after World War II, even the prolific Congressman Francis Walter of Pennsylvania (co-sponsor of the McCarran-Walter Act) submitted private bills admitting barely 350 Japanese and American-Japanese children for adoption.[32] In addition to the grasp of civics required of a serviceman, his relatives, or interested families to initiate and monitor the process, some members of Congress vigorously opposed the tactic. In the spring of 1947 arch-segregationist Representative John Rankin of Mississippi, responding to rumors that 5,000 British brown babies (half the purported total) would be shipped to the United States, took to the floor of the House to condemn the entry of "a lot of illegitimate half-breed colored children from England." They were, he sneered, "the off-spring of the scum of the British Isles," likely having inherited "the vices of both races and the virtues of neither."[33]

Four years later Rankin protested consideration of a private bill to admit an American-Japanese orphan adopted by a couple stationed in Japan. "It is about time we put a stop to flooding our country with foreigners in this way," he thundered. Admittedly unaware of the specifics of the case, Rankin insisted that by "going beyond the quota limit and bringing in these people, this country is being literally flooded with un-American elements, a vast number of whom are today undermining and trying to wreck this Government and to destroy the American way of life." When a colleague patiently explained that the child was only three years old, hardly of an age to take part in subversive activities, Rankin held fast: "They always have some kind of excuse for going around the immigration law and bringing these people in." Two weeks later, after an outpouring of censure and ridicule, Rankin relented. However, he gave notice of his continued vigilance over "infiltration" by such "riff-raff": "I am going to watch all these cases from now on and try to stop the flood of undesirable aliens who are now being admitted into this country, many of whom have wormed their way onto the Federal payroll." The dispute was one of several developments that, particularly in the months to come, gave pause to those favoring the adoption of Afro-Asian children.[34]

———

A series of events in 1952 and 1953 largely determined the children's future. The miniscule quotas for Asian immigration imposed by the McCarran-Walter Act seemed to preclude mass adoption. Among the Japanese, the end of the occupation enabled them to vent their pent-up frustrations. The peace treaty's terms, which ensured that American bases and military personnel would remain on the archipelago indefinitely, generated considerable irritation and anger often sublimated into hostility toward biracial, and especially Afro-Asian, children. In South Korea, the end to active combat increased fraternization between GIs and Korean women, while geopolitical considerations and a shaky armistice guaranteed the American military's long-term presence. In both nations it became clear that as hosts to U.S. servicemen they would bear the brunt of responsibility for mixed-race offspring. However, black–Korean children appeared in substantial numbers after the African American media had begun to lose interest in the status of Afro-Asians overseas. They were also more likely than their Japanese counterparts to be confined to the shadows of the innumerable camptowns ringing American bases. Meanwhile, African Americans' domestic priorities and the uneven racial logic of the Cold War crippled the case for Afro-Asian adoption.

One of the first undertakings of the post-occupation Japanese government was to conduct a formal census of American-Japanese children, precisely what SCAP had long prohibited. On the eve of the April 1952 transfer of sovereignty, Tokyo's *Yomiuri* newspaper, the nation's largest, claimed that American servicemen had fathered 200,000 offspring, a wildly exaggerated figure that nonetheless captured the imagination of readers and much of the Japanese media.[35] Part of the problem in acquiring an accurate count was that after years of near anonymity these children and their mothers were difficult to track down; another was their dispersal throughout the home islands, notwithstanding the large number concentrated in the Toyo-Yokohama area.[36] The Japanese Children's Bureau completed the first official census that spring, with a final tally of 5,002 biracial children (in August the Ministry of Welfare produced a similar result). That figure, although likely an undercount, was considerably more accurate than others, and it increased steadily as the American military presence endured, an outcome the Japanese bitterly anticipated. "The number of half-breeds will be on the increase," complained the *Tokyo Times* in 1952, "in view of the stationing of United States forces in Japan for a relatively prolonged period."[37]

In the more frank post-occupation atmosphere, public attention immediately turned to the fate of GI babies, particularly those of African American ancestry. One debate, appearing in the pages of the academic monthly *Jidō shinri* (roughly "child psychology"), featured uncommon criticism of proposals to transfer black–Japanese children to the United States. According a chronicler of the discussion, one participant argued that "once sent 'back' to the United States, [they] would very likely be absorbed into black society, remaining forever segregated from white society and persecuted by it. Since Japanese people are also colored, . . .

the Japanese might have a better chance of successfully merging these half-black children into the mainstream."[38] Conversely, *Jet* magazine reported that the same influential Japanese newspaper promoting the figure of 200,000 GI babies—one third of them allegedly fathered by black servicemen—was urging "that these waifs 'with blue eyes or black faces' be sent to the U.S." The paper insisted that since "America is a melting pot of races . . . these orphans would not be as forlorn there as here in Japan."[39]

The latter argument proved more convincing, since few Japanese were willing to forgo a commitment to ethno-racial homogeneity. One representative human-interest piece emphasized biological obstacles to mainstream society's absorption of Afro-Asian offspring. Its author, a Japanese professor, began by pondering why the children's mothers—"almost exclusively 'women of the streets' "—had been attracted to black servicemen. The problem lay in their confusion of African Americans with the admirable qualities of American life: "Suppose those negro soldiers . . . had come direct from their original home, Africa, without the background and support of American culture, would they have appealed to the Japanese girls . . . ? Certainly not." These "untutored, unschooled, unfortunate girls of postwar Japan" had mistakenly "taken it for granted" that since black soldiers wore American uniforms "they are not much worse than the white ones." The author shuddered at the demographic implications of "the black blood [that] now runs in the veins of some children." The number of these individuals, he predicted, "though very small at present, is bound to follow the Malthusian law. What would happen in one hundred, two hundred, five hundred years? God knows."[40] Such popular alarm received the imprimatur of official Japanese science in 1954, when the Ministry of Welfare's Institute of Population Problems released a report confirming the view that racial intermarriage produced intellectually deficient offspring.[41]

Nineteen fifties Japanese popular culture also made it more likely that Afro-Asian children would be relegated to the margins of society. On the one hand, evolving terminology for biracial individuals appeared to signal a more tolerant attitude. The occupation-era expression *ainoko* ("a child of sex") was considered derogatory and could be applied to both humans and animals, evoking notions of impurity, illegitimacy, and destitution. It was gradually replaced by the more neutral *konketsuji* ("mixed-blood child"), although the "problem of the konketsuji"—their unwelcome and allegedly disreputable existence—was routinely cited as evidence of the social problems caused by the American military presence. On the other hand, new cultural products reinforced perceptions of black peoples as residing beyond the boundaries of national inclusion. SCAP played a supporting role in this development. In early 1952 officials at occupation-sponsored Civil Information and Education Libraries prominently advertised the acquisition of *The Story of Little Black Sambo*, much to the consternation of African American observers.[42] Helen Bannerman's book, introduced to Japan decades earlier, captured enormous attention the following year, when a Japanese publisher released a wildly popular version "complete with 'pickaninny' illustrations."[43] Its caricatures meshed well with the popular epithet *kuronbo* ("a black one"), a belittling and derogatory term whose diminutive suffix connotes childishness.[44]

Post-occupation Japan therefore appeared a particularly inhospitable environment for the black-Japanese. Even former SCAP officials voiced concern. As a onetime Chief of Labor Education pleaded in 1953, "If any of the mixed-blood children of the Occupation should be adopted it is these Negro-Japanese mixed-blood children—and as rapidly as possible before they are scarred too deeply by racial exclusion." He urged that they be endowed with "special American citizenship" and placed "in selected areas" of the United States, since in Japan "they seem to be marked for bias and discrimination." The children could thereby reach adulthood "inside a multi-lingual, multi-cultural, multi-national"—and thus presumably more welcoming—society. "While America is no Heaven for obviously Negro children," he concluded, "I am sure their fate will be happier."[45]

Miki Sawada agreed. She had endured numerous threatening protests against her efforts on behalf of American-Japanese children. Thugs stoned Sawada and an employee as they walked through town one evening, and an outraged schoolmaster burst into the Saunders Home to deliver a tirade of abuse, accusing Sawada of "shamelessly contributing to the delinquency of his students."[46] When seventeen Saunders children (including three black-Japanese) reached school age in the spring of 1952, a public outcry effectively prevented their entry into the local school system.[47] The following autumn, after an initial rebuff from American officials, Sawada set out for a three-month fund-raising and lobbying tour of the United States. During her planning she emphasized outreach to the African American community, and arranged meetings with such prominent black figures as Rev. Mordecai Johnson, the president of Howard University.[48] The tour cemented her carefully cultivated image as the representative at large for the interests of American-Japanese and Afro-Asian children.[49] However, she was notably unsuccessful in a more tangible pursuit: immigration officials denied her request to bring along ten black-Japanese youngsters for adoption.[50]

In a letter of introduction to the NAACP's Walter White, written on the eve of her arrival, Sawada revealed much about her intentions and prejudices. She began by calling for "definite action" on behalf of children "abandoned by their irresponsible parents." Sawada hoped to raise funds for technical-education scholarships and to secure an expansion of the immigration quota for Japan, then set at 185 per year. Not only had the convoluted overseas adoption procedures severely limited the number of Saunders Home children placed with American families, but the "public attitude in Japan has changed toward these children from the very day the Occupation ended. People who had awakened to the fact that they had mistaken degenerated morals for democracy do not hesitate to give vent to their feelings by turning their wrath on these unfortunate children," whose number Sawada now placed at over 100,000. She also enclosed transcripts from her Japanese radio speeches, in which she described "miserable half-breed children," "born of sin, of ignorance, of carelessness" and "a nuisance to the whole world." As for the "chocolate-colored infant"—"never before known in Japanese history"—its birth had been a "hair-raising sight." Sawada further warned her Japanese audiences that such mixed-race individuals were criminally inclined. The only viable course of action was to segregate the children from Japanese society and to send them elsewhere as soon as possible.[51]

In most respects Sawada's American tour was a failure. Despite receiving donations and publicity, she was unable to surmount "the hard wall of the Immigration Laws," as she complained in a letter to African American Congressman William L. Dawson of Illinois. Non-military couples and American orphanages remained legally prohibited from accepting American-Japanese children, despite the willingness of several to care for them.[52] "Would it not be possible," she suggested to the NAACP's Roy Wilkins, to draft legislation "naming eight or ten children from my orphanage—instead of just one baby, thus hastening their entry? Would it not be possible to have a separate quota for children born during the OCCUPATION?"[53] Sawada also failed in her attempt to enlist the United Nations in her cause, since, as *Jet* magazine reported, "The UN says such illegitimate babies were left by armies all over the world and there is no reason to make a special case . . . of the problems of Japanese-American babies." Nonetheless, upon her return to Japan Sawada voiced cautious optimism that the incoming Eisenhower administration might relax immigration restrictions. Legislative action was all the more pressing because the United States clearly intended to maintain a sizable number of troops in Japan. As Sawada reminded Roy Wilkins in late 1952, enormous new American airbases were depriving many Japanese farmers of their livelihoods: "These farmers are unfit to earn their living by another trade. Now they have learned it is far more lucrative to send their daughters away to these airbases. . . . This means the babies still continue to come."[54]

The following summer Congress, reacting in part to Soviet propaganda denouncing American intervention in Korea, enacted the Admission of Orphans Adopted by United States Citizens and Refugee Relief Acts. Together they authorized nonquota immigrant visas for up to 4,000 "orphans," children under the age of ten deserted by one or both parents or surrendered for adoption (they need not officially have been declared refugees). Unlike previous acts, these authorized adoption beyond the confines of Europe and appeared to supersede the private-bill system. However, 4,000 was a miniscule figure considering the total number of adoptable children—fathered by servicemen or not—living within the bounds of the American military's far-flung reach. Nine months later American families had adopted only 300 GI babies from Japan. Not until 1957 did amendments to the Immigration and Nationality Act authorize unlimited entry for alien orphans adopted by American citizens through June 1959, at which point the provisions were renewed for another year.[55] The unprecedented availability of these children set off an East Asian adoption boom. These congressional acts "permanently shifted the primary countries of origin from Europe to Asia"; by 1963 Americans had adopted nearly 9,000 Asian children, the majority of them from war-torn South Korea.[56]

This surge in popularity centered on Korean War orphans (in the literal sense of the term), and considerably less on American-Korean, American-Japanese, or, very rarely, Afro-Asian children.[57] White Americans exhibited virtually no interest in adopting Afro-Asians, and African Americans had become much less responsive to appeals for their help. *Ebony* reported in 1955 that 300 Korean brown babies, "offspring of Oriental-Negro romances that flowed between battles and faded with the first hint of an armistice," had recently been cleared for adoption. "Not only would the youngsters benefit enormously by coming to the

U.S.," the author remarked, "but, in the words of a Foreign Service aide in Korea, their adoption 'would effectively counteract any drop in America's prestige in this part of the world.'"[58] The anemic use of strategic considerations is noteworthy. Despite the occasional reference to American "prestige" in Asia by those discussing Afro-Asian adoption, Cold War logic did not require assuming responsibility for children fathered by nonwhite Americans. That same year, an official in charge of East Asia for the Refugee Relief Program wrote to Walter White to discuss the growing number of GI babies. There were hundreds, perhaps thousands in South Korea, where, he claimed, "racial discrimination is said to be more pronounced than anywhere else in the world. About fifty percent of the children are negroid [sic] and it has been extremely difficult to find [them] American homes." Like the Foreign Service aide quoted in *Ebony*, the author added a lackluster appeal to Cold War concerns: "Apart from the very pressing need of the children . . . , immeasurable goodwill would be generated throughout Free Asia." Given white Americans' lack of interest in adopting black-Koreans, the author suggested (as he had during a conversation with Congressman Adam Clayton Powell, Jr., of Harlem) that the NAACP make use of its contacts in African American communities across the country to publicize the children's availability for adoption.[59] Three years later famed author Pearl Buck, who had recently adopted a black-Japanese girl, took to the pages of *Ebony* to bemoan the fact that "half-Negro children will have the most difficult time" in South Korea and Japan, since the "evil of prejudice has drifted across the seas, or was there already." "We need many more Negro families, willing and eager to adopt them," she pleaded, in an attempt "to awaken the hearts" of black readers.[60]

These increasingly urgent appeals for help reflected the fact that by the mid-to-late 1950s most African Americans had lost interest in the East Asian brown baby crisis. In addition to the economic obstacles to international adoption, the fading media coverage of Afro-Asian offspring, and the lack of a direct connection between their predicament and American credibility abroad, a vigorous campaign had emerged to encourage domestic black adoption. It began at precisely the moment Sawada initiated her awareness-raising offensive and the Refugee Relief Act inspired sporadic hopes for a massive babylift. Some African Americans had by then become exasperated with appeals for their assistance (and, perhaps, with Asian peoples' emphasis on maintaining their supposed racial purity). One New York woman wrote to the *Pittsburgh Courier* in late 1952 to air her displeasure: "I am thoroughly disgusted with Negro publication[s] continually wailing over the plight of 'brown babies' in . . . Japan. Aren't we tired of other races making ours the dumping ground of the world?" That same year the *Chicago Defender* ran a four-part series championing the adoption of African American orphans. Its inaugural story quoted a social worker who estimated there were between 30,000 and 50,000 black children in need of permanent homes. A photo caption in the final installment explained that the father shown had served in Japan and Korea before adopting an African American child in Chicago. *Ebony* joined the campaign with an article entitled "Why Negroes Don't Adopt Children," in which the author lamented the fact that "only 3,000 Negro babies (only 4 per cent of the total U.S. adoptions) are adopted each year." The Urban League also took up the cause, making domestic black adoption a priority from 1953 to 1958. The Executive Director of the League's Pittsburgh branch tackled the imbalance between an abundance of black orphans and the relatively small number of financially qualified black applicants. He remarked, with more than a hint of resentment, that the "concept of an 'over-supply' of Negro children" was true only to the extent that black couples were considered the sole appropriate adopters of black orphans. "It is an interesting commentary on prevailing American attitudes on race that white families are able to adopt across international racial lines, for example the fairly widespread adoption of Korean war orphans," he observed, "but it is not yet possible to give serious or widespread consideration to domestic interracial adoption." By the late 1950s and early 1960s, with black interest in international adoption having largely dissipated, the first generation of Afro-Asian children reached the age at which they became inadmissible as orphans under American law.[61]

As a result, they confronted an adolescence and early adulthood marked by harassment and discrimination in Asia. South Korean orphanages generally refused to care for mixed-race children. A mother's assumed, prior, or ongoing work as a "prostitute engaged with American soldiers" (*yang saeksi*) enhanced the stigma attached to her children. Most black-Koreans grew up and congregated in the camptowns that flourished alongside American bases, hidden in plain sight. A study of 1,300 American-Korean adolescents and young adults found "a great deal of pimping and blackmarketeering among the Amerasians, especially around the military compounds, and many of the youths make their living this way." The daughters of a Korean War–era prostitute and two black servicemen, for example, became prostitutes themselves at an early age. Although indistinguishable from their fellow Koreans in speech, customs, and habits, they rarely ventured beyond the camptown in which they worked and lived. In Japan, by contrast, the number of prostitutes catering to U.S. troops declined steadily as the nation rebounded economically, and few American-Japanese individuals became commercial sex workers. Nonetheless, they too endured discrimination in education and employment, often relegated to menial work at low wages on or near American bases. The Japanese media portrayed their lives as disreputable, if not sordid. Mainstream society treated the black-Japanese as pariahs, close to the hereditary *eta* ("full of filth") caste, and, like survivors of the atomic bomb, ritually polluted.[62]

With most Asian communities overtly hostile and Americans seemingly indifferent, those charged with providing for Afro-Asian children and adolescents hit upon emigration elsewhere. The South Korean government established diplomatic relations with several South American nations, forging agreements in the hopes of establishing expatriate agricultural communities. No records exist of the number of black-Koreans able to take advantage of these opportunities, but given their urban backgrounds and educational disadvantages few would have met host nations' requirements that applicants be proficient in agriculture, mechanics, or engineering. For this reason one church-based social worker proposed a program "to recruit the physically fit young Amerasians into the U.S. Army and then channel them . . . into full [American] citizenship." The idea was both ironic, given these individuals' parentage, and perceptive, considering the long-standing ties between military service and claims on citizenship in the United States.[63]

In Japan, proposals to send GI children to South America were more substantive, in part because of the government's long-standing practice, dating to the turn of the century, of facilitating migration there.[64] (The selection of South America as a site for mixed-race resettlement may also have stemmed from the tendency, beginning in the early 1930s, to dismiss migrants to the region as "human discards" [*kimin*].)[65] As early as 1952, the Japanese media circulated rumors of a move to send groups of occupation children to Brazil for adoption by Japanese farmers. More than a decade later Miki Sawada pioneered a quixotic scheme to hack a pepper plantation out of the Amazon basin for American-Japanese emigrant laborers.[66] When the unrealistic project failed—among other things the Brazilian government, for reasons unclear, denied the black-Japanese entry—African American observers scoffed. One derisively remarked: "Looking for an easy solution, the Japanese seized upon immigration as the perfect panacea for its mixed-blood problem. . . . But that myth exploded this summer when Mrs. Sawada was turned down after three attempts to send part-Negro boys there." Allowing that neither Japan nor the United States had welcomed Afro-Asian children with open arms, the author insisted the Japanese bore the weight of liability: "The first responsibility and the lasting solution lie with Japan where the problem started; where the problem is. Not with . . . the United States, for the mores of these young adults are set; their language, culture and habits are Oriental."[67]

By the late 1960s several thousand Afro-Asian children, teenagers, and young adults clung to a precarious existence overseas.[68] Despite ongoing discrimination, poverty, and neglect, a handful enjoyed brief moments of celebrity. Notably, their success occurred most often in entertainment and athletics, fields traditionally providing occupational outlets for minorities in the United States. Biracial Koreans became closely linked in the public imagination with an inborn talent for music and acting. Nonetheless, most black-Koreans, male and female, remained ensnared by the vice economies that surrounded American military installations, catering to another generation of servicemen. Within these camptowns, mixed-race young adults divided along Western racial lines, with black-Korean women relegated to the bottom of the prostitution industry. Japan too witnessed a "mixed-blood boom" (*konketsuji bumu*), limited to a few fortunate individuals. The abandoned daughter of an African American military policeman, for example, excelled in high school track and field and aspired to represent Japan at the Olympics. The vast majority of black-Japanese, however, lived as members of a disdained class on the fringes of respectable society.[69]

As the United States intensified its war in Vietnam, the black press revisited Japan's mistreatment of its black-Japanese citizens. For instance, *Ebony*'s September 1967 cover story, "Japan's Rejected," contained a litany of criticisms similar to those voiced by African American observers fifteen years earlier. It began with the story of nineteen-year-old Kayoko, a black-Japanese domestic working in the home of an African American serviceman and his wife. The couple had once considered adopting Kayoko, but her age disqualified her from "orphan" status, while a lack of education and limited occupational skills rendered her an unlikely candidate for immigration. As "social outcasts that no Japanese will wed [and] that few [Japanese] employers will hire," individuals like Kayoko were "fighting a hopeless battle in a hostile world." Japan remained "a racially monolithic nation; its people a closed society" that clung to an "attitude of race and class superiority." Indeed, the country was one in which life itself was unappreciated: "In Japan, where abortion is both cheap and legal, where disgrace is worse than death, countless thousands of [American-Japanese] infants were murdered during the occupation." Those Afro-Asians who managed to survive suffered "the curse of being labeled *kuronbo* (nigger) and *hitokui kinshu* (cannibal), as well as 'Yank.'" "Aliens on both sides of the Pacific," the author concluded, they faced "an adulthood that is a dead-end street."[70]

Black readers were appalled. The director of an adoption program for American-Korean children and Korean orphans sought to exploit the African American backlash, agreeing that most black-Japanese were "already hurt to a cruel degree," while "many younger children . . . can be helped in Korea . . . [and] learn 'love' instead of 'rejection.'" One African American reader, who recalled "a series of recent articles in newspapers and magazines nationally extolling the virtues of the Japanese," commended *Ebony* for showing "the second side of the coin. It's not very pleasant!" He called for a letter-writing campaign to Japanese diplomatic personnel, along with threats of economic retaliation. "Japan is seeking dollars to bolster its economy and its foreign exchange," he observed, while "black people here in America especially are consumers on a grand scale of things Japanese." The mere "hint of a boycott of Japanese merchandise in the U.S. similar to the Jewish boycott of German goods in the 1930s," he reasoned, "could help re-mold the attitude of the Japanese toward these children who through no fault of their own are victims of prejudice."[71] Strong emotions were easily rekindled fifteen years after the occupation came to a close.

In the quarter century following the landing of the first black occupationaire, African Americans reacted to the growing number of Afro-Asian individuals and their difficulties abroad with two strikingly different responses: anger at America's Asian subjects and allies, which resurfaced in the late 1960s; and an intervening period of disinterest, which helped obscure a major human toll of America's indefinite military presence in the region. By the time black attention returned to the Afro-Asians, not only were the young adults ineligible for adoption, but most African

Americans now viewed the care of abandoned children of black military personnel in Asia as an essentially Asian concern, rather than one that demanded international cooperation. The Japanese had from the start received greater African American scrutiny and censure, in part because of the smaller and less visible group of black-Korean children. This imbalance was also the result of a different focus among black servicemen, the African American press, and their stateside audiences in the early 1950s. Rather than emphasize romantic relations with Korean women or the misfortunes of biracial Korean offspring, they instead foregrounded the role of black GIs in a military conflict pitting them against Asian men, women, and, on occasion, children. Black soldiers and civilians vigorously debated the racial politics of war on the Korean peninsula, where for the first time in half a century African Americans directly participated in the mass slaughter of an Asian adversary.

Chapter 5

The Race of Combat in Korea

"Today France is using the black Senegalese to conquer Viet-Nam, and Britain has used troops of every race and hue to hold the remains of her empire," charged W. E. B. Du Bois in 1952. "Perhaps worst of all today is the use of American Negro troops in Korea." The effect on African Americans—"almost forced to be the dumb tools of business corporations" coveting Asia and "in a sense compelled to murder colored folk who suffer from the same race prejudice"—would inevitably exacerbate black–white enmity at home. Most lamentably, the war was "bound to leave a legacy of hate between yellow nations and black."[1] Du Bois's allegations were wide of the mark on two counts. First, the initial proximity of black troops to Korea was the result of no economic conspiracy. African Americans' keen interest in military service and policymakers' desire to keep them out of postwar Europe channeled black soldiers to Japan and, from there, to a war that caught the United States off guard. Second, American intervention on the Korean peninsula generated neither widespread black protest nor an appreciable uptick in black–white conflict at home. Du Bois's suggestion of a Korean legacy of Afro-Asian antagonism, however, was prophetic. Intervention in Korea—where black soldiers clashed wholesale with Asians for the first time since the turn-of-the-century Filipino insurrection—aggravated the racial tensions festering within America's East Asian military empire and brought the question of Afro-Asian cooperation or conflict to a head.[2]

African Americans at home and abroad passionately argued over the racial politics in play in the conflict, many of whose features foreshadowed subsequent American wars. Was Korea, as several prominent activists claimed, a race war pitting a "white," imperialist United States against fellow people of color? Did the presence of large numbers of black troops negate these allegations? Cold War propaganda and domestic suppression of dissent certainly contributed to an acceptance of American intervention, but many African Americans sincerely believed in the necessity of military action against what appeared flagrant communist aggression. Even more important were characterizations of Korea and its people by black servicemen and the correspondents who covered them, characterizations that took shape before army integration commenced in earnest in the spring of 1951. During the conflict's first months, black journalists and other observers spent considerable time introducing those at home to life on a peninsula unfamiliar to most Americans. Their preoccupations with alleged Asian cruelty, Korean poverty, and South Korean fecklessness on the battlefield did much to alienate a home-front audience from enemy and ally alike.

By the time an armistice was signed, more than 25,000 black soldiers were stationed in Korea, 15 percent of the army's strength there.[3] Over the previous three years, some 600,000 African Americans had served in all branches of the military.[4] Caught in the midst of a brutal civil war turned international conflict, where the lines separating friend from foe and combatant from civilian were porous, most black soldiers were quick to view all Koreans with suspicion and contempt. American counterinsurgency tactics, along with an apparent South Korean apathy toward, if not clandestine collaboration with, their ostensible opponents, exacerbated servicemen's distrust of Koreans. Among troops on the ground, the military's embrace of firepower to counter a North Korean and Chinese manpower advantage fostered a dehumanization not only of the enemy but of the United States' Asian allies. Altogether, black military service in Korea further encouraged African Americans to hold racialized attitudes toward Asian peoples, while increasing their support both for the war and for their nation's growing military empire in Asia.

———

In the predawn hours of June 25, 1950, 135,000 troops of the Korean People's Army (KPA) attacked South Korea across the 38th parallel, the arbitrary border agreed upon by the United States and the Soviet Union at the conclusion of World War II.[5] Many of the KPA's soldiers and officers were veterans of the Chinese Civil War, having helped defeat Chiang Kai-shek's Nationalists. There were <u>482 American military advisers</u> in the Republic of Korea (ROK) at the time, remnants of an occupation that had arranged separate elections in the South, trained and armed the South Korean military, and assisted President Syngman Rhee (an authoritarian anticommunist educated in the United States) as he suppressed a popular left-leaning nationalist movement. The KPA, fighting a smaller, ill-equipped, and poorly motivated South Korean army, took the southern capital of Seoul in seventy-two hours. It appeared poised to conquer all of South Korea in a matter of weeks.[6]

Within days the Truman administration chose to intervene. Unwilling to seek a congressional declaration of war, it obtained United Nations Security Council sanction for military assistance to South Korea and then persuaded Britain and France to introduce a resolution establishing a unified military command (the Soviet Union was temporarily boycotting the world body over its refusal to seat the People's Republic of China). This command, ostensibly subject to UN authority and operating under the UN flag, was in effect an American enterprise.[7] Under the generalship of Douglas MacArthur, it consisted of military units from only sixteen of the UN's sixty member nations, and the United States provided most troops on the ground. Excepting the Republic of Korea, the American military commitment was ten times that of all other coalition members combined.[8]

The United States' overwhelming commitment to the war did not, however, guarantee that sacrifice fell equally upon all Americans. This was a "limited war," a "police action" as President Truman inopportunely characterized it. The first Americans to arrive on the peninsula, including those of the all-black 24th Infantry Regiment, came directly from occupation duty in Japan. As of July 1, 1950, there were more than 80,000 enlisted army men serving as occupationaires; one month later that figure had plunged to 45,000, roughly equal in number to those then fighting in Korea. As soldiers from the United States entered the Korean pipeline, Japan became the American staging area for the war, and the number of occupation personnel rebounded. <u>One year later</u> the <u>totals for the army in Korea</u> and Japan <u>were 215,000 and 100,000, respectively, numbers that held steady for much of the war.</u> Mobilization of the re- *working-class ?* serves <u>began less than a month into the conflict</u>, at first <u>voluntarily</u> but by early August on <u>a compulsory basis</u>, as the need for bodies outpaced

the number of volunteers. Truman authorized the armed forces to operate the machinery of Selective Service for whatever level of manpower
might prove necessary. In five months the army doubled in size; by June
1951 it had swollen to 1.6 million men.[9]

The introduction of the draft notwithstanding, those assigned to fight
were remarkably homogeneous in demographic background. Korea was
primarily a working-class war. College-student deferments remained
available throughout the conflict. Soldiers on the ground were relatively
young and poorly educated, particularly after the war's first year when
recalled veterans of World War II rotated home. Few were over twenty-
one years of age; less than a third had high school diplomas. Reporter
Edward R. Murrow joined a growing chorus branding Korea a "poor
man's war" when he charged in the spring of 1951 that American draft
policies favored an "intellectual elite." Former Assistant Secretary of
Defense John Hannah later conceded that too often "the son of the well-
to-do family goes to college and the sons of some of the rest go to Korea." The issue became so contentious that a pair of Illinois draft board
members resigned in protest of a deferment policy they deemed "un-
American" and a form of "class discrimination." Such claims received
quantitative backing shortly after the war. The "number of Detroiters
who died, were captured, or were reported missing in Korea," two social
scientists observed, "varied directly with the relative economic or racial
standing of the city areas from which the men stemmed."[10]

Whatever their deprivations relative to other Americans, these soldiers enjoyed comfortable wealth compared to the Korean civilians they
encountered. The city of Pusan, on the southeastern coast, became the
primary entry point for American servicemen. Before the war it was a
bustling port city of 400,000 inhabitants. An influx of refugees caused its
population to swell to three times that number in a matter of weeks.
Homeless and impoverished, they constructed sprawling shanty towns
on the city's outskirts, in which some lived ten or more to a room without
running water. Cooking took place outside, often adjacent to a commu-
nal privy. Where no facilities existed, they had no choice but to relieve
themselves in stagnant, vermin-infested gutters. The war, in effect, had
transformed Pusan into an enormous slum. One black correspondent
deemed the city a "cesspool" due to its odor and "human depravity."
American personnel claimed they smelled Pusan from miles out at sea,
well before it came into view. Once they set foot on the docks the combined sensory effect could be overwhelming. An African American

serviceman later recalled witnessing "fathers with their daughters . . . using them to get food. . . . I'd never seen a person kill . . . or go down in a garbage pit for food." Although he and his family and friends were by no means wealthy, "we didn't have to do that. We still had our morals."[11]

Adding to the disorienting juxtaposition of foreign poverty and American abundance, the military continued to emphasize personal consumption among soldiers, even in the midst of a war that U.S. forces appeared at first to be losing. As in Japan, commanders sought to maintain morale through appeals to material self-interest. Less than two months into the conflict the army opened its first Korean post exchange. The three-story facility in Pusan, formerly occupied by South Korean military police, was dedicated with an official ribbon-cutting ceremony. Its stock of food, reading material, toiletries, and other personal items, explained a soldier-journalist, expanded daily. Throughout the war, in response to ongoing concerns about troop motivation, commanders assigned combat units their own mobile PXs, which lugged tax-free goods from one battle to the next.[12]

As the first wave of Americans moved north to meet the new enemy, their optimism was sorely tested. The weather was sweltering, the hottest Korean summer in memory. Lacking a steady supply of clean water, some GIs resorted to drinking from rice paddies fertilized with human excrement. The resulting intestinal ailments exacted an alarming toll. Especially troubling was the performance of America's South Korean allies. The ROK army of 100,000 disintegrated to less than 20,000 after the fall of Seoul, as soldiers deserted or simply dropped their weapons and surrendered. American servicemen moving up the peninsula encountered streams of South Korean troops headed in the opposite direction, some in appropriated American vehicles. The result was an abiding bitterness among officers and enlisted men who believed they were fighting and dying for a people too cowardly—or too disloyal—to do the same.[13]

Partly in response to the ROK army's disappointing performance, MacArthur in August ordered field commanders to integrate South Koreans into their units. (The policy was announced much to the disgust of African Americans well aware of ongoing military segregation; the *Pittsburgh Courier* declared it an "insult" to every black citizen.) By war's end more than 20,000 ROK troops were serving in American combat units. Despite reports that South Korean replacements would "in general do everything the GIs do and [be] treated identically," in practice they were exempt from kitchen police duties and not required to go out on often dangerous patrols, angering many American servicemen. The South Korean government also established a paramilitary service corps to provide laborers for each unit on the front lines. Its members, known to their GI overseers as "chogie bearers," were routinely forced to carry punishing supply loads. Where these laborers could not be found, American troops simply dragooned able-bodied Korean civilians to serve as porters.[14]

Despite its members' disdain for both South and North Korean martial prowess, the outgunned and outmanned American military quickly found itself fleeing headlong down the peninsula. Its actions during the war's first three months consisted of, in one observer's estimation, "frantic retreat amid savagery." The civil and revolutionary nature of the conflict and the North's use of guerrilla tactics helped ensure it would be a very dirty war. So too did the American decision to reintroduce its World War II policy of destroying civilian targets to prevent their real or potential use by the enemy. GIs routinely encountered peasants, women and children included, "retreating" along their flanks as if refugees, only to bring down withering fire on American positions with weapons concealed beneath their clothing. Local partisans organized roadblocks and ambushes to entrap withdrawing UN forces. The KPA "fought a total war, using every resource to turn Korean weakness into strength," notes the preeminent historian of the conflict. "Sometimes this meant using little kids to ferry ammunition; sometimes it meant driving weeping refugees into American lines to cover an infantry assault." American forces retaliated by burning suspect villages to the ground. Larger communities believed to harbor leftist elements were forcibly evacuated, their populations driven south at gunpoint.[15]

Among American servicemen, confusion, anger, and resentment registered through disparaging characterizations of Korea and its people. Many bitterly complained of the nation's underdevelopment. "I'll fight for my country," remarked one corporal from Chicago, "but I'll be damned if I see why I'm fighting to save this hell hole."[16] Use of the term "gook" was ubiquitous from the start. The epithet has a lengthy pedigree in the history of American interventions in Asia and the Pacific. A linguistic cousin of "goo-goos," which was employed by servicemen to refer to Filipino insurgents at the turn of the century, it emerged in its current form in Korea.[17] One journalist reported that if American troops remarked upon "a dead Korean body of whatever sex, uniformed or ununiformed, it was simply 'dead Gook' or 'good Gook.'" Indiscriminate use of such racial slurs, noted another, was problematic at a time when UN forces were engaged in "a combination of war and revolution" that required securing the sympathies of the populace. MacArthur's Tokyo headquarters issued a circular that compared servicemen using the term to "the small minority of Americans" who uttered racial epithets at home, both groups "unwittingly guilty of 'Giving aid and comfort to the enemy.'" Such admonitions, reiterated throughout the war and after, had little effect.[18]

With UN forces pushed to a defensive perimeter in Korea's extreme southeast awaiting reinforcements, American military commanders opted to rely on air power, generating tremendous casualties.[19] Napalm became a weapon of choice. A jellied mixture designed to burn into the skin for hours, it first saw use toward the end of World War II. In Korea, one American chemical officer enthused, "napalm mix has really come into its own." Pilots, several of them African American, began dropping enormous quantities on targets across Korea, executing a policy in effect throughout the war. In three months of fighting, the United States expended nearly eight million gallons of napalm, in addition to 97,000 tons of conventional explosives. The following March an officer blithely explained that on an "average good day" American forces used more than 60,000 gallons both as an anti-tank weapon and against "enemy personnel."[20] Few pilots expressed unease with their assignments, in part because every Korean seemed a potential combatant.[21] Napalm was also quite popular with troops on the ground. Black combat engineer Robert Chappel later explained that seeing American jets make daily napalm strikes was almost like "watching a football game": "Every afternoon . . . our jets would come in and hit those valleys. And we'd watch . . . and rave and clap our hands. . . . It [was] just a thrill to see American planes come in . . . and hit those hills and that fire just roll." The Korean people, of course, had misgivings. In late 1952, the National Christian Council of Korea pleaded in vain that to protect civilians—and "from the religious standpoint"—the American military's indiscriminate use of napalm be "reconsidered."[22] All told, in three years the United States dropped more than 30,000 tons of napalm on a peninsula about the size of Minnesota.[23]

Following an amphibious landing behind enemy lines in mid-September 1950, UN forces broke out of their defensive positions and advanced on Seoul, destroying much of what remained standing along the way. "The war was fought without regard for the South Koreans," observed a contemporary British military almanac, "and their unfortunate country was regarded as an arena rather than a country to be liberated." American soldiers, reclaiming a South Korean city, belted out an irreverent tune: "The last time we saw Taejon, it was not bright or gay, / Now we're going back to Taejon, to blow the goddam place away!" Troops encountering the slightest resistance during the push north called in planes, tanks, and artillery to blot out entire villages before moving in to liberate them. In late September Seoul endured the same treatment, despite American promises to the contrary. "The coolness of the welcome received by the liberators," explained a dispatch from the city, "is understandable in the light of the millions of dollars worth of damage" (not to mention the loss of civilian life).[24] The war for the South was all but over, at a cost of 20,000 American casualties: approximately 3,000 dead; nearly 14,000 wounded; and 3,877 missing in action. The KPA lost perhaps 70,000 troops. The statistics for South Korea were staggering: 110,000 soldiers and civilians killed; 106,000 wounded; 57,000 missing; 314,000 homes destroyed; and 244,000 damaged.[25]

Flush with victory, MacArthur and the Truman administration made a fateful decision: American forces would invade North Korea, despite Chinese warnings that it considered any drive to its border a hostile act. The goal was to unify the peninsula under a government friendly to the United States, a move that, if accomplished quickly enough, would render moot any UN inclination to restore the *status quo ante*. Thus did the United States make its first attempt at Cold War "rollback" (as opposed to mere containment). In early October, American troops crossed into North Korea and made a dash for the border with China. The apparent disintegration of the KPA seemed to promise an end to the war by Christmas. All of Korea appeared in reach. Then came the crash. In late 1950 a partially reconstituted KPA, plus several hundred thousand members of a new Chinese People's Volunteer Army, surprised and proceeded to rout the UN coalition. A despondent Secretary of State Dean Acheson called it the "worst defeat of U.S. forces since Bull Run."[26]

With the United States forced into a second embarrassing retreat, officers and enlisted men responded with stepped-up attacks on Korea and its people. Enemy tactics again contributed to the destruction. In addition to hiding among the wandering columns of refugees, North Korean and Chinese troops occupied isolated villages far behind the front lines—after herding the inhabitants into the surrounding hills—and set up ambushes. Wary American commanders responded by ordering the obliteration of several ostensibly "friendly" villages, producing yet more refugees.

Many soldiers, already distrustful of their Korean allies, blamed the "gooks" for the humiliating sight of a military that had defeated Imperial Japan being routed by a peasant-based and presumably inferior force. The country's meager infrastructure became one object of their resentment. Troops used the windows of Korean buildings, costly power-line insulators, and scarce livestock for target practice with their rifles. Attacks on civilians reached alarming proportions. Across the front and well to the rear there were near nightly incidents of looting, assault, and rape. One disturbing outbreak occurred in Seoul, quashed only by a curfew and the firm assistance of American MPs.[27] General Matthew Ridgway, commander of the Eighth Army in Korea, released a statement condemning the attacks, with instructions that it be read aloud to every serviceman at least once a month.[28] Meanwhile, in early January 1951, Seoul fell once again to the enemy.

As a crisis atmosphere enveloped Washington, respected policymakers suggested conducting nuclear, chemical, or biological strikes on North Korea and mainland China. The Truman administration may have come closest to using atomic weapons in April. Two months later the Joint Chiefs discussed deploying tactical nuclear warheads to the battlefield. These bipartisan proposals enjoyed growing support among Americans frustrated by the lack of a decisive victory. A Gallup poll conducted the following November found that 51 percent of respondents agreed with dropping atomic weapons on "military targets" in Korea, up from 23 percent at the start of the conflict. Although the nuclear bombs never fell, once China intervened General MacArthur ordered the elimination from the air of every "installation, factory, city, and village" between the border and his retreating troops, rendering most of North Korea a wasteland.[29]

UN forces eventually rallied, fighting their way to a shifting front roughly along the 38th parallel, where the war began. As before, they treated South Korea more as a combat arena than a land and a people to defend, its population centers potentially hostile territory. One South Korean communiqué summarized the accumulated damage: "Fifty-two of our fifty-five cities are missing." UN forces again bombarded Seoul, once home to one-and-a-half million people, before recapturing it in mid-March 1951. Investigators reported that South Korea's capital, having changed hands four times, was at least 50 percent destroyed. "It was just about as inert as a city could become," explained one correspondent, "short of altogether ceasing to exist."[30] A physicist on secret assignment for the Defense Department, pondering Seoul's destruction in the course of saving it, wondered if it was possible to eliminate a city's inhabitants without obliterating its infrastructure. He later invented the neutron bomb.[31]

During the spring and summer of 1951 both sides consolidated their positions, and the conflict settled into static, trench-warfare slaughter. In June the UN command signaled its willingness to discuss truce terms, but the contentious negotiations dragged on for two years. In the meantime, enormous conventional armies were reduced to lobbing world-war levels of ordnance at each other. By 1953 more artillery shells had been fired than in all of World War II. The United States continued to deploy its superior air power, while ground forces fought savage battles for limited objectives along an essentially stable front. "This is the damndest war," exclaimed one lieutenant. "We can't win, we can't lose, and we can't quit." The incoming Eisenhower administration was not sure it wanted the bloodshed to end at once, despite public claims to the contrary. Secretary of State John Foster Dulles, asked in private how he would feel about an immediate armistice, answered, "We'd be worried. I don't think we can get much out of a Korean settlement until we have shown—before all Asia—our clear superiority by giving the Chinese one hell of a licking."[32]

The transition to stalemate brought its own difficulties for American servicemen. Infiltration and guerrilla warfare continued to plague the south. One popular quip held it was the Republic of Korea during the day but North Korea at night. Enlisted men routinely conducted "skunk hunts," rounding up all civilians without proper credentials for a given area. (The American command moved to wipe out resistance for good in late 1951 with a counter-insurgency operation revealingly dubbed Rat Killer.)[33] A black market in military supplies thrived, abetted by U.S. troops' reliance on Korean "houseboys" to attend to laundry, housecleaning, and other chores.[34] Drugs such as heroin, freely available throughout South Korea, were becoming popular among servicemen.[35] However, leaving American bases to venture into South Korean towns in search of drugs, commercial sex, or more wholesome diversions was often physically dangerous. Officers instructed their men not to walk streets alone at night and required them to carry loaded weapons at all times. Some GIs reported being stoned by irate civilians. "These days it is more dangerous for Americans in South Korean cities than on the front-lines," a soldier wrote home late in the war. Servicemen attempted to make light of their circumstances, facetiously asking why their allies seemed implacably hostile despite the fact that, with American firepower, "their fields have been plowed, their trees have been pruned, and their houses have been air-conditioned."[36]

So continued a war that Senator Albert Gore, Sr., called a "meat grinder of American manhood." It finally came to a close in July 1953, with the signing of an armistice (the two Koreas technically remain at war). The meat grinder consumed nearly 35,000 American lives. For the Chinese and Koreans it was a catastrophe. Estimates of the number of Chinese soldiers killed range from one to three million. South Korea lost perhaps 1.3 million soldiers and civilians. The North, which endured the heaviest and most sustained bombing in history until the war in Vietnam, emerged with roughly two million civilian dead, or 20 percent of its prewar population, a proportion higher than that of Poland or the Soviet Union during World War II. For the entire peninsula civilians accounted for 70 percent of total casualties (by comparison, the figures for World War II and Vietnam were 40 percent and 28 percent, respectively). In just three years more than three million Koreans perished.[37]

While most Americans attempted to ignore the mess in Korea, black citizens followed the conflict and the contributions of African American personnel with keen interest. (The emphasis here is on the black public sphere; determining aggregate black opinion on the war presents several difficulties, chief among them African Americans' significant underrepresentation in opinion polls of the time.)[38] At the outbreak of hostilities a contentious debate erupted over the war's racial aspects. The North Koreans played no small part in stoking the controversy, seizing every opportunity to highlight the racial composition of the opposing forces. They littered the peninsula with pamphlets charging, among other things, that "under the orders of a Southern U.S. President [i.e., Truman of Missouri], U.S. planes are bombing and strafing COLORED PEOPLE in Korea."[39] The introduction and widespread use of segregated, all-black units provided excellent propaganda fodder for "Seoul City Sue," the North Korean radio equivalent of World War II's "Tokyo Rose" and "Axis Sally." The announcer targeted African American troops, asserting in at least one early broadcast—which made the front page of the *Pittsburgh Courier*— that black soldiers should desert or refuse to fight since "we are all of the colored race." White officers circulated apocryphal rumors that a black military chaplain had advised his men not to attack an enemy of "color," indicating the interracial mistrust that North Korean appeals helped perpetuate. Moreover, in the war's first weeks some North Korean troops used the disorienting tactic of donning captured American uniforms, darkening their faces, and attempting to pass as black servicemen in order to infiltrate American positions.[40]

The decision to intervene provoked fierce attacks on the Truman administration from a portion of the black left hostile to American Cold War foreign policy. Some framed it as an imperial undertaking. At a Madison Square Garden rally sponsored by the Civil Rights Congress in late June 1950, the activist and entertainer Paul Robeson proclaimed that "the Negro people . . . know that if we don't stop our armed adventure in Korea today—tomorrow it will be Africa." One columnist, observing the arrival of American military advisers in Vietnam the same year, incredulously asked, "Will Americans be dying there next?" Most criticism, however, emphasized the racial politics involved. Among black periodicals, the *California Eagle* served as the primary organ for those declaring Korea a war of color. One of its commentators accused the United States of seeking "to enforce its racial theories throughout the world," its servicemen "inoculated with the virus of color hatred." Another decried an "irony of ironies, the land of jimcrow [*sic*] . . . using colored troops to shoot down other colored folk seeking their freedom!"[41] Arguments to the contrary elicited harsh rebukes from these critics. An editorial in the *Eagle* accused African Americans who downplayed the question of race in the war of "passing for white . . . mentally."[42] The American editor of *The Korean Independence* condemned "a large section of the Negro press [for] daily propagandizing the Negro people" with "jingoism designed to inculcate . . . support for the American invasion of Korea."[43]

Private black citizens also labeled the war an imperial, racist endeavor, especially during its first months. One of the milder protest letters contemplated the long-term consequences of "our trigger-happy haste to rush into Korea." Its author, observing that many South Koreans appeared reluctant to resist their northern countrymen, inquired if intervention might precipitate a global "war of the color line." Others were more acerbic. One woman took the *Chicago Defender* to task for portraying certain criticisms of American policy as communist propaganda, bluntly calling the paper's arguments "white washed lies." The presence of black troops in Korea was dismissed by some as camouflage for malevolent intent. According a resident of Brooklyn, their use was an example of "the crassest hypocrisy of a white supremacist, imperialist, American government." A Bostonian flatly declared, "No Negro who has done any thinking would desire to go overseas and kill people who, like himself, have been exploited for centuries." Even a few black servicemen agreed. Following the war's first anniversary, anonymous members of an all-black laundry company—a service unit that, significantly, had remained stateside—insisted that the United States could not "possibly bring freedom to colored people in other countries [when] we are not free at home."[44]

On the other hand, a larger (or at least more vocal) segment of the black public championed American intervention and dismissed talk of a race war during the summer and fall of 1950. This support came primarily from a broad swath of liberal and centrist opinion, and stemmed in part from a desire to appear patriotic in light of a crystallizing Cold War consensus on American foreign policy. Yet it also reflected a strong conviction that Korea represented an unprovoked attack against a peaceful ally. The labor leader A. Philip Randolph appeared at a July pro-war rally in Harlem and reportedly called upon "Negroes throughout the country to give the United States and the United Nations moral and material support to halt the march of communism toward world conquest." The *Cleveland Call and Post* argued that "only the most stupid American Negro" would side with his or her nation's Asian adversaries, since the United States' "history eloquently supports its claim that it has no major imperialistic dreams" in the region. The Republican-leaning editorial page of the *Pittsburgh Courier,* although it eventually came to oppose American intervention as the war dragged on, insisted in August that in the interest of "national survival," the United States "must oppose the new slavery of totalitarianism just as it . . . drowned the slave system in blood on its own soil."[45]

The extensive participation of African American combat troops in the conflict provided crucial political ammunition to a range of war supporters. The *Chicago Defender* repeatedly emphasized their significance. One columnist maintained that black soldiers were "putting color into what otherwise would be a war of whites against colored." Two front-page articles stressed the strategic benefits that would accrue to the United States if it commissioned an African American general and assigned him to the battlefield. The *Afro-American* reprinted a Japanese editorial that emphasized how important it was for "the whole world to know that Americans with dark skin are helping put down Communist aggression."[46]

Ebony magazine devoted its sole editorial for October 1950 to the question "Is It a War of Color?," succinctly replying, "Color is not involved." Again the deployment of black soldiers was key. "The Negroes of the courageous 24th Infantry Regiment," it argued, "gave the most dramatic reply to Communist 'war of color' propaganda and 'Negroes-won't-fight-Russia' claims by Paul Robeson." "The Communists are not the first in their attempt to use race" as a "propaganda device," it added, for in World War II "the Japanese tried the same technique" with "a call for the solidarity of colored peoples." However, then as (*Ebony* believed) now, "the vast majority of Negroes saw the 'war of color' propaganda for what it was—a flimsy curtain behind which hid the ugly specter of . . . militarism intent on world conquest."[47] Reader response to *Ebony*'s stance was overwhelmingly positive, particularly among black military personnel serving abroad. For example, one soldier wrote from Korea to express "how much the fellows and myself appreciated" the magazine's argument, noting that "we all read and commented on it." An airman stationed in Honolulu applauded the editorial, calling its emphasis on the participation of black troops in Korea one of "our most potent weapons against race prejudice."[48] The South Korean government anxiously monitored these public discussions and was pleased with what it saw. It too recognized the symbolic value of black military service. Its consul general to the United States paid a friendly visit to the offices of the *Afro-American*, which approvingly paraphrased his claim that the "gallant participation of colored American fighting men in the Far Eastern conflict gives the lie" to claims Korea "is a 'race war' " (see figure 5.1).[49]

African American war supporters could also gesture to the supposed dignity of a military death, as opposed to the racial violence, industrial accidents, and street crime that claimed the health and lives of so many black men.[50] In a time of the infamous legal executions of Willie Mc-Gee and the Martinsville Seven, of race riots in Cicero, Illinois, and Milledgeville, Georgia, and of terror bombings across the South, to perish in combat provided the dead and their kin with claims to honor and respect.[51] Private Edward Cleaborn of Memphis, Tennessee, received the Distinguished Service Cross after being killed in Korea. More than 2,500 blacks and whites attended the ceremony, where, according to one account, the "mayor and other civil leaders paid tribute to the 18-year-old martyr and Memphis dailies parted with tradition to

It Seems Like Only Yesterday When He Went Away

5.1 The arrival of thousands of African American troops in Korea, where a small number of black service units had landed with American forces five years earlier, was celebrated in this editorial cartoon published three weeks into the war. Note the American air power looming in the distance. *Afro-American*, 15 July 1950. Courtesy of the Afro-American Newspapers Archives and Research Center.

refer to the youth's mother and father as 'Mr. and Mrs.'" A housing project, which still stands, was named in Cleaborn's honor.[52] Americans also celebrated the courage of Ensign Jesse Brown, the first black naval officer to die in combat. One report noted that "both Negro and white" residents of his hometown of Hattiesburg, Mississippi—"where

long time period
?

nine Negroes have been lynched since 1890"—"came to express their sympathy and offer help."[53] The *Chicago Defender* profiled Sergeant Cornelius Charlton of the Bronx, who was posthumously awarded the Congressional Medal of Honor, the nation's highest military decoration. (Charlton and Private William Thompson, who also died in Korea, were the first African Americans since the Spanish-American War to receive the award.) Charlton's father, a porter, spoke of his son's bravery "with quiet pride," and declared that "the death of my boy in combat" made "a liar" out of those like Robeson who insisted that "Negroes will not fight for our country."[54]

Despite this contentious public debate, black observers across the political spectrum were initially anxious to deplore the use of racially charged language, especially by white Americans, to describe the enemy. Racial epithets—"gook" in particular—drew the most criticism. One editorial complained that the term, "coined to indicate utter contempt . . . not for the Russians who may be backing them, but for the little brown men alone," was "being popularized." It added, erroneously, that American soldiers had for the time being stopped short of applying the epithet to their South Korean allies. Other accounts more accurately described its indiscriminate use by servicemen in Korea. *The Crisis* magazine lamented that "such phrases as these fall easily from the lips of our soldiers." A September 1950 pronouncement from General MacArthur declaring "gook" an insult to Asian peoples helped mollify such critics, although as one bitingly suggested, "While he is about it, he might frown on any and all epithets applying to race." On the other hand, by that point many black correspondents and servicemen had become perfectly willing to denigrate the enemy. A reader of the *Pittsburgh Courier*, responding to articles adopting the language of the mainstream press to describe "hordes" and "swarms" of Asian troops, lamented a few months into the war that a growing number of African Americans were "applying derogatory epithets and terms to other colored peoples. . . . Only recently, a black American soldier . . . referred to the North Koreans as 'savages.' "[55]

Indeed, as the trickle of reported African American casualties became a grim stream, portrayals of the Asian enemy increasingly assumed a disparaging tone. Because black personnel at first constituted more than one in four of those on the front lines, newspaper rolls of the dead, wounded, and missing included unprecedented numbers of African Americans. (Black soldiers were overrepresented among ground forces throughout the war, and their casualty rates remained disproportionately high; according to one estimate, at least 5,000 were killed in action.)[56] Tales of North Korean atrocities abounded, along with reports that their soldiers were fueled by drugs. Black correspondents searching for ways to describe the enemy began employing terms such as "treacherous," "ruthless," "crafty," and "fanatical." One article recounted bloody hand-to-hand fighting between members of the all-black 24th Infantry Regiment and a unit of "slant-eyed North Korean Reds." Another quoted a Tennessee private who described enemy soldiers scaling the rugged Korean hills "like monkeys." Once the Chinese entered the conflict, they too were routinely caricatured. Dispatches began to speak of a distinctive, and utterly foreign and uncivilized, Asian way of war. According to one, for "Oriental Peoples" "the enemy is an enemy, and they treat him accordingly, indifferent to the nice conventions with which Western peoples are familiar." Claimed another, "There's something about Asiatic concepts of fighting that impels them to come whooping down hillsides in great hordes." Unsurprisingly, these wartime stereotypes insinuated themselves into black popular culture. A January 1953 blues recording, in the words of one scholar, portrayed the Chinese as "ruthless rice-eating killers."[57]

White attacks on the performance of all-black units prompted celebratory accounts of African American military exploits, which in turn further dehumanized the Asian enemy. White officers and the mainstream press routinely accused black soldiers of "bugging out"—fleeing in the face of the enemy—and mocked the 24th Infantry Regiment as the "Running 24th" and the "Bugout Brigade." (The term had racial overtones, for it was rarely if ever used to describe the disorganized retreats of white troops.) One story that made the rounds claimed members of the regiment composed and sang with pride their "official song," the "The Bugout Boogie" ("When them Chinese mortars begin to thud, the old Deuce-Four begins to bug . . ."). Allegations of cowardice and insubordination contributed to, and were fed by, a spate of courts-martial during the war's desperate early months, when twice as many black as white servicemen faced military tribunals. Lieutenant Leon Gilbert became the public symbol of unequal justice in Korea. For refusing a direct order to lead what he thought a suicide mission, Gilbert was charged with desertion before the enemy and sentenced to death. Civil rights groups organized a massive petition to have the case reviewed, and in November 1950 President Truman reduced Gilbert's sentence to twenty years (he served five). Thirty-nine other black soldiers convicted of serious infractions requested assistance from the NAACP, which dispatched counsel Thurgood Marshall to investigate. He and his colleagues eventually succeeded in reversing the convictions or reducing the sentences of most of the men. However, as one black columnist complained, African American GIs were still being "booted by the dozen . . . at the dropping of a helmet" by white officers determined "to discredit their heroic performances."[58]

African American observers responded to these pervasive attacks by extolling the military prowess of black combat troops. One mark of esteem for soldiers under the microscope was the ability to generate a high enemy body count. The *Pittsburgh Courier,* one of the largest and most influential black newspapers, splashed its front pages with such headlines as "MOWS DOWN 30 REDS IN ONE DAY," "EAGLE EYE GI SHOOTS 55," and "TAN GIS KILL 200." The last article included a soldier's macabre account of a Korean human-wave attack: "There were some cut in two and others with their heads and hands blown off. But they kept coming until we nearly shot all of them up."[59] The paper heralded Sergeant Arthur Dudley, a recipient of the Distinguished Service Cross "credited with killing nearly 100 Red troops," as the "No. 1 Hero" of the war. The *Chicago Defender* lauded the "prodigious" Dudley and directed readers to a *Collier's* magazine story, in which the sergeant spoke of his personal "quota" of "dead gooks." *Jet* featured a Silver Star–winning private from Louisiana who "single-handedly killed Chinese Communists 'right and left' while protecting his white Georgia battalion commander." The private, in an interview with the *Afro-American,* explained that during the battle he had "used the same method I learned while shooting deer," "waiting for the Guks [sic] to raise their heads out of the trenches so that I could blast them off."[60] One gruesome dispatch described soldier Curtis Pugh's deadly encounter with a small band of North Koreans: "The first of the four enemy troopers was shot by Pugh at a distance of less than ten feet. The second one had his rifle taken away from him by Pugh, who shot him in the head; the third suffered a bashed-in skull with a rifle butt, and the fourth was strangled to death." The final killing earned two additional paragraphs of graphic description.[61]

The contributions of African American support units attracted positive attention as well. Given the American military's scorched-earth policies and its multiple retreats in the early going, these accounts centered on the destruction of Korean property, regardless of provenance. In

September 1950 a correspondent profiled an engineering unit responsible for destroying the South Korean community of Yechon, "a city about the size of Santa Monica." The black lieutenant in charge stressed that while it was not standard army practice to wantonly destroy civilian assets, everything of potential military and commercial value, food included, had to be burned. The author, noting that "Koreans virtually live on rice," described how the engineers put the torch to 300,000 tons, enough to feed the city for a year. The unit proceeded to level most of Yechon's 40,000 buildings, along with its lumber yard and hydroelectric plant. The article's tone, however, was more matter-of-fact than mournful. "Every GI in embattled South Korea," it explained, "would like to burn one of the squalid enemy infested villages."[62]

Indeed, early characterizations of South Korea and its destitute population were often as disparaging as those of the enemy. Among black journalists the most popular trope for the physical environment was an alienating concoction of decay, wretchedness, and affliction. African Americans at home encountered a rash of articles in the summer and fall of 1950 highlighting the traditional Korean use of human waste as fertilizer. The "infamous sugar carts"—as GIs dubbed vehicles collecting the yields of outhouses—reportedly "prowl[ed] the streets at all hours of the day." Another dispatch described ubiquitous open sewers lazily emptying their contents into rice paddies, where, in the author's estimation, "the real filth of Korea begins." Not only could one supposedly smell a Korean village from hundreds of yards away, but soldiers were forced "to march knee-deep in mud and human excreta." Another piece quoted a veteran describing his fellow black soldiers' disgust with the peninsula's "filth and disease." The weather was a "literal hell," made worse through "bombardments by lice, bugs and leeches." Korean living arrangements appeared to promote infestation (fleas were routinely cited). One headline unequivocally deemed Korea the "FILTHIEST PLACE IN [THE] WORLD."[63] Another sensationally claimed, "STORY OF KOREA IS SHOCKING SAGA OF A NATION LIVING IN THE PAST." Its content is worth quoting at length for what it reveals about the tenor of these exposés: "What do UN troops think of Korea? They put it this way: All the world is a pig. And Korea is that portion of the hog covered by the pig's tail. . . . The villages [and] huts of these people . . . are worse than anything found in the ghettoes of Chicago, Detroit, or New York. The interior of the homes are bare when compared with the plantation shacks of Dixie. . . . Due to lack of sanitation, almost every village or city emits a nauseating smell. . . . GIs fighting in the country have no love for the hell-hole."[64] To African Americans arriving from Japan's Little Americas and their consumerist bonanza, and to a lesser extent from the inner-city North and Jim Crow South, Korea appeared truly godforsaken.

The alienating features of this impoverished landscape appeared inextricable from its inhabitants. One report declared the peninsula "much more filthy than Arabia. . . . What makes this true? The Koreans themselves." "As for personal habits," claimed another, "the Koreans win the honor of being worst."[65] Most African American coverage of the Korean people characterized them variously as barbaric, cunning, or ungrateful. Correspondents routinely fell back upon imagery of the American West and Native Americans. (The comparison was common among white observers as well.)[66] One simply declared Koreans "semi-primitive," "immature economically [and] politically." An apparent Korean indifference or brutality toward one another seemed especially inhuman. A journalist writing for the *Afro-American* and the *Chicago Defender* provided two variations on the theme that black servicemen believed Koreans to be "cruel, mean and backward" and therefore "do not respect the Koreans, north or south, that they meet." As one of his headlines declared, they were a "CRUEL PEOPLE: 'RATHER BE NEGRO IN ALA[BAMA] THAN KOREAN IN SEOUL,' SAYS GI." Most were also not to be trusted. Accounts of attacks by "friendly" civilians, even elderly women, were common. "You don't know who is who," complained a soldier, "until you shoot one and find that he has been hanging around your unit all the time as a friend."[67]

Above all, most South Koreans appeared unappreciative of American sacrifices. One newly arrived black journalist was surprised by the vehemence with which his African American military escort immediately began "denouncing all Koreans as a bunch of thieves and scoundrels." However, after losing several fountain pens, a flashlight, and his only pair of pants to local pickpockets and burglars, he informed readers of his full conversion to the soldier's "I Hate Koreans Cult." Other black correspondents found the South Koreans' "questionable value as allies" and the absence of a suitable welcome in cities retaken from the enemy particularly unsettling. The "Korean attitude toward Americans is so hostile," alleged the *Pittsburgh Courier*, "that they follow Americans in the streets and spit at their heels." A journalist and his colleagues were taken aback to discover "a significant number" of those the United States was supposedly rescuing "unanimous in one thing: They wanted American troops, regardless of color, to get out of Korea!" Contradictorily, some accused the South Koreans of needlessly prolonging the conflict—and generating additional African American casualties—out of greed or sloth. In late 1952 an embittered black veteran insisted the South Koreans "don't want the war to end as they 'never had it so good.' Instead of the thirty cents a day they once made, they now get seventy cents to a dollar."[68] The American military's extensive use of indigenous labor, although it provided a meager income to the impoverished population, often led to abuses. Black servicemen routinely supervised gangs of Asian workers (as in occupied Japan), with all the attendant conflicts over productivity and accusations of malingering.[69] The greatest difficulty for a sergeant from New Orleans was "getting work out of his Korean laborers," since they "have no sense of patriotism so far as this war is concerned." "Sometimes I have to get real tough," he calmly explained to a reporter, since "I am determined that these Gooks are not going to mess up my schedule and cost me" a military promotion.[70] These and myriad other accounts of daily life on the peninsula informed stateside audiences just how infrequently the identities and interests of black servicemen and their Korean allies coincided.

As late as October 1952, readers of the *Pittsburgh Courier* could contemplate a rare letter claiming that most black citizens held a "sneaking admiration" for the North Koreans—"a non-white people"—whose ongoing struggle against the United States "tends to boost our racial self-respect."[71] In other words, Korea was indeed a race war, one that obliged African Americans to support their nation's Asian adversaries. This was a position that, if measured by media content, by then enjoyed meager support. African Americans on the home front had heard little from the black press and the servicemen it profiled lending credence to earlier claims of a "war of color." Among the tens of thousands of black soldiers fighting on the front lines, playing cat and mouse with guerrillas, and patting-down suspect civilians, the argument would have appeared absurd.

For the men of the all-black 24th Infantry Regiment, the redeployment from Japan to Korea got off to a rocky start.[72] A few came close to rioting when their commanders initially denied them permission to bid farewell to their Japanese girlfriends and children. As the men began streaming into the port of Moji, Japan, en route to the conflict, chaos reigned. An unknown number, abruptly uprooted from their comfortable lives as occupationaires and unsure of what to expect, slipped away for one last night on the town. Vague but alarming reports reached division head-quarters that drunk and disorderly soldiers were assaulting civilians. Local police lodged a formal complaint, but since the men rejoined their units and departed for Korea on schedule (and, presumably, because the incidents were low on military officials' list of concerns at the time), their commanders were disinclined to pursue the matter. A hastily arranged investigation dismissed the complaints.[73]

Soldiers of the 24th and other black units stepped onto the Korean peninsula brimming with confidence that an American military that had helped crush the Axis war machines would make short work of an up-start peasant army. "This policing of the commies of North Korea," boasted a veteran of World War II, "should end almost as abruptly as it started."[74] Their optimism soon faltered. The sight of South Korean troops fleeing to the rear as black units moved up to defensive positions provoked disgust, as well as concern. Instead of cheering crowds, taciturn civilians stared ominously as they passed. Supposed refugees began attacking from the rear.[75] Many black servicemen soon felt nothing but contempt for al-lies who failed to behave the way America's dominant Cold War narra-tive insisted they would. And in Korea contempt could be lethal. Lieu-tenant Charles Bussey, whose unit would shortly destroy the city of Yechon, witnessed one of his men snipe an elderly South Korean on a bet. Although "murder had been committed," Bussey chose not to report the incident. "I could see the press and the holier-than-thou rear-echelon officers browbeating another 'nigra soljuh,'" he remarked years later, "and smearing this crime on every other Negro in the theater of opera-tions. . . . I felt for the old Korean man lying dead in the road ahead of me, but in my order of priorities it was his life against the lives of ten thousand black soldiers who didn't deserve the ignominy."[76] The decision was painful to make, certainly, but it did nothing to counter a growing sense that, when push came to shove, Korean lives were expendable.

Similarly disturbing encounters with Korean civilians occurred throughout the war (see figure 5.2). One seventeen-year-old black GI arrived in December 1950 to find the Chinese routing American forces and colder weather than he had ever experienced, the "winter air heavy with the smell of burning flesh, garlic, and gunpowder." He and his fam-ished comrades scoured the countryside for food during the retreat south. While manning a roadblock to screen for guerrillas, they were approached by a group of refugees using an ox to transport their meager belongings. The teenage soldier ordered them at gunpoint to unload the animal and

5.2 An African American soldier keeps his weapon at the ready and others look on as Korean civilians, suspected of being guerrillas, are interrogated. *Pittsburgh Courier*, 26 August 1950. Courtesy of the Pittsburgh Courier Archives.

then shot it. His platoon butchered the ox and cooked it along with some confiscated rice. They discarded the intestines, which the starving Koreans scrambled to eat raw. Fearing a riot, he and several other black soldiers threatened to shoot them on the spot.[77]

Soldier-civilian relations remained tense and often dangerous as the war settled into a stalemate. Sergeant Charles Berry was assigned to a trucking company hauling supplies from Pusan to the front lines. One day a Korean boy ran up to one of the vehicles calling out "GI!" and, raising his arms, dropped two grenades. The explosions killed everyone inside. Following the young suicide bomber's attack, Berry ordered the men in his squad to use lethal force if approached by suspicious civilians. Military authorities "told us to be nice and stuff," he later explained. "But I told my people . . .'if they come up, shoot 'em.' I said, 'Your life is worth more than theirs.'"[78] Outwardly friendly civilian laborers could prove just as threatening. Years after the war one black veteran recalled a South Korean who was "staying there in our tent, washing our clothes, you know, our houseboy." Another member of his unit eventually found a map of the entire camp on the young man, implicating him as a spy. He was taken in custody to the rear and likely executed by his American captors or South Korean personnel.[79]

Attitudes toward the official enemy were more antagonistic, of course, although some black servicemen made a qualitative distinction between their Chinese and North Korean adversaries. "This was indeed a strange war," one remarked, for "there were no noble ideals to defend. . . . Our mission was to carry out orders, to survive and to return home." From December 1950 forward the primary order was, as another understood it, "to kill as many Chinese as possible." However, Chinese troops earned a modicum of respect for their conformity to standard military techniques. Although they persisted in "com[ing] off the hill[s] like Indians"—drug use, again, was the prime suspect—they were "normal soldiers, in the sense that when they saw they couldn't do something they'd pull back." The North Korean combatant, on the other hand, was despised for his guerrilla tactics and apparent fanaticism. A sergeant with the 24th Infantry Regiment, wounded by machine gun fire two months into his tour at the front, denounced the Korean enemy as "tricky" and "hateful."[80] North Korean commanders had little use for prisoners during the initial drive to unite the peninsula, and black servicemen witnessed or read of a disturbing number of GIs discovered bound and executed.[81] One combat engineer recounted that, for the remainder of the war, "they still had

Koreans . . . taking communication wire and catching guys on guard
duty and choking them . . . [and] riddl[ing] their bodies with barbed
wire."[82] During open combat, explained a lieutenant, "they'd come
right into your [fox]hole, try and shoot you or stab you or bite you if they
didn't have a weapon. Just fanatical as hell." The North Koreans, he declared, "were vicious people. They mutilated bodies. They shot prisoners. Just nasty, nasty people."[83]

Some black enlisted men were thus disinclined to treat prisoners of
war humanely. Although Curtis Morrow claimed he never heard his fellow soldiers express hatred for the enemy—"although some may have
done so"—they openly pondered whether or not to accept an enemy
combatant's surrender (see figure 5.3). Aware of the value army intelligence placed on acquiring captives to interrogate, Morrow reasoned he
"might not kill him if there happened to be an officer around." All the
same, he recoiled at the thought of a hypothetical prisoner "sitting the rest
of the war out in some prison camp while I am still up here fighting."
"When discussing the question with members of my squad," he continued, "all agreed that under the same circumstances they too would kill
the prisoner."[84] For others the topic was less speculative. After stumbling
upon several GIs shot execution-style, individuals in Samuel King's unit
vowed to retaliate in kind. "A lot of times when we captured the enemy," he later admitted, "we didn't take them back to no concentration
camp. Took them to the side over here." King, insisting he never directly
participated in the killings, remembered that one soldier in particular
"would always volunteer to take the prisoners back, and they would always jump [him] and try to take his gun" and wind up dead. Everyone
knew the soldier's claims were bogus, but "he always had a story and nobody ever investigated." King, given what he had seen of the enemy's
methods, was not one to judge his fellow serviceman harshly.[85]

By the end of the war, most black soldiers had come to identify with
American military power in Korea and to eschew a race-based interpretation of U.S. policy in the region. One veteran explained that "although
we were considered second-class citizens, we were still fighting for our
country."[86] Another, asked to describe the men who served in Korea,
replied, "Blacks, poor whites, Mexicans and inner-city kids fought that
war. . . . And I don't care how you talk about race, there has never been
a race war."[87] James Thompson, who had served in the Pacific during
World War II, was captured in Korea and detained by the Chinese for
more than two years. As one of the more than seven thousand Americans

On Their Way to Prison Compound Behind Lines

5.3 An African American corporal and his partner take two Korean prisoners, one of whom appears to be a child, to the rear at gunpoint. *Afro-American*, 9 September 1950. Courtesy of the Afro-American Newspapers Archives and Research Center.

taken prisoner during the war, and unlike many who remained on the front lines, he found the Chinese particularly brutal. "I had little experience with people of Chinese ancestry" before Korea, Thompson later noted. He was surprised to conclude that "mild mannered, innocent looking, polite little Chinese civilians"—such as the few he had seen in American movies or encountered in San Francisco's Chinatown—"become vicious fanatical maniacs during times of war." Thompson likened this intellectual reorientation to his thoughts on the Japanese. Conflating the experiences of the small number of black soldiers who saw combat in the World War II Pacific and the much larger cohort pitted against Asian troops in Korea, he explained,

> Japanese and black soldiers on the battlefields didn't lay their weapons down, run and embrace each other, and begin discussing the solidarity of Third World Peoples. When those little suckers came running through those jungles shouting "Banzai" they were after [anyone's] ass, black or white, [who] wore an American uniform. That Third World stuff is fine for radicals preaching on the streets of New York, but on the battlefields

it isn't worth a god damn. Anyone who has ever witnessed a group of Communist Chinese running fanatically down a slope in Korea knows all too well they aren't making color distinctions. . . . It was ass kicking time, not an ethnic reunion.[88]

There were, evidently, no internationalists in American foxholes.

Such Afro-Asian antagonism, due perhaps just as much to black citizens' direct participation in the projection of American power as to actual combat, long outlasted the war.[89] Three years after the signing of an armistice, for example, a young black private was assigned to one of the American bases dotting South Korea. Shortly after arriving, he took time off from his duties to write a letter home describing daily life on and around his post. Race relations, he explained, were "curious": "The difficulties are not white-negro so much as American-Korean." Although open conflict with the South Koreans working on the base was infrequent, the soldier noted with surprise that American personnel, regardless of race, failed to "show that appreciation, sympathy, understanding, and respect for Koreans which our presence as guests and our role as allies ought to require." Indeed, everything he had observed in his short time there indicated that African American servicemen were "not a whit more appreciative of Koreans and their problems than whites are." This disregard and mutual distrust seemed to him all the more unfortunate since, as evidenced by the substantial American presence on numerous military installations, U.S. troops appeared likely "to serve here for many, many years."[90]

Epilogue

Military Desegregation in a Militarized World

The Korean War entrenched America's national security state. This culmination was most apparent in the maintenance of an enormous global military apparatus. The number of citizens under arms provides one metric for grasping the extent of American militarization. During the war the army more than doubled in size to 3.5 million men and women, supported by an annual military budget that jumped from $15 billion in 1950 to some $50 billion by 1953. Despite an inevitable decline in personnel following the armistice, the army in the late 1950s remained 50 percent larger than its prewar incarnation. The total for all branches of the armed forces thereafter held steady at approximately 2.5 million personnel, stationed around the world, through the start of America's war in Vietnam.[1] Korea also precipitated or crystallized military, economic, and political commitments throughout Asia, including aid to the French in Indochina, to the Filipino government in its struggle against a communist insurgency, to the Nationalist Chinese government on Taiwan, and to an economically resurgent but militarily subordinate Japan.[2] Finally, massive national security expenditures (the Pentagon was by then the world's largest employer), along with the Eisenhower administration's ostensible commitment to fiscal restraint, precluded any substantial expansion of New Deal social programs.[3] The United States had become a full-fledged warfare-welfare state, its armed forces and defense industries providing critical employment opportunities to disadvantaged citizens.

The war and its enduring consequences sustained African Americans' socioeconomic dependence on militarization, an empire of bases (and their claims on local resources), and foreign intervention. (This finding likely holds true for other minority groups, Latinos in particular.) Annual black earnings relative to whites had fallen five points, to 52 percent, during post–World War II reconversion. They rebounded only through the militarized economic boom of the Korean War era, reaching 56 percent by 1953.[4] Some black observers counseled wariness of the correlation. Shortly into the war one columnist pronounced himself "gravely alarmed at the growing dominance of the military in the affairs of this nation." However, only weeks later (and on the same editorial page), a second countered that after years of declining black fortunes, war-production plants again beckoned: "Here is a golden opportunity for the colored worker to gain new laurels . . . and better his own condition." Indeed, in states such as Ohio, employment centers were reporting the most robust industrial job market since World War II. The *Cleveland Call and Post* observed that opportunities for black workers to acquire steady employment were the "best in years" and predicted that such gains would endure given both the war and the "extended period thereafter needed to keep us well armed against foreign aggression." The *Afro-American* exhibited a related shift in understanding. Its editorial cartoon for mid-August 1950 represented a traditional distinction between martial endeavors and economic opportunity (see figure 6.1). A second cartoon, published one month later, reflected a new reality, in which a "Major Preparedness Program" meant that militarization and employment proceeded hand-in-hand (see figure 6.2). The accompanying editorial called for federal legislation to tackle employment discrimination, in light of the "pressing need for speed in our re-armament program."[5]

Enlistment remained the most direct way to take advantage of militarization's opportunities. A veteran from South Carolina, who enlisted in the army at the height of the Korean War, described the appeal of a military career despite the obvious dangers: "I appreciated whatever happened because . . . being a sharecropper and a farmer, I had no other way of going in life." He served for over two decades. African American enthusiasm for voluntary service continued to distress military commanders,

If First in One, Why Not in the Other?

6.1 Guns versus jobs. *Afro-American*, 19 August 1950. Courtesy of the Afro-American Newspapers Archives and Research Center.

notwithstanding the recruitment challenges posed by an era of economic expansion. "What worries me," admitted a brigadier general following the armistice, "is that a military career for a Negro is now about the top he can get. It worries me whether we are going to have a predominantly Negro military service." The armed forces attempted to stave off the

AN FEPC WOULD HALT THIS SUBVERSIVE ACT

6.2 Guns as jobs. *Afro-American*, 23 September 1950. Courtesy of the Afro-American Newspapers Archives and Research Center.

possibility by discharging black personnel at a rate well out of proportion to their numbers. For example, in 1957–58 African Americans accounted for over 40 percent of army discharges. However, a decade later, and with the added effect of Selective Service, more than one in ten soldiers was black. The trend outlasted Vietnam and the draft: in 1984, 20 percent of those serving in the military were African American; six years later, black citizens, including a growing number of women, made up an astonishing 32 percent of enlisted army personnel.[6]

The rapid desegregation of the army in Korea nourished this professional interest, although the military initially attempted to keep the program under wraps.[7] High-ranking officers recognized that their orders to desegregate would be less difficult to carry out in Asia—where there were no off-base Jim Crow laws and few opportunities for black-white heterosexual intimacy—than in the United States or Europe.[8] Military expediency in the face of mass casualties also dictated the process. Limited integration of combat units began two months into the war, as commanders accepted individual black replacements to plug holes in the front lines. (A cartoonist for the *Pittsburgh Courier* gently lampooned the privilege afforded black servicemen of sitting "right up in front" of a war zone.)[9] This haphazard policy accelerated and became quietly routinized in the winter and spring of 1951; by May, 61 percent of the Eighth Army's combat infantry companies along the front were integrated. Desegregation was also spreading to stateside basic training (from which many inductees were sent directly to Korea), and soon extended to the 30,000 black troops recently deployed to Europe. In a July 1951 press release the army disclosed its intention to disband the 24th Infantry Regiment and to desegregate the entire Far East Command.[10] Fifteen months later the Assistant Defense Secretary declared the process complete. By war's end, more than 90 percent of the 200,000 black army personnel stationed across the globe served in integrated units, alongside more than 100,000 black servicemen in the integrated air force, navy, and marines. (The last all-black army unit disappeared in October 1954.) Desegregation was encompassing servicemen's dependents as well. Months before the Supreme Court's ruling in *Brown v. Board of Education*, the military successfully integrated all federally funded, on-base elementary schools, even those in the Jim Crow South. (A sympathetic white observer tentatively suggested that the military's "smoothly functioning non-segregated schools . . . could temper the southern reaction to a Supreme Court decision against segregated education."[11]) Of course, a war was required to effect this revolution in military affairs. General Omar Bradley, among others, granted that Korea hastened integration by more than a decade. Nonetheless, in just over four years one of the nation's most conservative and undemocratic institutions achieved complete desegregation—and ahead of schedule at that—unexpectedly launching itself into the vanguard of civil rights reform.[12]

This is not to suggest that integration came off without a hitch in Korea. Prior to the war some black civilians objected to the idea for fear of harassment by white officers and enlisted men.[13] Once in the service many remained wary of their new comrades in arms. An African American soldier from Texas, having been "brought up in a segregated society," was surprised and more than a little uneasy to find himself assigned to an integrating unit.[14] Others doubted any interracial goodwill would outlast the conflict. "It might work in Korea," allowed one, since a "white man is your friend as long as you're protecting his ass. [But] [i]n the States . . . it's different." Remarked another, decades later: "We knew then, as now, that outside of combat we could never depend on whites for support."[15] Adding to these doubts—in addition to reports of interracial violence stateside—were ubiquitous signs of white racism. The Confederate flag quickly spread throughout Korea as a popular symbol of resistance to integration in the fall of 1951.[16] (The NAACP's Walter White reported with grim humor that enemy snipers, unaware of the flag's history, assumed it signified the presence of a high-ranking officer and responded accordingly.)[17] Desegregation clearly had not rendered the army an interracial utopia.

Nonetheless, African Americans within and without the military increasingly viewed their nation's armed forces as a model for civilian society. In early 1951 Raymond Brown of Georgia, then "engaged in the offensive against Chinese aggression," explained to the *Chicago Defender* that "since I have been in the army, it has been my grateful privilege to experience . . . relief from complete racial servitude as exists in the South." Nine months later Sergeant Paul Shaw pointed to the "remarkable and unbelievable change [that] has occurred in race relations during the short period" of military integration as evidence that "we Americans are at last learning to live in peace and harmony with one another."[18] The striking juxtaposition created by on-base integration in the South strengthened the case for the military as a guide for civilian life. In response to a September 1954 *Ebony* story on Fort Benning, Georgia, a soldier stationed in North Carolina asked, "If we can work, sleep, eat and play together on an Army post—why not in town?"[19] The harmonious military portrayed in the article, wrote a resident of Muskegon, Michigan, constituted "real DEMOCRACY." "I can't understand why the state of Georgia or Washington, D.C., or even my home Muskegon," he protested, "isn't the same as [that] army camp" (see figure 6.3).[20]

A chorus of African American commentators echoed these sentiments, further popularizing an idealized conception of the integrated

He's Got A Good Left, But No Right

6.3 A fighting Uncle Sam's muscular, integrated military points the way for his weak and divided home front. *Afro-American*, 18 April 1953. Courtesy of the Afro-American Newspapers Archives and Research Center.

military as a bastion of racial harmony. The *Afro-American* editorialized that Korea had enabled black Americans "for the first time" to serve their nation "as first-class citizen soldiers." Black and white GIs in Korea had become "completely relaxed in each other's company," it reported, in contrast to released American prisoners of war, whose black members had "received daily dosages of race hate doctrine" from their Asian captors in segregated camps. Another correspondent acknowledged that the "costly achievement" of army integration was "not born altogether of plan, but of necessity," yet he hailed the "tragic Korean conflict" as "another milestone in the forward march of the Negro . . . toward complete integration in the democratic way of life."[21] The author had previously cast warfare itself as "the purgative of race hate among comrades on the front lines" and argued that Korea proved black and white Americans could "work together and fight shoulder to shoulder—and LIKE IT, IF LEFT ALONE."[22] Indeed, the black press routinely emphasized the interracial brotherhood supposedly born of the conflict (see figure 6.4). One dispatch described an integrated airbase in Japan, from which pilots were flying devastating sorties against Korean targets, as "one of the most peaceful and democratic communities that Americans have ever lived in." Although "no one likes the idea of benefiting through war and the misery it brings to millions of people," explained the *Chicago Defender*, Korea had proven to all Americans that "colored and white men can work and fight side by side to their mutual benefit."[23] This realization was expected to bear societal fruit as well. When word of the army's formal integration program reached the United States, it immediately raised African American hopes for advances on the domestic front. The NAACP's Roy Wilkins, speaking before a New York audience in October 1951, argued that after ten years of "either open war or a war economy" the line separating military from civilian affairs was vanishing: "When millions of young men wear the same uniform, train together . . . and learn through the rating system . . . to recognize individual merit rather than mere color, the carry-over to civilian life and activities will be tremendous."[24]

In fact, despite—or rather because of—subsequent lulls in civil rights advances during the Eisenhower and Kennedy administrations, military desegregation ushered in a more than decade-long era of good feelings between black Americans and the armed forces. Although prejudice and discrimination persisted, not only military officialdom but much of the general public deemed the program an unconditional triumph.[25] Civil rights organizations and the black press, historically the most vociferous critics of racism in the armed forces, were reluctant to find fault with a formally integrated institution during an era of white campaigns of "massive resistance" against desegregation. One newspaper, surveying the state of military race relations in May 1960, spoke only of "great strides" since the

"Look, A Strange Light!

6.4 Two soldiers, perhaps nearing death on the battlefield, are surprised to find themselves purged of racial animosity in Korea. *Chicago Defender,* 3 March 1951. Courtesy of the *Chicago Defender.*

late 1940s.[26] This reticence was not, however, merely the product of willful ignorance. Through the mid-1960s the armed forces endured none of the large-scale protests and race riots that had erupted with grim regularity before Korea. Military and other government officials received the fewest complaints of discrimination since the early days of World War II. Black servicemen had once sent Congressman Adam Clayton Powell, Jr., of Harlem some 5,000 letters of protest annually. By the mid-1960s that figure had plummeted by 70 percent, and most pertained to conditions off-base. Relative racial tranquility and opportunities for African American advancement made the military a perennial recourse for black men facing a dubious civilian job market. In 1965 the African American reenlistment rate stood at more than 45 percent, three times the rate for whites.[27] This situation in turn made it that much easier for the Department of Defense to meet its recruitment and retention targets, suggesting that black enlistments went far in enabling the United States to maintain a global military empire without resort to universal, and hence socially disruptive, conscription.

Finally, the maintenance of a robust military presence in Asia perpetuated the attendant strains on Afro-Asian social relations. In 1960 African American Congressman Charles Diggs, Jr., of Michigan toured military installations in Japan, Okinawa, and the Philippines. He returned denouncing the discrimination practiced by local communities. "Typical charges" from African American servicemen, he reported, included "shabby and offensive treatment . . . in clubs and bars, [and] outright refusal of service." In one Okinawan town white servicemen and their Asian hosts enforced racial segregation "through a system of reprisal, intimidation, and physical violence." His recommendation that unit commanders place offending establishments off-limits to all enlisted men fell on deaf ears. Three years later, black personnel stationed near Misawa, Japan, took matters into their own hands, staging sit-ins to end discrimination at the city's forty-two entertainment venues that refused to serve black customers. The Japanese proprietors retaliated by threatening to hire local toughs to forcibly eject the protestors. Although the standoff ended peacefully when the owners relented, patron-proprietor relations remained tense.[28] As one black soldier complained to *Ebony* in 1969, "When it comes to hate and prejudice towards the Afro-American military man, Japan ranks 'head and shoulders' at the top of the list."[29]

Many of the historical actors examined in these pages served through America's war in Vietnam, a conflict that reprised controversies generated by African American service in Japan and Korea.[30] Rampant prostitution and commanding officers' disinclination to permit interracial marriages, for example, inevitably led to another brown baby crisis. By the early 1970s the estimated number of black-Vietnamese children ranged from an official count of less than 500 to several thousand. A black sergeant who attempted to return to the United States with his daughter encountered endless red tape and daunting legal fees and, according to one report, was obliged to pay off "the money-minded Vietnamese mother of his child to the tune of '$6,000 or $7,000.'" ("Although less hung up on racial purity than the Japanese and Koreans," added the author, "Vietnamese admit privately that their people are prejudiced against dark skin.")[31] Because "many Vietnamese" disliked African Americans, explained *Ebony*, the Afro-Asian children left behind were bound to endure harassment and discrimination in education and employment, the "girls who cannot become entertainers . . . likely to become prostitutes," the boys either entertainers or "soldiers in the Vietnamese army."[32] Asian prejudice seemed once again to doom a generation of Afro-Asian children to physical, economic, and emotional exploitation.

Although prominent African Americans criticized the war and expressed solidarity with the Vietnamese people, black servicemen vigorously defended their role in the conflict.[33] Martin Luther King, Jr.'s April 1967 call for African Americans to avoid serving in Vietnam appeared in *Stars and Stripes*, prompting reporter Mike Wallace to ask a black officer for his response. "I don't react favorably to that statement," he replied, "because as a career officer, United States Army, I certainly am here because I want to be here. I believe in what the Army stands for, and I'm solidly behind what they're doing here." He also firmly rejected King's assertion that the war was hindering progress on civil rights at home. Enlisted men offered nearly identical reactions. "I think this war is worthwhile," explained a soldier from Hattiesburg, Mississippi, "and I think we should stay over here and see this thing out."[34] African American journalist Wallace Terry, on assignment for *Time* magazine that same year, discovered remarkably similar attitudes among black troops in Vietnam. King, the boxer and draft resister Muhammad Ali, and the black-power advocate Stokely Carmichael were harshly rebuked for their opposition to the war. Said one soldier of King and Carmichael, "They live in a free country and somebody has to pay for it." Protested another: "If King had any pride in his race, he ought to do what he can to support us." It was only after King's assassination and the Tet Offensive in early 1968, Terry concluded, as racial violence flared in the military, the war grew in unpopularity, and African American conscripts outpaced volunteers, that a majority of black servicemen began to speak of Vietnam as a race war in which they should take no part.[35] The 1973 transition to an all-volunteer service, of course, removed such disgruntled conscripts from the military. By decade's end, the number of African Americans as a percentage of the armed forces' enlisted strength reached an all-time high.[36]

Afro-Asian social relations remain to this day highly militarized. Given residential and occupational segregation in the United States, ongoing African American overrepresentation in the armed forces, and the maintenance of American installations across Asia, overseas bases and their surrounding communities continue to be primary sites of Afro-Asian encounters.[37] Physical proximity under these circumstances, as evidenced in occupied Japan and war-torn South Korea—and by ongoing incidents of serious misconduct by American soldiers in Asia—has rarely contributed to greater empathy and affinity between armed guest and reluctant host.[38] Rather, mutual indifference, suspicion, or hostility has been the norm. African Americans' lived experiences with this empire of bases, one that emerged with the Cold War but outlasted it, largely precluded alliances with Asian peoples and instead encouraged an embrace of the opportunities afforded by the global projection of American power. One of this story's central ironies is that many African Americans enjoyed the privileges of first-class, consumption-based citizenship when serving abroad in an authoritarian institution dedicated to the use of force. Robert Chappel, a black veteran of Korea, stressed "the lifestyle, the money" he acquired during his twenty-one years with the army, stationed around the world. Indeed, he not only "enjoyed the service" and "reaping [its] benefits" but found that soldiering quickly became "a way of life."[39] This militarized outlook, one shared by thousands of other black servicemen after World War II, underscores the difficulties encountered by those who have sought to put notions of international solidarity into everyday practice in an age of American military empire.

Notes

Introduction

1. Miles Xian Liu, ed., *Asian American Playwrights: A Bio-Bibliographical Critical Source-book* (Westport, Conn.: Greenwood Press, 2002), 103; Duane Noriyuki, "Still Searching for Acceptance," *Los Angeles Times*, 1 May 2000; Elfrieda Berthiaume Shukert and Barbara Smith Scibetta, *War Brides of World War II* (Novato, Calif.: Presidio Press, 1988), 225.

2. Curtis James Morrow, *What's a Commie Ever Done to Black People?: A Korean War Memoir of Fighting in the U.S. Army's Last All Negro Unit* (Jefferson, N.C.: McFarland, 1997), 1, 41, 77.

3. Michael Lee Lanning, *The African-American Soldier: From Crispus Attucks to Colin Powell* (Secaucus, N.J.: Carol Publishing Group, 1997), 241; *U.S. Census of the Population: 1950*, vol. 2, part 1, *United States Summary* (Washington, D.C.: U.S. Government Printing Office, 1952), 87; Anni P. Baker, *American Soldiers Overseas: The Global Military Presence* (Westport, Conn.: Praeger, 2004), 53; Donna Alvah, *Unofficial Ambassadors: American Military Families Overseas and the Cold War, 1946–1965* (New York: New York University Press, 2007), 45.

4. The ongoing and often contentious debate over claims that the United States was and is an imperial power shows no signs of abating. For two measured takes on the question, see Charles S. Maier, *Among Empires: American Ascendancy and Its Predecessors* (Cambridge: Harvard University Press, 2006); and Bernard Porter, *Empire and Superempire: Britain, America, and the World* (New Haven: Yale University Press, 2006).

5. Okinawa, whose administration the United States grudgingly relinquished in 1972, after twenty-seven years, is the exception to the postwar rule. John W. Dower, *Embracing Defeat: Japan in the Wake of World War II* (New York: W. W. Norton, 1999), 23 ("the last

immodest exercise"); John W. Dower, "Peace and Democracy in Two Systems: External Policy and Internal Conflict," in *Postwar Japan as History*, ed. Andrew Gordon (Berkeley: University of California Press, 1993), 10–11; Chalmers Johnson, *The Sorrows of Empire: Militarism, Secrecy, and the End of the Republic* (New York: Henry Holt, 2004), 199.

6. Eiji Takemae, *Inside GHQ: The Allied Occupation of Japan and Its Legacy* (London: Continuum, 2002), 51, 500; Bruce Cumings, "Is America an Imperial Power?" *Current History* 102, no. 667 (Nov. 2003), 355–360; Johnson, *Sorrows of Empire*, 1–2, 199–203. See also Bruce Cumings, *Parallax Visions: Making Sense of American–East Asian Relations at the End of the Century* (Durham, N.C.: Duke University Press, 1999), chap. 8. As historian Michael S. Sherry observes, "much that emerged by 1950," including the maintenance of military bases around the world, was "planned, desired, or foreseen" by American leaders by 1945. Sherry, *In the Shadow of War: The United States since the 1930s* (New Haven: Yale University Press, 1994), 125.

7. At the beginning of the twenty-first century, the United States maintained nearly 200 bases in Japan and South Korea, installations housing 80,000 troops and 50,000 dependents of military personnel and employing tens of thousands of local civilians. Johnson, *Sorrows of Empire*, 91, 202.

8. For a collection of essays examining recent popular movements to shut down overseas American bases, see Catherine Lutz, ed., *The Bases of Empire: The Global Struggle against U.S. Military Posts* (New York: New York University Press, 2009).

9. For an analysis of this dynamic at work during the United States' turn-of-the-century conquest of the Philippines, see Paul A. Kramer, *The Blood of Government: Race, Empire, the United States, and the Philippines* (Chapel Hill: University of North Carolina Press, 2006), 2–7, 124–129.

10. One military study conducted during World War II, for example, noted the "tremendous influence" wielded by the black press among African American servicemen, observing that "76% of the troops read a paper of the *Afro-American* chain, while 56% read the *Pittsburgh Courier*." "Participation of Negro Troops in the Post-War Military Establishment," memorandum, 27 December 1945, Folder 291.2, Box 32, RG 165, Records of the War Department General and Special Staffs, Special Planning Division, Security— Classified General Correspondence, 1943–46, National Archives II.

11. In order to access servicemen's perspectives I draw upon the innumerable interviews and accounts of their activities that appeared in African American periodicals. In so doing, I bear in mind that the black press at this time functioned first and foremost as an advocate for African Americans and their interests. I also employ military records, memoirs, and oral history collections to help uncover the daily lives of black soldiers in Asia. For profiles of some of the African American journalists mentioned in the text, see Gene Roberts and Hank Klibanoff, *The Race Beat: The Press, the Civil Rights Struggle, and the Awakening of a Nation* (New York: Alfred A. Knopf, 2006). While the research for this book is restricted to English-language sources, I hope this limitation will encourage scholars to pursue answers to similar questions in foreign-language archives.

12. The term is from George Lipsitz, "'Frantic to Join . . . the Japanese Army': The Asia Pacific War in the Lives of African American Soldiers and Civilians," in *The Politics of Culture in the Shadow of Capital*, ed. Lisa Lowe and David Lloyd (Durham, N.C.: Duke University Press, 1997), 327.

13. For examples of works advancing such arguments, see Ernest Allen, Jr., "When Japan Was 'Champion of the Darker Races': Satokata Takahashi and the Flowering of Black Messianic Nationalism," *The Black Scholar* 24, no. 1 (1994): 23–46; Reginald Kearney, *Afri-*

can American Views of the Japanese: Solidarity or Sedition? (Albany: State University of New York Press, 1998); Marc Gallicchio, *The African American Encounter with Japan and China: Black Internationalism in Asia, 1895–1945* (Chapel Hill: University of North Carolina Press, 2000); Gerald Horne, "Tokyo Bound: African Americans and Japan Confront White Supremacy," *Souls* 3, no. 3 (Summer 2001): 17–29; Gerald Horne, "The Asiatic Black Man? Japan and the 'Colored Races' Challenge White Supremacy," *Black Renaissance* 4, no. 1 (Spring 2002): 26–38; Gerald Horne, *Race War: White Supremacy and the Japanese Attack on the British Empire* (New York: New York University Press, 2004); and Marc Gallicchio, "Memory and the Lost Found Relationship between Black Americans and Japan," in *The Unpredictability of the Past: Memories of the Asia-Pacific War in U.S.–East Asian Relations*, ed. Marc Gallicchio (Durham, N.C.: Duke University Press, 2007). Historian George Lipsitz is one of a few to emphasize Afro-Asian solidarity in the postwar era, arguing that the ongoing American military presence in Asia instigated "unexpected alliances and affinities across communities of color." He asserts that one black soldier, who served in Japan and Korea before becoming a community activist, encountered "Japanese and Korean citizens who seemed . . . refreshingly nonracist compared to the white Americans he had known." Lipsitz, " 'Frantic to Join,' " 343–344. See also George Lipsitz, *A Life in the Struggle: Ivory Perry and the Culture of Opposition* (Philadelphia: Temple University Press, 1988), 40. For a study that emphasizes solidarities between African American members of the 93rd Infantry Division and Filipino civilians during World War II's final months and immediate aftermath, see Robert F. Jefferson, "Staging Points of African American Identity in the Southwest Pacific Theater and the Politics of Demobilization," *Contours: A Journal of the African Diaspora* 1, no. 1 (Spring 2003): 82–100.

14. Penny M. Von Eschen, *Race against Empire: Black Americans and Anticolonialism, 1937–1957* (Ithaca: Cornell University Press, 1997), 2–3, 146–147. For related arguments, centered on groups such as the National Association for the Advancement of Colored People, the Civil Rights Congress, and the Council on African Affairs, see Gerald Horne, *Black and Red: W. E. B. Du Bois and the Afro-American Response to the Cold War, 1944–1963* (Albany: State University of New York Press, 1986); Brenda Gayle Plummer, *Rising Wind: Black Americans and U.S. Foreign Affairs, 1935–1960* (Chapel Hill: University of North Carolina Press, 1996); Mary L. Dudziak, *Cold War Civil Rights: Race and the Image of American Democracy* (Princeton: Princeton University Press, 2000); Carol Anderson, *Eyes off the Prize: The United Nations and the African American Struggle for Human Rights, 1944–1955* (New York: Cambridge University Press, 2003); and Jonathan Rosenberg, *How Far the Promised Land?: World Affairs and the American Civil Rights Movement from the First World War to Vietnam* (Princeton: Princeton University Press, 2005).

15. A recent study concludes that even the best-crafted political indoctrination "failed to budge soldiers' opinions on issues closest to their immediate self-interest." Christopher S. DeRosa, *Political Indoctrination in the U.S. Army from World War II to the Vietnam War* (Lincoln: University of Nebraska Press, 2006), xii.

16. In weaving together a history of these interactions I have found the notion of the "everyday," where macro-level phenomena such as foreign policy and military strategy are put into practiced and lived, especially useful. My approach is informed by historian Thomas C. Holt's discussion—inspired by the work of sociologist Henri Lefebvre—of "the concept of a study of everyday life and 'everydayness' " as a tool to bridge the global and the local. Holt adds a valuable caveat: "It is important, moreover, not to confuse the everyday with the merely popular or non-elite. Every institution, class, or power also has its 'everyday'; it is a level of experience and analysis, not an aspect of social hierarchy." Holt, "Marking:

Race, Race-making, and the Writing of History," *American Historical Review* 100, no. 1 (Feb. 1995): 7–10.

17. My approach in these two chapters is to treat postwar military history as labor history. For an analysis of the importance black Americans placed on access to sites of consumption as a sine qua non of American citizenship during and after World War II, see Lizabeth Cohen, *A Consumers' Republic: The Politics of Mass Consumption in Postwar America* (New York: Alfred A. Knopf, 2003), 83–84, 90–95, 166–167. My interpretation of black volunteers' motives parallels historian Christian G. Appy's findings on those induced to enlist some twenty years later. See Appy, *Working-Class War: American Combat Soldiers and Vietnam* (Chapel Hill: University of North Carolina Press, 1993), chap. 2.

18. Alvah, *Unofficial Ambassadors*, 92.

19. See, for example, Milton J. Bates, *The Wars We Took to Vietnam: Cultural Conflict and Storytelling* (Berkeley: University of California Press, 1996), 61.

20. Kevin Gaines, "Historians Reflect on the War in Iraq: A Roundtable," Organization of American Historians, 5 April 2003, http://www.oah.org/meetings/2003/roundtable/gaines.html.

1. Reconversion Blues and the Appeal of (Re)Enlistment

1. Charles M. Payne, *I've Got the Light of Freedom: The Organizing Tradition and the Mississippi Freedom Struggle* (Berkeley: University of California Press, 1995), 30. Numerous scholars have recorded the more loathsome experiences of black military personnel during the war and the impact of their anger and frustration on civil rights activism. See, for example, Richard M. Dalfiume, *Desegregation of the U.S. Armed Forces: Fighting on Two Fronts, 1939–1953* (Columbia: University of Missouri Press, 1969); John Dittmer, *Local People: The Struggle for Civil Rights in Mississippi* (Urbana: University of Illinois Press, 1994); Gerald Astor, *The Right to Fight: A History of African Americans in the Military* (Cambridge, Mass.: Da Capo Press, 1998); Martha Biondi, *To Stand and Fight: The Struggle for Civil Rights in Postwar New York City* (Cambridge: Harvard University Press, 2003); and Steve Estes, *I Am a Man!: Race, Manhood, and the Civil Rights Movement* (Chapel Hill: University of North Carolina Press, 2005).

2. Bernard C. Nalty, *Strength for the Fight: A History of Black Americans in the Military* (New York: Free Press, 1986), 218; Sherry, *In the Shadow of War*, 145; "The Army Stumbles On," *The Crisis*, February 1950, 101 ("two years"). In this and subsequent chapters the terms "army" and "the military" are used interchangeably unless otherwise noted. The reasoning is twofold: first, the army was by far the largest branch of the armed forces and contained the highest number of African Americans in uniform; second, black citizens paid greatest attention to the army as a site of both conflict and opportunity. For specific information on African Americans in the navy, air force, and marines, see Sherie Mershon and Steven Schlossman, *Foxholes and Color Lines: Desegregating the U.S. Armed Forces* (Baltimore: Johns Hopkins University Press, 1998), 135, 139; Nalty, *Strength for the Fight*, 234; and Dalfiume, *Desegregation*, 53.

3. "Army's Recruiting Wins Elks' Backing," *New York Times*, 11 July 1946.

4. "Truman Limits Army Draft to Take Only Men 19 to 29," *New York Times*, 17 July 1946.

5. Dalfiume, *Desegregation*, 202.

6. Claude A. Barnett to "Pat," letter, 15 August 1945, Folder 13: "Home Front—World War II—Correspondence, 1940–45," Box 316, Claude A. Barnett Papers, Chicago Historical

Society ("celebrating the Peace"); "Victory: Not without Sadness," *New York Amsterdam News*, 25 August 1945 ("strangely quiet"); Abe Hill, "Workers Fear Loss of Jobs on Heels of End of the War," *New York Amsterdam News*, 25 August 1945 ("cessation of hostilities"); "Peace and a Jobless Minority," *Chicago Defender*, 8 September 1945 ("color caste").

7. Robert Lucas, "50,000 Lose Jobs Here!: Big Dodge Engine Plant Shuts Down," *Chicago Defender*, 18 August 1945.

8. Ted Graham, "Job Famine May Sweep Nation: Reconversion to Throw Thousands Out of War Jobs, *Pittsburgh Courier*, 25 August 1945; "Unemployment Is Here," *Pittsburgh Courier*, 25 August 1945.

9. "Mayor Backs Plans for Reconversion," *New York Times*, 29 August 1945; George Lipsitz, *Rainbow at Midnight: Labor and Culture in the 1940s* (Urbana: University of Illinois Press, 1994), 73.

10. National Urban League, "Racial Aspects of Reconversion," 27 August 1945, Folder 291.2, Box 32, RG 165, Records of the War Department General and Special Staffs, Special Planning Division, Security—Classified General Correspondence, 1943–46, National Archives II. See also "Anti-Bias Laws Urged on Truman," *New York Times*, 13 September 1945; and Anderson, *Eyes off the Prize*, 66.

11. Ben Burns, "V-J Unemployed Forced to Take Low-Paying Jobs," *Chicago Defender*, 25 August 1945.

12. Morris J. MacGregor, Jr., *Integration of the Armed Forces, 1940–1965* (Washington, D.C.: Center of Military History, United States Army, 1981), 152; "Discharge Bias Charged," *New York Times*, 19 August 1945 ("unbelievable violence"); "Survey of 50 Cities Reveals Negro Vets Denied Jobs, Training," *California Eagle*, 11 April 1946.

13. Donald R. McCoy and Richard T. Ruetten, *Quest and Response: Minority Rights and the Truman Administration* (Lawrence: University Press of Kansas, 1973), 25–26.

14. Lipsitz, *Rainbow at Midnight*, 99, 115, 338.

15. Guido van Rijn, *The Truman and Eisenhower Blues: African-American Blues and Gospel Songs, 1945–1960* (New York: Continuum, 2004), 14–15.

16. "Not since the fight to pass the civil war amendments," it added, "has there been such a clear-cut fight against feudalism, racism and reaction." "The Battle of the Century," *Pittsburgh Courier*, 2 February 1946.

17. Jacquelyn Dowd Hall, "The Long Civil Rights Movement and the Political Uses of the Past," *Journal of American History* 91, no. 4 (March 2005): 1248; "The FEPC Is Dead," *Chicago Defender*, 16 February 1946; "Closure Defeated, FEPC Sidetracked," *New York Times*, 10 February 1946.

18. "FEPC's Life Ends with No Hope Held for Early Revival," *New York Times*, 1 July 1946.

19. "Nearly [sic] Fourth of Veterans Unemployed in 26 Southern Areas, Survey Shows," *Afro-American*, 24 May 1947; "Spectre of Joblessness," *Chicago Defender*, 20 September 1947; "Urgent Need Seen to Train the Negro," *New York Times*, 27 March 1947 ("dismal picture").

20. Several factors contributed to the low enrollment figures, including government racism and indifference, black distrust of state intentions, and fly-by-night operators' schemes to secure government funds. Charlie Cherokee, "National Grapevine," *Chicago Defender*, 4 December 1948; Mark D. Van Ells, *To Hear Only Thunder Again: America's World War II Veterans Come Home* (Lanham, Md.: Lexington Books, 2001), 142.

21. Risa Goluboff, "'Let Economic Equality Take Care of Itself': The NAACP, Labor Litigation, and the Making of Civil Rights in the 1940s," *UCLA Law Review* 52 (June 2005): 1395–1468. See also Robert Korstad and Nelson Lichtenstein, "Opportunities Found

and Lost: Labor, Radicals, and the Early Civil Rights Movement," *Journal of American History* 75, no. 3 (Dec. 1988): 800–801, 811; Lipsitz, *Rainbow at Midnight*, 157, 255; and Biondi, *To Stand and Fight*, 17, 98, 260, 269–270.

22. "Unemployment Rates Twice as High for Colored Group, Census Shows," *Afro-American*, 20 December 1947; "Our DP Problem," *Chicago Defender*, 17 April 1948 ("displaced persons"); "Unemployment on Steady Rise throughout Nation," *Pittsburgh Courier*, 12 February 1949 ("little is seen"); "Negro Joblessness Reported on Rise," *New York Times*, 24 February 1949 ("depression"); McCoy and Ruetten, *Quest and Response*, 199.

23. MacGregor, *Integration*, 152; Samuel A. Stouffer et al., *Studies in Social Psychology in World War II, Volume 1, The American Soldier: Adjustment during Army Life* (Princeton: Princeton University Press, 1949), 542.

24. Historians have debated the merits of this policy, with some maintaining it represented a good-faith effort by the Board and military commanders to ensure a representative number of African Americans in the armed forces. Intentions aside, the policy functioned as a limiting quota. For detailed discussions of the Gillem Board's hearings, deliberations, and conclusions, see Astor, *The Right to Fight*, 310–313; Jack D. Foner, *Blacks and the Military in American History: A New Perspective* (New York: Praeger, 1974), 177–178; Dalfiume, *Desegregation*, 149–152; and Bernard C. Nalty and Morris J. MacGregor, eds., *Blacks in the Military: Essential Documents* (Wilmington, Del.: Scholarly Resources Inc., 1981), 168.

25. "Truman Limits Army Draft to Take Only Men 19 to 29," *New York Times*, 17 July 1946.

26. Morris J. MacGregor and Bernard C. Nalty, eds., *Blacks in the United States Armed Forces: Basic Documents*, vol. 8, *Segregation under Siege* (Wilmington, Del.: Scholarly Resources Inc., 1977), 36; "187,300 in Army May 1 This Year," *Afro-American*, 22 June 1946; McCoy and Ruetten, *Quest and Response*, 38; "Army to Weed Out Negroes," *California Eagle*, 22 August 1946; "Halts Negro Army Enlistments, Bars WACs from Overseas Duty," *California Eagle*, 18 July 1946.

27. MacGregor and Nalty, *Basic Documents*, vol. 8, 80, 90–91 ("Army Talk"); Mershon and Schlossman, *Foxholes and Color Lines*, 150.

28. Horace Mann Bond, letter to the editor, *New York Times*, 12 August 1946 ("well known fact"); R. Latimer to President Truman, telegram, 22 July 1946, Folder 11, B File 20, Desegregation of the Armed Forces, Center for the Study of the Korean War; Venice T. Spraggs, "Army Ducks Suit; Takes Educated Negro Enlistees," *Chicago Defender*, 12 October 1946; "The Inquiring Photographer," *New York Amsterdam News*, 7 December 1946 ("learn and earn," "an opportunity").

29. Venice T. Spraggs, "Army Ducks Suit; Takes Educated Negro Enlistees," *Chicago Defender*, 12 October 1946; "Negro Suit Charges Segregation in Army," *New York Times*, 19 December 1946; "Justice Dep't to Defend Army Suit," *Pittsburgh Courier*, 1 March 1947.

30. For more on the Truman administration's attempts to create a program of compulsory military training and the often contentious debates generated by the proposal, see Michael J. Hogan, *A Cross of Iron: Harry S. Truman and the Origins of the National Security State, 1945–1954* (New York: Cambridge University Press, 1998), 119–158.

31. Congress had authorized slightly more than one million personnel, but the army was then losing an average of 385 men per day. "Army Again Asks Negroes," *New York Times*, 19 July 1947.

32. MacGregor and Nalty, *Basic Documents*, vol. 8, 704, 710.

33. Charley Cherokee, "National Grapevine," *Chicago Defender*, 14 June 1947 ("face facts"); "What about Conscription?" *Pittsburgh Courier*, 15 February 1947; "Brass Hats and Jim Crow," *Pittsburgh Courier*, 10 January 1948 ("colored citizens"). Labor leader A. Philip Randolph led the most publicized opposition to universal military service. As national treasurer of the Committee against Jim Crow in Military Service and Training, he appeared before a Senate panel investigating UMT and various short-term draft proposals in the spring of 1948. Randolph testified he was "not beguiled by the Army's use of the word 'temporary,' " because no UMT program could avoid becoming permanent "since the world trend is toward militarism." He called for a mass civil disobedience campaign, sparking a national uproar, with various African American leaders appearing before the Senate Armed Services Committee either to support or to condemn his proposal. In the end, the UMT went down to defeat in Congress, and debates over a civil disobedience campaign quickly became moot. MacGregor and Nalty, *Basic Documents*, vol. 8, 653–655 ("not beguiled"); C. P. Trussell, "Congress Told UMT Racial Bars Would Unleash Civil Disobedience," *New York Times*, 1 April 1948; "Bars Negro War Protest," *New York Times*, 2 April 1948.

34. Morris J. MacGregor and Bernard C. Nalty, eds., *Blacks in the United States Armed Forces: Basic Documents*, vol. 11, *The Fahy Committee* (Wilmington, Del.: Scholarly Resources Inc., 1977), 1228–1229, 1252–1256 ("that excess"), 1314–1317 ("33 percent"); Foner, *Blacks and the Military*, 188; McCoy and Ruetten, *Quest and Response*, 197; Dalfiume, *Desegregation*, 196.

35. See, for example, "Weakest Link in Nation's Defense Chain," *Afro-American*, 3 June 1950.

36. Leo Bogart, ed., *Project Clear: Social Research and the Desegregation of the United States Army* (New Brunswick, N.J.: Transaction Publishers, 1992), xxx; "25,000 Negroes Face Draft!" *Pittsburgh Courier*, 22 July 1950 ("were swarming"); "War Floods Army with Enlistments," *Cleveland Call and Post*, 15 July 1950 ("swamped"); Mershon and Schlossman, *Foxholes and Color Lines*, 223.

37. Foner, *Blacks and the Military*, 180, 182; Clay Blair, *The Forgotten War: America in Korea, 1950–1953* (New York: Times Books, 1987), 28; "Draft Law Triples Enlistments," *Chicago Defender*, 26 June 1948.

38. West eventually obtained a commission and served long enough to see action in Vietnam. Norvel Phillip West interview, "Korea: The Unfinished War," a project of American RadioWorks, documentary unit of American Public Media.

39. Jessie Brown interview, "Korea: The Unfinished War."

40. Clentell Jackson interview, "Korea: The Unfinished War." Servicemen were of course subject to authoritarian control in the military, but the legal machinery was strictly standardized and judicial proceedings for enlisted personnel gradually improved. As one African American advocate for universal military training argued, "The Army court-martial is fairer than trial by your so-called peers in many parts of the country." Horace R. Cayton, "Conscription: Nicodemus Has Good Words for Universal Military Training," *Pittsburgh Courier*, 3 April 1948.

41. "Shape of Things to Come," *Afro-American*, 17 November 1945 ("vocational training"); Horace R. Cayton, "Conscription: Nicodemus Has Good Words for Universal Military Training," *Pittsburgh Courier*, 3 April 1948 ("against military training").

42. Photograph with caption, *California Eagle*, 24 January 1946 ("Army life"); "Two Tenth Cavalry Vets Help Ex-Buddy Reenlist in Army," *California Eagle*, 7 February 1946 ("sold"); "Two Here Choose Career in U.S. Army," *California Eagle*, 20 November 1947 ("best boss"); "For a Fifth Freedom," *Afro-American*, 28 September 1946.

43. Walter White, "People, Politics and Places," *Chicago Defender*, 18 May 1946.

44. Norvel Phillip West interview, "Korea: The Unfinished War" ("offered"); Rudy Tomedi, *No Bugles, No Drums: An Oral History of the Korean War* (New York: John Wiley & Sons, 1993), 182 ("no better institution"); Isaac Gardner, Jr. interview, "Korea: The Unfinished War" ("mountain boy").

45. Ollie Stewart, "Segregation Hurts Army," *Afro-American*, 17 July 1948.

46. Robert Bruton collection (AFC/2001/001/54254), Veterans History Project, American Folklife Center, Library of Congress.

47. "24th Inf. Soldiers Give $3,770 to NAACP," *Afro-American*, 4 September 1948.

48. Charles Berry collection (AFC/2001/001/5950), Veterans History Project.

49. Lipsitz, *Life in the Struggle*, 38–41.

50. Ira Neal collection (AFC/2001/001/1189), Veterans History Project; the income-equivalency estimate appeared in Eric Larrabee, "The Peacetime Army: Warriors Need Not Apply," *Harper's Magazine*, March 1947, 240–241. See also Yvonne Latty, *We Were There: Voices of African American Veterans, from World War II to the War in Iraq* (New York: Harper Collins, 2004), 63; "Philly Father of Eight Finds Civilian Pay Too Low, Reenlists," *Afro-American*, 27 April 1946; and Shedrick Burk Collection (AFC/2001/001/9554), Veterans History Project.

51. Philip Dodd, "Truman Calls Probe in Reich Unnecessary," *Chicago Daily Tribune*, 4 December 1946.

52. Lee Nichols, *Breakthrough on the Color Front* (New York: Random House, 1954), 186. Rape allegations against Americans in Germany peaked at 501 in April 1945 and then leveled off at forty-five per month for the rest of the year. Petra Goedde, *GIs and Germans: Culture, Gender, and Foreign Relations, 1945–1949* (New Haven: Yale University Press, 2003), 85.

53. Truman K. Gibson, Jr., "Meader's Report Seeks to Remove GIs," *Pittsburgh Courier*, 14 December 1946 ("resentful"); Louis Lautier, "Integration Will Solve Problem: Ray Discredits Meader Report on GI Misconduct in Germany," *Pittsburgh Courier*, 28 December 1946; Goedde, *GIs and Germans*, 64–65.

54. "Suppressed Report on Germany Lays Immorality to U.S. Forces," *New York Times*, 2 December 1946 ("large portion"); C. B. Alexander to Dwight Eisenhower, letter, n.d., Folder "291.2 Race 6–1–46–6–30–46," Box 719, RG 407, Records of the Adjutant General's Office, Army-AG Decimal File, 1946–48, National Archives II ("moved elsewhere"); Carl T. Curtis to James Forrestal, summary of letter sent 16 November 1948, Folder "291.2 Negroes 7-1-48," Box 71, RG 335, Records of the Office of the Secretary of the Army, General Correspondence, July 1947–Dec. 1950, National Archives II ("Advises that").

55. Memorandum, 14 June 1946, Frame 784, Reel 12, Series A, Part 9, *Papers of the NAACP* ("discontinue shipment"); Louis Lautier, "Army Places Ban on Negroes for ETO," *Pittsburgh Courier*, 6 July 1946 ("only overseas theatre"). See also Jean Byers, "A Study of the Negro in Military Service" (June 1947), 262, Folder "291.2 Negroes 2–9–50," Box 71, RG 335, Records of the Office of the Secretary of the Army, General Correspondence, July 1947–Dec. 1950, National Archives II. The ban on new black assignments to Europe, after evidently being lifted in late 1946 or 1947, was reinstated in early 1948. See Ashton Williams, "'For White Only' Signs Raised by Army Again," *Afro-American*, 28 February 1948.

56. Bill Smith, "Blue Discharges for Disliked GIs?: Army 'Big Shots' Speed 'Purge' Of Race Troops from Germany," *Pittsburgh Courier*, 9 November 1946; Allan Bérubé, *Coming Out under Fire: The History of Gay Men and Women in World War Two* (New York: Plume, 1991), 139–141; William Smith, "Chopped Off by Army: Half of Tan GIs Leaving Germany," *Pittsburgh Courier*, 21 December 1946; "Half of ETO Discharges Non-White," *Pittsburgh*

Courier, 4 January 1947; "Many Backing 'Blue Discharge' Outrage Now Face Army Trials," *Pittsburgh Courier*, 22 February 1947 ("carefully checked"). See also "1,000 Tan Yanks Shipped Home after Armed Clash with White Troops in Italy," *California Eagle*, 5 December 1946.

57. "122,037 Tan Yanks Listed in U.S. Army on First of Year," *Afro-American*, 8 March 1947; Cliff Mackay, "Europe's Most Beautiful Women Give Their Affection to Generous Tan Yanks," *Afro-American*, 17 April 1948; Vernon W. Stone, "German Baby Crop Left by Negro GI's," *The Survey*, November 1949, 580. The number of black servicemen in Europe rebounded to 9,000 by the start of the Korean War, and then, amid fears that Korea was a feint to disguise Soviet moves on Western Europe, to more than 27,000 by the end of 1951 (as part of a general tripling of American strength in the theater). Nalty, *Strength for the Fight*, 260.

58. The northern United States was the primary alternative, and by 1947 the majority of black soldiers serving in the United States were stationed outside the South. Jean Byers, "A Study of the Negro in Military Service" (June 1947), 262, Folder "291.2 Negroes 2-9-50," Box 71, RG 335, Records of the Office of the Secretary of the Army, General Correspondence, July 1947–Dec. 1950, National Archives II.

59. For two examples, from May 1947 and December 1948, of identical use of this language, see MacGregor and Nalty, *Basic Documents*, vol. 8, 115; and FEC Report, Folder "291.2—Races," Box 88, RG 554, Records of General HQ, Far East Command, Supreme Commander Allied Powers, and United Nations Command, Assistant Chief of Staff, G-1, General Correspondence, Unclassified, 1949, National Archives II.

2. The American Dream in a Prostrate Japan

1. James L. Hicks, "What Will Happen If Russia Conquers U.S.: Way We Treat Japan a Warning," *Afro-American*, 18 November 1950.

2. See, for example, the numerous works on Afro-Asian solidarity cited in the introduction. Mutual white-Japanese racial hatreds are extensively documented in John W. Dower, *War without Mercy: Race and Power in the Pacific War* (New York: Pantheon, 1986).

3. As one historian notes, the Japanese "sold cherry-blossom visions of Japan to help them revive their prewar tourist industry and downplay their militant wartime reputation." Naoko Shibusawa, "America's Geisha Ally: Race, Gender, and Maturity in Refiguring the Japanese Enemy, 1945–1964" (Ph.D. diss., Northwestern University, 1998), iv. See also Naoko Shibusawa, *America's Geisha Ally: Reimagining the Japanese Enemy* (Cambridge: Harvard University Press, 2006).

4. This composite description of travel to and arrival in occupied Japan is drawn from John W. Dower, preface to Takemae, *Inside GHQ*, xxii; Jacob Van Staaveren, *An American in Japan, 1945–1948: A Civilian View of the Occupation* (Seattle: University of Washington Press, 1994), 3–8; Noel F. Busch, *Fallen Sun: A Report on Japan* (New York: D. Appleton-Century, 1948), 13 ("to Tokyo"); Cpl. Arthur Gottlieb, "Fresh from the States," *Pacific Stars and Stripes*, 8 September 1946, Sunday Comic and Feature Section; and Harry Emerson Wildes, *Typhoon in Tokyo: The Occupation and Its Aftermath* (New York: Macmillan, 1954), 20. See also Carmen Johnson, *Wave-Rings in the Water: My Years with the Women of Postwar Japan* (Alexandria, Va.: Charles River Press, 1996), 5–6, for a similar description of travel from the West Coast to occupied Japan, albeit from a civilian perspective.

5. Wildes, *Typhoon in Tokyo*, 2; Laura E. Hein, *Fueling Growth: The Energy Revolution and Economic Policy in Postwar Japan* (Cambridge: Harvard University Press, 1990), 53; Dower,

Embracing Defeat, 44 ("entire economic structure"), 45, 93; Simon Partner, *Assembled in Japan: Electrical Goods and the Making of the Japanese Consumer* (Berkeley: University of California Press, 1999), 46; Tiana Norgren, *Abortion before Birth Control: The Politics of Reproduction in Postwar Japan* (Princeton: Princeton University Press, 2001), 36–37; Takemae, *Inside GHQ*, xxxviii–xxxix, 77–78; Walter Rundell, Jr., *Black Market Money* (Baton Rouge: Louisiana State University Press, 1964), 63; Patricia L. Maclachlan, *Consumer Politics in Postwar Japan: The Institutional Boundaries of Citizen Activism* (New York: Columbia University Press, 2002), 59 ("bamboo shoot lifestyle").

6. Partner, *Assembled in Japan*, 47.

7. Mark Gayn, *Japan Diary* (New York: William Sloane Associates, 1948), 47. Japanese literary portrayals of postwar hustling may be found in Ishikawa Jun, *The Legend of Gold and Other Stories*, trans. William J. Tyler (Honolulu: University of Hawai'i Press, 1998); and Hisako Matsubara, *Cranes at Dusk*, trans. Leila Vennewitz (Garden City, N.Y.: Dial Press, 1985).

8. Billy Rowe, "Tan Yanks Invade Japan: Service Troops First to Occupy Enemy Homeland," *Pittsburgh Courier*, 1 September 1945 ("poised"); Charles H. Loeb, "Negro Service Troops Arrive in Japan," *Cleveland Call and Post*, 15 September 1945; Langston Hughes, "Here to Yonder," *Chicago Defender*, 9 February 1946 ("do not want"); Deton J. Brooks, Jr., "Troops Anxious to Move on Jap Capital," *Chicago Defender*, 1 September 1945 ("Strange").

9. Vincent Tubbs, "Jungle-Weary Tan Yanks Feel Sorry for Japanese," *Afro-American*, 29 September 1945 ("mere soldiers"); "The Japs and 'Supremacy,'" *Afro-American*, 29 September 1945 ("sneering insinuation").

10. Emphasis in the original. "Look into an Uncle Tom's Eye," *Afro-American*, 22 September 1945. The paper returned to this theme one year later, arguing that "some day the Russians, the Chinese, the Africans or some other group with a birth rate higher than ours will conquer America. The Uncle Toms of that day will not be Japanese, but white Americans." "How Uncle Toms Are Made," *Afro-American*, 19 October 1946.

11. See, for example, Brian Masaru Hayashi, *Democratizing the Enemy: The Japanese American Internment* (Princeton: Princeton University Press, 2004), 39.

12. Vincent Tubbs, "Sign Language Used by GI's to Boss Jap Stevedores on Yokohama Docks," *Afro-American*, 13 October 1945. For similar accounts of black supervision of Japanese workers, see Charles H. Loeb, "Japs Disinterested in JC Ideas—GI's," *Afro-American*, 13 October 1945; and Charles H. Loeb, "Jap Friendliness to GIs Increases," *Afro-American*, 13 October 1945.

13. Peyton Gray, "First Tan Yanks in Tokyo Assigned to Guard Duty," *Afro-American*, 3 November 1945; Billy Rowe, "GI Bigotry Threatens U.S. Plan in Japan," *Pittsburgh Courier*, 27 October 1945, second news section ("flagrant insult"); "Even in Japan!" *Pittsburgh Courier*, 3 November 1945; "Nazi Methods Employed by Americans in Japan, Marines Reveal," *Afro-American*, 12 January 1946. Black observers also bristled at news of reforms, such as the abolition of sharecropping, instituted for the benefit of the Japanese but denied in the United States. See, for example, "Democracy Abroad; Slavery at Home" and "Somewhere in the U.S.A.," *Chicago Defender*, 29 December 1945.

14. "Join the Eighth Army to See Japan and Bon Voyage Soldier," *Pacific Stars and Stripes*, 3 November 1945.

15. The IOU was signed "Johnsood Sim Dupree Sineon John Roy Peep Leo Smith." Reports on Misconducts [*sic*] of American Soldiers, Folder "250–1 #2," Box 433, RG 331, Records of the Supreme Commander for the Allied Powers (SCAP), Adjutant General's Section, Operations Division, Mail & Records Branch, Decimal File, 1945–46, National Ar-

chives II. On the other hand, some black servicemen were appalled by the misery they witnessed. James Rutledge later remembered seeing countless "little kids on crutches" with missing limbs. When ordered back to the United States, he felt "glad to leave 'cause I couldn't stand seeing much of that anymore." James Rutledge collection (AFC/2001/001/30996), Veterans History Project.

16. R. P. Dore, *City Life in Japan: A Study of a Tokyo Ward* (Berkeley: University of California Press, 1958), 162. Another study reports that Japanese crime rates doubled following surrender. Meirion Harries and Susie Harries, *Sheathing the Sword: The Demilitarization of Japan* (New York: Macmillan, 1987), 34.

17. Takemae, *Inside GHQ*, 57, 67. See also Robert L. Eichelberger, with Milton Mackaye, *Our Jungle Road to Tokyo* (New York: Viking, 1950), 273–274, for an account of an assault on two GIs and the American military's harsh response.

18. Letter Digests, 22 December 1945 and 6 December 1946, Folder "250–1 #2," Box 433, RG 331, Records of the Supreme Commander for the Allied Powers (SCAP), Adjutant General's Section, Operations Division, Mail & Records Branch, Decimal File, 1945–46, National Archives II.

19. SCAP issued its pre-censorship rules on 10 September 1945. Takemae, *Inside GHQ*, 67.

20. Ibid., 68.

21. Frank Kelley and Cornelius Ryan, *Star-Spangled Mikado* (New York: Robert M. McBride, 1947), 148. Japanese historian Yuki Tanaka has written the fullest account of the RAA's origins, confirming the figure of at least two million in 1945 dollars. Tanaka, *Japan's Comfort Women: Sexual Slavery and Prostitution during World War II and the US Occupation* (New York: Routledge, 2002), 142–143.

22. Michael S. Molasky, *The American Occupation of Japan and Okinawa: Literature and Memory* (New York: Routledge, 1999), 105; Charles H. Loeb, "Loeb Looks at Japan," *Cleveland Call and Post*, 29 December 1945; John LaCerda, *The Conqueror Comes to Tea: Japan under MacArthur* (New Brunswick, N.J.: Rutgers University Press, 1946), 51; Theodore Cohen, *Remaking Japan: The American Occupation as New Deal*, ed. Herbert Passin (New York: Free Press, 1987), 126; Kelley and Ryan, *Star-Spangled Mikado*, 150, 152.

23. "Recommendation for support of military police function in Tokyo City," memorandum, 17 September 1945, Folder "250–1 #2," Box 433, RG 331, Records of the Supreme Commander for the Allied Powers (SCAP), Adjutant General's Section, Operations Division, Mail & Records Branch, Decimal File, 1945–46, National Archives II.

24. "Where Tan Yanks Are Located in Japan," map with caption, *Afro-American*, 6 April 1946; Vincent Tubbs, "Reveal 14,866 Tan GI's in Tokyo Area: Troops Attached to 75 Service Outfits," *Afro-American*, 15 December 1945; Vincent Tubbs, "Functions of Occupation Troops in Japan Outlined," *Afro-American*, 19 January 1946.

25. Tamotsu Shibutani, *The Derelicts of Company K: A Sociological Study of Demoralization* (Berkeley: University of California Press, 1978), 366; Helen Mears, "You in Tokyo," *New Yorker*, 23 November 1946, 90–91 ("new arrival"); Gayn, *Japan Diary*, 303 ("carpetbagger's dream").

26. Walt Sheldon, *The Honorable Conquerors: The Occupation of Japan, 1945–1952* (New York: Macmillan, 1965), 108; Mears, "You in Tokyo," 90–91; LaCerda, *Conqueror Comes to Tea*, 120–121; Ollie Stewart, "Definite Advantage Seen in Limiting of Occupation Troops to Service Units," *Afro-American*, 20 April 1946 ("as long as"). See also Jorge T. Teodoro, "Majority Still Confined to Service Jobs, Some GI's in Japan Given Special Work," *Afro-American*, 1 June 1946.

27. Helen Mears, *Mirror for Americans: Japan* (Cambridge, Mass.: Riverside Press, 1948), 256, 256–257n13; Dower, *Embracing Defeat*, 115.

28. John Curtis Perry, *Beneath the Eagle's Wings: Americans in Occupied Japan* (New York: Dodd, Mead, 1980), 176 ("high-school"); Cohen, *Remaking Japan*, 127.

29. Takemae, *Inside GHQ*, 75; Van Staaveren, *An American in Japan*, 10; FEC Report, Folder "291.2—Races," Box 88, RG 554, Records of General HQ, Far East Command, Supreme Commander Allied Powers, and United Nations Command, Assistant Chief of Staff, G-1, General Correspondence, Unclassified, 1949, National Archives II; Wildes, *Typhoon in Tokyo*, 326; Cohen, *Remaking Japan*, 122, 123 ("They keep trying"), 127.

30. For an example, from August and September 1945, of confusion among local commanders as to fraternization rules, see "Non-Fraternization Policy," memorandum, 12 September 1945, Folder "250–1 #2," Box 433, RG 331, Records of the Supreme Commander for the Allied Powers (SCAP), Adjutant General's Section, Operations Division, Mail & Records Branch, Decimal File, 1945–46, National Archives II.

31. Takemae, *Inside GHQ*, 75; "Public Display of Affection," memorandum, 23 March 1946, Folder "250–1 #2," Box 433, RG 331, Records of the Supreme Commander for the Allied Powers (SCAP), Adjutant General's Section, Operations Division, Mail & Records Branch, Decimal File, 1945–46, National Archives II ("public displays"); "Nisei GIs in Japan Included in Public Fraternization Ban," *Pacific Citizen*, 6 April 1946; "Neck in Private or Face Stockade!: 'Public Affection' between Soldiers, Jap Women Out," *Pacific Stars and Stripes*, 23 March 1946; Cohen, *Remaking Japan*, 128 ("not exactly illegal"); "An Old Southern Custom," *Afro-American*, 30 March 1946 ("after dark").

32. Margery Finn Brown, *Over a Bamboo Fence: An American Looks at Japan* (New York: William Morrow, 1951), 54 ("geared"); Busch, *Fallen Sun*, 25 ("most of the ordinary"); James L. Hicks, "MacArthur Backer of JC," *Afro-American*, 21 April 1951 ("Tokyo today"); Mitsu Yasuda, "In My Father's Japan," *Pacific Citizen*, 24 December 1949.

33. LaCerda, *Conqueror Comes to Tea*, 47–48.

34. "After World War II the value of Troop Information was no more widely accepted in the ranks than it had been during the conflict," observes one historian. "In fact, despite operating continuously from World War II through the Vietnam War, Troop Information never overcame its status as a new invention of dubious value." DeRosa, *Political Indoctrination in the U.S. Army*, 17, 74–75.

35. Cpl. Arthur Gottlieb, "Fresh from the States," *Pacific Stars and Stripes*, 8 September 1946, Sunday Comic and Feature Section.

36. Layle Silbert, "We Export—Race Prejudice to China," *The Crisis*, July 1948, 208; Declassified report, Folder "291.2, Section I, Cases 1–2," Box 171, RG 319, Records of the Army Staff, Plans and Operations Division, Decimal File, 1946–48, National Archives II ("exploit").

37. "Army Integrates Troops: Mixed Division Formed for Peace Duty in Japan," *Afro-American*, 1 February 1947; "Negro Unit Going to Japan," *New York Times*, 25 January 1947; "Praised by General: 24th Joining U.S. Forces in Japan," *Pittsburgh Courier*, 1 February 1947; L. Albert Scipio II, *Last of the Black Regulars: A History of the 24th Infantry Regiment (1869–1951)* (Silver Spring, Md.: Roman Publications, 1983), 79; Takemae, *Inside GHQ*, 442.

38. See, for example, "Army Integrates Troops: Mixed Division Formed for Peace Duty in Japan," *Afro-American*, 1 February 1947; P. L Prattis, "New Manpower Standards: Ray Proposals Plan to 'Equalize' Army," *Pittsburgh Courier*, 18 January 1947; and "24th Infantry to Police Japan," *Chicago Defender*, 1 February 1947. The author for the *Defender*, while accepting the military's professed motives, credited MacArthur more than the War Department.

39. Pfc. John Wesley Rankin, letter to the editor, *Chicago Defender*, 19 January 1946 ("even the people"); "Manila Posters Ask Ouster of Soldiers," *Chicago Defender*, 14 December 1946 ("armed Filipino gang"); Billy Rowe, "Manila Disorders Blamed on Army-Sponsored Segregation," *Pittsburgh Courier*, 19 January 1946; "Army Starts Probe of Manila Rioting," *Pittsburgh Courier*, 19 January 1946. See also E. T. Hall, Jr., "Race Prejudice and Negro-White Relations in the Army," *American Journal of Sociology* 52, no. 5 (March 1947): 406, which noted that Filipino men made references to "damn niggers." Similar incidents of anti-black discrimination reportedly occurred in both Guam and Hawaii. See, for example, Tech. Sgt. William Barnes, letter to the editor, *Ebony*, March 1947, 4; and "An American Soldier," letter to the editor, *Pittsburgh Courier*, 15 November 1947.

40. PHILRYCOM Troop Basis, confidential report, Folder "Conf. Oct.–Dec. 1947," Box 2, RG 554, Records of General HQ, Far East Command, Supreme Commander Allied Powers, and United Nations Command, Assistant Chief of Staff, G-1, General Records, Confidential, 1947–48, National Archives II.

41. "Policy for Negro Personnel, Clark Air Force Base, P.I.," memorandum, 14 June 1949, Folder "Conf. Book XI," Box 5, RG 554, Records of General HQ, Far East Command, Supreme Commander Allied Powers, and United Nations Command, Assistant Chief of Staff, G-1, General Records, Confidential, 1949, National Archives II.

42. Untitled confidential reports, Folder "Conf. 1948 Bk III," Box 3, RG 554, Records of General HQ, Far East Command, Supreme Commander Allied Powers, and United Nations Command, Assistant Chief of Staff, G-1, General Records, Confidential, 1948–49, National Archives II; "Analysis of the Program and Procedures Regarding Negro Troops Effective in the Far East Command," 3 January 1949, Folder "291.2—Races," Box 88, RG 554, Records of General HQ, Far East Command, Supreme Commander Allied Powers, and United Nations Command, Assistant Chief of Staff, G-1, General Correspondence, Unclassified, 1949, National Archives II. At the end of World War II, a limited number of black troops arrived with American forces in Korea. However, two years later a soldier complained that he was one of only one hundred or so African American personnel stationed on the entire peninsula. Billy Rowe, "4 QM Companies Land in Korea," *Pittsburgh Courier*, 22 September 1945; Billy Rowe, "43 Tan Yanks with Malaria Control Unit in Free Korea," *Pittsburgh Courier*, 6 October 1945; Kenneth Latimer, letter to the editor, *Pittsburgh Courier*, 23 August 1947.

43. Blair, *The Forgotten War*, 48.

44. R. L. Eichelberger, letter to the editor, *Time*, 5 August 1946, 12 ("When I saw"); "General Eichelberger Gives Report on First Year of Jap Occupation," *Pacific Stars and Stripes*, 1 September 1946 ("the most pleasant").

45. ". . . the First Year," special magazine, *Pacific Stars and Stripes*, 2 September 1946.

46. "Army Is Studying Question of Bringing Wives to Japan," *Pacific Stars and Stripes*, 15 November 1945.

47. "Army Plans Overseas Housing for Families," *Pacific Stars and Stripes*, 4 February 1946. For information on the armed forces' evolving attitudes toward and policies regarding American military families overseas before and after World War II, see Alvah, *Unofficial Ambassadors*, 39–40, 61–62.

48. "MacArthur Hopes All EM Can Get Wives to Japan," *Pacific Stars and Stripes*, 12 February 1946.

49. See, for example, "First Army Families to Be on Way in June," *Pacific Stars and Stripes*, 25 May 1946; and Sheldon, *The Honorable Conquerors*, 115.

50. Cynthia Enloe has pioneered understandings of the importance of women to military endeavors abroad. Particularly relevant here are her observations that "wives' dissatisfaction with military life can produce worrisome manpower shortages," while "keeping soldiers happy on a foreign base requires keeping soldiers' wives happy." Enloe, *Bananas, Beaches, & Bases: Making Feminist Sense of International Politics* (Berkeley: University of California Press, 1990), 71–72.

51. "Reconstruction of Tokyo Proceeding at Slow Pace; Materials Black Marketed," *Pacific Stars and Stripes*, 1 March 1946. The requisitioning of local resources for housing and other facilities continued for years. By 1949 it had swallowed up one third of Japan's iron and cement, one fifth of its steel, and one tenth of its lumber and glass. Sheldon, *The Honorable Conquerors*, 114.

52. "Tokyo-Yokohama Dependent Housing under Construction," *Pacific Stars and Stripes*, 23 June 1946; Russell Brines, *MacArthur's Japan* (Philadelphia: J. B. Lippincott, 1948), 290.

53. "Officers and EM Get Same Housing," *Pacific Stars and Stripes*, 25 March 1946 ("an equal number"); Cpl. Sam Lester, "A Home Away from Home: Army Families Will Live in Style," *Pacific Stars and Stripes*, 31 March 1946 ("typical home").

54. Michael Schaller, *The American Occupation of Japan: The Origins of the Cold War in Asia* (New York: Oxford University Press, 1985), 125. Most of the larger American bases in operation today retain this suburban flavor. See, for example, Mark L. Gillem, *America Town: Building the Outposts of Empire* (Minneapolis: University of Minnesota Press, 2007).

55. John Rich, "GI Dependents to Arrive in May: Two Big Projects in Tokyo Will House U.S. Families," *Pacific Stars and Stripes*, 25 March 1946 ("complete communities"); "GI Dependents in Japan to Get Full Medical Care," *Pacific Stars and Stripes*, 30 May 1946; "Dependents' Children to Get Baby Foods," *Pacific Stars and Stripes*, 19 June 1945 ("powdered"); Busch, *Fallen Sun*, 22–23. Occupationaires and their dependents were largely unaffected by the rapid postwar rise in domestic food prices. See, for example, "Occupation Foods Cost Rise to Be Slower Than U.S.," *Pacific Stars and Stripes*, 2 November 1947.

56. Mears, "You in Tokyo," 92 ("the Army"); Takemae, *Inside GHQ*, 75; Sheldon, *The Honorable Conquerors*, 113, 115; Van Staaveren, *An American in Japan*, 80 ("to portray").

57. "New Tokyo PX Officially Opens, Largest in World," *Pacific Stars and Stripes*, 22 October 1946 ("largest"); James L. Hicks, "GI's in Tokyo Lavish Gifts on Jap Girls, Shun Own Clubs," *Afro-American*, 2 September 1950, magazine section ("PX in Tokyo"); "Army PX System Is Big Enterprise," *Pacific Stars and Stripes*, 11 May 1947, Sunday Comic and Feature Section; "PX Bought Gifts to Go Duty Free," *Pacific Stars and Stripes*, 7 September 1947; "No Duty Limit on PX Gifts to U.S.," *Pacific Stars and Stripes*, 9 September 1947.

58. "P-X-Train," *Pacific Stars and Stripes*, 8 December 1946, Sunday Comic and Feature Section.

59. Interview with Lt. Col. Charles Bussey, National Security Archive, George Washington University, www.gwu.edu/~nsarchiv/coldwar/interviews/episode-5/bussey1.html.

60. "Dependent Priority Change Announced for Army, WDC's," *Pacific Stars and Stripes*, 8 July 1947.

61. Charley Cherokee, "National Grapevine," *Chicago Defender*, 1 March 1947.

62. Ralph Matthews, "GI's Ponder Peace Moves," *Afro-American*, 22 September 1951 ("the saddest people"); "Every GI a King in Japan," *Ebony*, April 1953, 36, 40 ("easy, plush life").

63. *Foreign Relations of the United States, 1949*, vol. 7, *The Far East and Australasia*, part 2 (Washington, D.C.: United States Government Printing Office, 1976), 660–661.

64. Sheldon, *The Honorable Conquerors*, 65.

65. This summary of the origins of the Kobe disturbances is based on Takemae, *Inside GHQ*, 462–463. For General Eichelberger's account of this and other "wild Korean outbreaks," see Eichelberger, *Jungle Road to Tokyo*, 274.

66. "Outbreak Seen as Red Inspired," *New York Times*, 26 April 1948.

67. "Negro Troops in World Trouble Areas," *Norfolk Journal and Guide*, 1 May 1948; Takemae, *Inside GHQ*, 463–464; Emmanuel Duncan interview, "Korea: The Unfinished War"; Shibusawa, *America's Geisha Ally*, 168; Scipio, *Last of the Black Regulars*, 81. The black press repeatedly highlighted the fact that Japanese citizens had greater access to the ballot box than African Americans did in the South. See, for example, "Charity Begins at Home," *Afro-American*, 3 November 1945; and "Democracy vs. Democracy!" *California Eagle*, 25 July 1946.

68. "Staff Section Report of G-1 Section, GHQ, FEC, for 1 January–31 October 1950," Box 12, RG 554, Records of General HQ, Far East Command, Supreme Commander Allied Powers, and United Nations Command, Assistant Chief of Staff, G-1, General Records, Secret, 1949, National Archives II ("an attitude"); Wildes, *Typhoon in Tokyo*, 329–330 ("to establish," "Army installations"); "Staff Section Report of G-1 Section, GHQ, FEC, for 1 January–31 October 1950," Box 12, RG 554, Records of General HQ, Far East Command, Supreme Commander Allied Powers, and United Nations Command, Assistant Chief of Staff, G-1, General Records, Secret, 1949, National Archives II; Cohen, *Remaking Japan*, 134; Takemae, *Inside GHQ*, 80.

69. Emphasis in the original. Ira Neal collection, Veterans History Project.

70. Yukiko Koshiro, *Trans-Pacific Racisms and the U.S. Occupation of Japan* (New York: Columbia University Press, 1999), 52.

71. "X.Y.Z.," letter to the editor, *Afro-American*, 24 May 1947. The 24th's zone of responsibility during the occupation, centered on Gifu, encompassed four prefectures with a population of six-and-a-half million Japanese. Louis Lautier, "Lautier Says Gen. MacArthur Not to Blame for Jim Crow Policies," *Afro-American*, 28 April 1951.

72. Jessie Brown interview, "Korea: The Unfinished War"; Selika Marianne Ducksworth, "What Hour of the Night: Black Enlisted Men's Experiences and the Desegregation of the Army during the Korean War, 1950–1951" (Ph.D. diss., Ohio State University, 1994), 129.

73. "Tan Yanks Help Nip Tokyo Black Market," *California Eagle*, 2 January 1947; "Brooklyn GI Captures 7 Jap Black Marketeers [sic]," *Afro-American*, 22 May 1948; Charley Cherokee, "National Grapevine," *Chicago Defender*, 13 March 1948 ("these boys").

74. Charles Berry collection, Veterans History Project ("We didn't"); Jessie Brown interview, "Korea: The Unfinished War" ("life was good"); "Around the World," *California Eagle*, 26 January 1950 ("theatres").

75. A historian of the 24th Infantry Regiment notes that facilities at Camp Gifu "included the Easly Theater, which featured USO shows in addition to regular movies. The American Red Cross Club provided enlisted men with a lounge, waiting room, game room, photographic laboratory, library, craft shop, canteen, a 'Little Theater,' and a patio." Scipio, *Last of the Black Regulars*, 81. For a similar description of Camp Gifu, see William T. Bowers, William M. Hammond, and George L. MacGarrigle, *Black Soldier, White Army: The 24th Infantry Regiment in Korea* (Washington, D.C.: Center of Military History, United States Army, 1996), 50. By contrast, one author maintains that "white troops generally were well looked after, with their snack bars, swimming pools, barber shops, and clubs. Black troops often lacked these amenities." Perry, *Beneath the Eagle's Wings*, 171.

76. Sheldon, *The Honorable Conquerors*, 150.

77. Alfred A. Duckett, "Japs Teach Americans Democracy, GI Reports," *Afro-American*, 22 April 1950 ("pleasure"); Takemae, *Inside GHQ*, 130 ("get out at night"); Perry, *Beneath*

the *Eagle's Wings*, 171; "1940th Engineer Aviation Utilities Company," letter to the editor, *Chicago Defender*, 6 July 1946 ("Lily-White"); "C.B.S.," letter to the editor, *Afro-American*, 13 April 1946 ("shooting gallery"). See also Jimmie Cagney Akias, letter to the editor, *New York Amsterdam News*, 19 January 1946.

78. "Japan Intrigued Jersey Girl," *Afro-American*, 13 October 1951, magazine section ("the greatest concentration"); Ira Neal collection, Veterans History Project.

79. The NAACP demanded of the Secretary of the Army "an immediate investigation of the manner in which Negro troops are treated in Tokyo and the elimination of racial discrimination so persistently reported to presently exist." Roy Wilkins to Frank Pace, Jr., 21 July 1950, Folder "291.2 Negroes (Jan '50 to [illegible])," Box 71, RG 335, Records of the Office of the Secretary of the Army, General Correspondence, July 1947–Dec. 1950, National Archives II. The Japanese American newspaper *Pacific Citizen* editorialized that "one cannot dismiss the report lightly," but argued "if the people of occupied Japan adopt the more obvious habits of discrimination, as practiced by some of our troops, they can hardly be blamed for wanting to take on the customs of the conqueror." "Prejudice for Export," *Pacific Citizen*, 12 August 1950.

80. Emmanuel Duncan interview, "Korea: The Unfinished War."

81. Ira Neal collection, Veterans History Project.

3. The Public Politics of Intimate Affairs

1. "The Inquiring Reporter," *Afro-American*, 15 September 1945. Historian Reginald Kearney has employed the same poll to posit a "historical affinity for the Japanese" among many black Americans, one that rendered them "natural supporters of a liberal policy of occupation." Kearney, *African American Views*, 123.

2. Elder H. Russell, "Why American Soldiers Will Get Along with Japanese Girls," *Afro-American*, 22 September 1945.

3. "The Race War That Flopped," *Ebony*, July 1946, 3. Interestingly, the Japanese American newspaper *Pacific Citizen* admiringly reported on and extensively excerpted from the *Ebony* story, yet completely ignored its sexualized and marital imagery. "Ebony Magazine Tells about 'The Race War That Flopped,'" *Pacific Citizen*, 13 July 1946.

4. Lipsitz, "'Frantic to Join,'" 347 ("fables"); Shibusawa, "America's Geisha Ally," 30 ("Japanese women"). See also Shibusawa, *America's Geisha Ally*, 4; and Christina Klein, "Family Ties and Political Obligation: The Discourse of Adoption and the Cold War Commitment to Asia," in *Cold War Constructions: The Political Culture of United States Imperialism, 1945–1966*, ed. Christian G. Appy (Amherst: University of Massachusetts Press, 2000), 37–38. This development was also encouraged and sustained through a demonization of the People's Republic of China. "The war hates and race hates of World War Two," notes a historian, "proved very adaptable to the cold war." The Chinese, "heralded by Americans during the war for their individualism and love of democracy," "suddenly inherited most of the old, monolithic, inherently totalitarian raiments the Japanese were shedding." Dower, *War without Mercy*, 309.

5. Intimate relations between black servicemen and Asian women have received little scholarly attention despite the numbers involved. The historian Alex Lubin, in his study of the politics of interracial sex between the end of World War II and the Supreme Court's 1954 *Brown* decision, admits that he "struggled to understand race by moving beyond the black/white binary" to consider Afro-Asian relations. However, he argues, "the kind of

interracial intimacy that most concerned policy makers, the NAACP, and cultural workers after the war involved white bodies." He further notes that "more ethnographic work needs to be done on black soldiers' intimate relations while serving abroad." Lubin, *Romance and Rights: The Politics of Interracial Intimacy, 1945–1954* (Jackson: University Press of Mississippi, 2005), xx–xxi, 167n10.

6. Paul R. Spickard, *Mixed Blood: Intermarriage and Ethnic Identity in Twentieth-Century America* (Madison: University of Wisconsin Press, 1989), 43. Two venerable proverbs—"a white skin compensates for many deficiencies" (*iro no shiroi wa shichinan kakusu*) and "in rice and women, the whiter the better" (*kome no meshi to onna wa shiroi hodo yoi*)—testify to this traditional preference. The proverbs and their translations appear in John Russell, "Race and Reflexivity: The Black Other in Contemporary Japanese Mass Culture," *Cultural Anthropology* 6, no. 1 (Feb. 1991): 5.

7. Frank Dikötter, "Introduction," in *The Construction of Racial Identities in China and Japan: Historical and Contemporary Perspectives*, ed. Dikötter (London: Hurst, 1997), 2, 6.

8. Russell, "Race and Reflexivity," 5. A historian agrees: "Given that Japan was consciously modeling its behavior in other spheres of activity on its European and North American contemporaries, it is hardly surprising that Japanese 'racial' thought drew much of its inspiration from the most advanced Western nations and developed in response to it." Michael Weiner, "The Invention of Identity: Race and Nation in Pre-war Japan," in *The Construction of Racial Identities in China and Japan*, ed. Dikötter, 104–105.

9. Dikötter, "Introduction," 7.

10. See, for example, Russell, "Race and Reflexivity," 20.

11. Tanaka, *Japan's Comfort Women*, 146–147 ("The women"); Hiroshi Wagatsuma, "Mixed-Blood Children in Japan: An Exploratory Study," *Journal of Asian Affairs* 2, no. 1 (Spring 1977): 10 ("stain").

12. Molasky, *The American Occupation*, 75. To provide but one example, celebrated author Kenzaburō Ōe's award-winning short story "The Catch," published in 1958, features a captured black pilot described as a "gentle animal," a "dull-witted animal," and "as well-behaved as any domestic animal," with "a splendid, a heroic, an unbelievably beautiful phallus." Kenzaburō Ōe, "The Catch," in *The Catch and Other War Stories*, ed. Shoichi Saeki (New York: Kodansha International, 1981), 38, 41, 47.

13. Russell, "Race and Reflexivity," 23n5.

14. The historian John Dower explains that "initially, women designated for use by black soldiers were said to have been horrified—until they discovered that many black GIs treated them more kindly than the whites did." Dower, *Embracing Defeat*, 130.

15. "Summary of Censorship Information," 15 June 1946, unlabeled folder, Box 1225, RG 331, Records of the Supreme Commander for the Allied Powers (SCAP), Legal Section, Administrative Division, Miscellaneous Subject File, 1945–50, National Archives II. The report contains a summary of "intercepts"—private letters and other materials seized and translated into English—generated by SCAP's Civil Censorship Detachment.

16. Black soldiers were not alone in these exchanges; white servicemen enthusiastically participated as well. A journalist for *Pacific Stars and Stripes* boasted, "The boys here say you can get an overnight wife for a chocolate bar." Ernest Hoberecht, "While Various Geisha Deals Prevail, No 'Wife-Buying' Found in Japan," *Pacific Stars and Stripes*, 13 January 1946, Sunday Comic and Feature Section.

17. Ironically, MacArthur publicly justified the ban on fraternization as a measure to prevent sexual encounters with "Japanese women of immoral character" and thereby lower rates of venereal disease among occupation personnel. Koshiro, *Trans-Pacific Racisms*, 60.

18. In June 1948 SCAP's Legal Section summarized its objections to outlawing all forms of prostitution: "SCAP will be severely criticized as attempting to impose American moral standards on a nation whose sexual mores are based on essentially different Oriental traditions." Two years later, the Government Section's chief of staff explained, "This Section has consistently held the view that the eradication of this practice is not a proper matter for Occupation concern but is a matter of social evolution within the Japanese community." Cold War imperatives played a crucial role in the chief of staff's reasoning: "From the standpoint of public relations abroad, the issuance of such a directive could not fail to invite the ridicule of the not too friendly foreign press which would in all probability characterize it as an effort on the part of the Occupation to shift the blame to the Japanese authorities for the Occupation's own failure in military discipline and moral guidance." Check Sheet, 15 June 1948, and "Prohibitions against Solicitation," memorandum, 14 April 1950, Folder "Solicitation of Troops for the Purpose of Prostitution," Box 2191, RG 331, Records of the Supreme Commander for the Allied Powers, Government Section, Central Files Branch, Miscellaneous Subject File, 1945–52, National Archives II.

19. Sheldon Garon, *Molding Japanese Minds: The State in Everyday Life* (Princeton: Princeton University Press, 1997), 198; Tanaka, *Japan's Comfort Women*, 155 ("no exaggeration"); "Is Vice Menacing Our GIs?" *Jet*, 8 May 1952, 16. As for the motives of Japanese prostitutes, the evidence is ambiguous. For conflicting historical data and interpretations, see Garon, *Molding Japanese Minds*, 197; Tanaka, *Japan's Comfort Women*, 155; and Scott R. Rohrer, "From Demons to Dependents: American-Japanese Social Relations during the Occupation, 1945–1952" (Ph.D. diss., Northwestern University, 2006), 231. Nonetheless, it seems reasonable to assume that economic necessity motivated most of these women.

20. Dower, *Embracing Defeat*, 132; Garon, *Molding Japanese Minds*, 198.

21. Tanaka, *Japan's Comfort Women*, 162; Donald Richie, *The Donald Richie Reader: 50 Years of Writing on Japan*, ed. Arturo Silva (Berkeley, Calif.: Stone Bridge Press, 2001), 31 ("Yurakucho Station"); Cohen, *Remaking Japan*, 129 ("GIs seeking").

22. As an Armed Forces Information and Education Division booklet explained, "The best rule in the Orient is a rule that makes sense anywhere: Keep away from prostitutes and pickups. That is the best way to avoid a venereal disease. The next best way is to use prophylaxis properly and promptly." *A Pocket Guide to Japan* (Washington, D.C.: U.S. Government Printing Office, 1950), 53. Japan legalized abortion through the 1948 Eugenic Protection Law, with SCAP's approval (American officials believed the measure would help rebuild the Japanese economy by controlling overpopulation). A 1949 revision to the law, which made Japan the first nation in the world to permit abortion for economic reasons, greatly increased the procedure's availability. Until the mid-1950s, however, access to contraception and adequate information regarding its use remained rare in Japan. Norgren, *Abortion before Birth Control*, 3, 43–44, 83.

23. C. Sarah Soh, *The Comfort Women: Sexual Violence and Postcolonial Memory in Korea and Japan* (Chicago: University of Chicago Press, 2008), 210.

24. Women who serviced American soldiers in 1945–46, according to one historian, "were dubbed *yang galbo* (Western whore). As militarized prostitution, American style, expanded throughout Korea, other terms were added: *yang gongju* (Western princess) and *yang saeksi* (Western bride)." These women were and are considered by Korean society "a necessary evil since their existence safeguards the chastity of the 'virtuous' women." Ji-Yeon Yuh, *Beyond the Shadow of Camptown: Korean Military Brides in America* (New York: New York University Press, 2002), 19–21.

25. Bruce Cumings, "Silent but Deadly: Sexual Subordination in the U.S.-Korean Relationship," in *Let the Good Times Roll: Prostitution and the U.S. Military in Asia*, ed. Saundra

Pollock Sturdevant and Brenda Stoltzfus (New York: New Press, 1992), 169. In the first forty years of America's presence on the peninsula, more than one million Korean women reportedly worked in the military sex industry. *The Women Outside: Korean Women and the U.S. Military*, DVD, directed by J. T. Takagi and Hye Jung Park (New York: Third World Newsreel, 1995).

26. "Yell for Action: Morale of Race GIs High," *Pittsburgh Courier*, 29 July 1950 ("fighting in Korea"); Milton A. Smith, "Korean Belles 'No Trouble,' Says Smith," *Afro-American*, 16 December 1950 ("many men"); Milton A. Smith, "GIs Spurn Korean Gals, Wait for Jap Lassies," *Chicago Defender*, 16 December 1950 ("the mechanics").

27. Ralph Matthews, "How Sex Demoralized Our Army in Korea," *Afro-American*, 5 August 1950.

28. Milton A. Smith, "GIs Spurn Korean Gals, Wait for Jap Lassies," *Chicago Defender*, 16 December 1950. A journalist similarly wrote of "the stinking straw-thatched, flea-ridden hovels from whence the women come." L. Alex Wilson, "Front Line Grapevine," *Chicago Defender*, 9 September 1950.

29. Milton A. Smith, "GIs Spurn Korean Gals, Wait for Jap Lassies," *Chicago Defender*, 16 December 1950.

30. Cynthia Enloe, "It Takes Two," in *Let the Good Times Roll*, ed. Sturdevant and Stoltzfus, 23; "Staff Section Report of G-1 Section, GHQ, FEC, for 1–28 February 1951," Box 12, RG 554, Records of General HQ, Far East Command, Supreme Commander Allied Powers, and United Nations Command, Assistant Chief of Staff, G-1, General Records, Secret, 1949, National Archives II; "Dictionary of Rice Paddy Lingo," Folder 1049, Box A.1025-A.1130, Center for the Study of the Korean War ("Rock and Ruin"); David H. Hackworth, with Julie Sherman, *About Face* (New York: Simon and Schuster, 1989), 170 ("Rape and Run"); E. J. Kahn, Jr., *The Peculiar War: Impressions of a Reporter in Korea* (New York: Random House, 1952), 12 ("Rape and Restitution"); Sheldon, *The Honorable Conquerors*, 239 ("I&I"). See also T. R. Fehrenbach, *This Kind of War: A Study in Unpreparedness* (New York: Macmillan, 1963), 503.

31. Bound report, March 1951, Folder "250–1 #1 Morals and Conduct FEC Secret 1951," Box 747, RG 554, Records of General HQ, Far East Command, Supreme Commander Allied Powers, and United Nations Command, Adjutant General's Section, Operations Division, Secret General Correspondence, 1951, National Archives II.

32. Approximately 1.8 million Americans served in the Korean theater during the war. "U.S. Military Korean War Statistics," http://koreanwarmemorial.sd.gov/U.S.Forces/MIA_KIA.htm.

33. Ralph Matthews, "GIs Sing 'Inflation Blues': Spiraling Cost of Love Is Joe's Biggest Gripe," *Afro-American*, 8 September 1951 ("commodity prices"); Ralph Matthews, "Fifth Avenue of Tokyo: The Ginza Most Fabulous Shopping Area in World," *Afro-American*, 12 January 1952 ("streetwalkers"); Ralph Matthews, "Matthews Writes of GIs in Japan: Soldiers from 18 States Are Found in Yokohama," *Afro-American*, 22 September 1951 ("favorite cruising beaches"); Ralph Matthews, "Wacs and Pom Poms Wage War in Yokohama: GIs Counter-Attack in Battle of Sexes," *Afro-American*, 22 September 1951 ("short-term leave," "becoming mercenary").

34. Molasky, *The American Occupation*, 6; Lloyd B. Graham, "Those G.I.'s in Japan," *Christian Century*, 17 March 1954, 330.

35. James A. Michener, "The Facts about the GI Babies," *Reader's Digest*, March 1954, 9 ("rough conditions"); Graham, "Those G.I.'s in Japan," 331 ("increasingly turning"); Wildes, *Typhoon in Tokyo*, 330 ("shocked"); "Is Vice Menacing Our GIs?" *Jet*, 8 May 1952, 14–16 ("prostitution menace").

36. One month after Japan's surrender, SCAP issued a circular on marriage and the implications of American immigration laws barring non-Chinese Asians. "Marriage of Military Personnel," memorandum, 2 December 1945, Folder "291–1 #1," Box 433, RG 331, Records of the Supreme Commander for the Allied Powers (SCAP), Adjutant General's Section, Operations Division, Mail & Records Branch, Decimal File, 1945–46, National Archives II. For more information on barriers to Asian immigration erected in the late nineteenth and early twentieth centuries, see Mae M. Ngai, *Impossible Subjects: Illegal Aliens and the Making of Modern America* (Princeton: Princeton University Press, 2004).

37. Fifty-four of the women were Okinawan, the rest from Japan's main islands. "Most of Summer Marriages between GIs, Japan Girls Not Faring Well, Says Writer," *Pacific Citizen*, 1 November 1947; Lucy Herndon Crockett, *Popcorn on the Ginza: An Informal Portrait of Postwar Japan* (New York: William Sloane Associates, 1949), 147.

38. The second window for immigration expired in February 1951. After a month-long interval, it was replaced with legislation that remained in force until March 1952. The only remaining option for enlisted personnel involved passage of a private law, specific congressional legislation for the benefit of a foreign individual or group of related foreigners. Rohrer, "From Demons to Dependents," 125–129; "President Signs Bill to Extend GI Brides Act," *Pacific Citizen*, 31 March 1951; Janet Wentworth Smith and William L. Worden, "They're Bringing Home Japanese Wives," *Saturday Evening Post*, 19 January 1952, 81; Graham, "Those G.I.'s in Japan," 330; Peter Kalischer, "Madam Butterfly's Children," *Collier's*, 20 September 1952, 17; Michener, "GI Babies," 7.

39. Howard C. Petersen to Joseph H. Ball, letter, 31 January 1947, Folder 291.1, Box 20, RG 107, Records of the Office of the Secretary of War, Asst. Sec. of War, Formerly Security-Classified Correspondence of Howard Petersen, Dec. 1945–Aug. 1947, National Archives II ("placing in jeopardy"); "Most of Summer Marriages between GIs, Japan Girls Not Faring Well, Says Writer," *Pacific Citizen*, 1 November 1947 ("no one will be reenlisted"); C. G. Blakeney to John C. Stennis, letter, 11 October 1949, Folder "291.1 1–1–49–31 Dec 49," Box 363, RG 407, Records of the Adjutant General's Office, Army-AG Decimal File, 1949–50, National Archives II ("experience in occupied countries").

40. Howard C. Petersen to Joseph H. Ball, letter, 31 January 1947, Folder 291.1, Box 20, RG 107, Records of the Office of the Secretary of War, Asst. Sec. of War, Formerly Security-Classified Correspondence of Howard Petersen, Dec. 1945–Aug. 1947, National Archives II. One scholar argues that the Japanese contributed to American thoughts on the matter. Opposition to intermarriage provided "yet another occasion for diplomatic collaboration in tolerating mutual racism. . . . Both countries looked upon mixed marriage as a social evil, a threat to public health, safety, morals, and the general welfare." Koshiro, *Trans-Pacific Racisms*, 159.

41. C. G. Blakeney to Claude Pepper, letter, 29 August 1949, Folder "291.1 1–1–49–8/31/49," Box 363, RG 407, Records of the Adjutant General's Office, Army-AG Decimal File, 1949–50, National Archives II ("very gregarious people"); Spickard, *Mixed Blood*, 135 ("prevent intermarriage"), 410n23 ("consistent policy"). See also Koshiro, *Trans-Pacific Racisms*, 198.

42. "Shades of 'Madam Butterfly,'" *Pittsburgh Courier*, 22 March 1947. The woman was elsewhere identified as "Chioko Payama." "GI, Jap Girl Die in Suicide Pact," *Afro-American*, 15 March 1947.

43. Charley Cherokee, "National Grapevine," *Chicago Defender*, 24 May 1947.

44. Charley Cherokee, "National Grapevine," *Chicago Defender*, 6 March 1948 ("feathering their nests") and 24 July 1948 ("Oriental custom").

45. George D. Brown to NAACP Legal Committee, letter, 20 November 1949, Frames 167–168, Reel 15, Series B, Part 9, *Papers of the NAACP*; Charles M. Bussey, *Firefight at Yechon: Courage & Racism in the Korean War* (McLean, Va.: Brassey's (US), 1991), 63, 65, 72–73.

46. Kalischer, "Madame Butterfly's Children," 17; Smith and Worden, "They're Bringing Home Japanese Wives," 81; Rohrer, "From Demons to Dependents," 125.

47. James L. Hicks, "Many 24th Men Eye Brides in Japan," *Afro-American*, 4 November 1950 ("an amazing number," "Some claim"); Robert Sloan, "Tan GI Tells Why: I Want a Japanese Wife," *New York Amsterdam News*, 11 November 1950; Robert Sloan, "Gifu Girls Say: 'We Make Better Wives,'" *New York Amsterdam News*, 18 November 1950 ("one of the Gifu"); L. Alex Wilson, "Why Tan Yanks Go for Japanese Girls," *Chicago Defender*, 11 November 1950, second news section ("would not be surprising").

48. James L. Hicks, "Officer Says Our Girls in Japan Not Attractive," *Afro-American*, 25 November 1950.

49. The author included a remark that black occupationaires "virtually own the Japanese girls," but it was their material support of girlfriends that caught readers' attention. James L. Hicks, "GI's in Tokyo Lavish Gifts on Jap Girls, Shun Own Clubs," *Afro-American*, 2 September 1950, magazine section. African American women, on the other hand, were said to eschew intimate contact with the Japanese. "An extensive check on the love affairs of American Negro women in Japan," explained a *Chicago Defender* correspondent, "revealed they spurn the Japanese men. Two very attractive women told me in a convincing manner that any thought of having a Japanese as a boyfriend causes cold chills." L. Alex Wilson, "Why Tan Yanks Go for Japanese Girls," *Chicago Defender*, 11 November 1950, second news section.

50. Emphasis in the original. L. Alex Wilson, "Why Tan Yanks Go for Japanese Girls," *Chicago Defender*, 11 November 1950, second news section.

51. For a summary of these feminist arguments of the late 1940s and early 1950s see Nancy MacLean, *Freedom Is Not Enough: The Opening of the American Workplace* (Cambridge: Harvard University Press, with the Russell Sage Foundation, New York, 2006), 122.

52. James L. Hicks, "Officer Says Our Girls in Japan Not Attractive," *Afro-American*, 25 November 1950.

53. See, for example, Douglass Hall, "Tan Yanks Nation's Best 'Good Neighbor' Envoy," *Afro-American*, 24 June 1950; and Milton A. Smith, "Tan GIs in Korea Envoys of Good Will," *Afro-American*, 3 March 1951. "We've said this before and we say it again," argued a 1950 booklet for occupationaires, "Americans abroad are the unofficial ambassadors of the United States." *Pocket Guide to Japan*, 58.

54. Sidney Joulon, "On Romance in Japan: Sergeant Defends Soldiers' Actions," *Afro-American*, 14 October 1950.

55. Frederick J. Bryant, letter to the editor, *Afro-American*, 4 November 1950.

56. Pvt. Elmer Neely, letter to the editor *Pittsburgh Courier*, 24 February 1951.

57. Payne worked for the *Chicago Defender* for twenty-seven years, routinely needled President Dwight Eisenhower, reported on civil rights activism from the Montgomery Bus Boycott to the 1963 March on Washington, traveled to Vietnam to cover the experiences of black soldiers, and in 1972 joined CBS, where for years she provided editorial commentary. Interview with Ethel Payne by Kathleen Currie, Women in Journalism oral history project of the Washington Press Club Foundation, 8 September 1987, 31–32, in the Oral History Collection of Columbia University and other repositories.

58. L. Alex Wilson, "Why Tan Yanks Go for Japanese Girls," *Chicago Defender*, 11 November 1950, second news section.

59. Payne gave her diary to a *Defender* correspondent who, upon his return to Chicago and without her permission, had an article published under her byline. After that, the "newspapers were just jumping off the stands. Circulation . . . boomed because people were fascinated by this. . . . It was just so explosive." Interview with Ethel Payne by Kathleen Currie, Women in Journalism oral history project, 31–32.

60. Ethel Payne, "Says Japanese Girls Playing GIs for Suckers: 'Chocolate Joe' Used, Amused, Confused," *Chicago Defender*, 18 November 1950. One might contrast these attitudes with those expressed in the wildly popular "Babysan" cartoons, which reflected a more benevolent economic paternalism increasingly common among white occupationaires. See, for example, Bill Hume and John Annarino, *Babysan: A Private Look at the Japanese Occupation* (Columbia, Mo.: American Press, 1953), 32.

61. "Most American Women Say: 'Let GIs Wed Japanese Girls,'" *Pittsburgh Courier*, 18 November 1950.

62. How this serviceman reached his conclusions is unclear. He may have previously served in Asia and witnessed the widespread prostitution surrounding American bases. On the other hand, he may simply have followed the lively public debate over Japanese motives and Afro-Asian intimacy. Pvt. Frank A. Topsail, letter to the editor, *Ebony*, December 1951, 8.

63. "Letters of a Dying Mother to Her Brown Baby," *Ebony*, July 1954, 16–17.

64. Morrow, *What's a Commie Ever Done*, 107–109, 121, 130–135.

65. Brown was discharged in 1953 and within six months married and began to raise a family in the United States. Jessie Brown interview, "Korea: The Unfinished War."

66. Kalischer, "Madame Butterfly's Children," 17.

67. This estimate is the result of applying an admittedly inexact rate of 10 percent to the range of figures provided by historians for all American-Japanese marriages during this period. See, for example, Lubin, *Romance and Rights*, 167n10; and Rohrer, "From Demons to Dependents," 534.

68. Yuh, *Beyond the Shadow of Camptown*, 47; Ralph Matthews, "1,000 Cheer Sarge and Korean Bride," *Afro-American*, 1 December 1951; "Tie Matrimonial Knot," photograph with caption, *New York Amsterdam News*, 1 December 1951.

69. Nothing more was written of the Porche family, although Miyo may eventually have obtained American citizenship after the McCarran-Walter Act became law. "With Little Daughter: Japanese Bride, GI Win Home," *Pittsburgh Courier*, 8 March 1952.

70. "Many Japanese War Brides in U.S. Unhappy, Says Editor," *Pacific Citizen*, 24 June 1950 ("Many of these"); Spickard, *Mixed Blood*, 137–138, 141.

71. As of September 1951, fifteen states—Arizona, California, Georgia, Idaho, Maryland, Mississippi, Missouri, Montana, Nebraska, Nevada, Oregon, South Dakota, Utah, Virginia, and Wyoming—had laws prohibiting marriages between whites and Asians. In 1948 the Supreme Court of California had ruled that state's law unconstitutional, but it remained on the books. "Outmoded Marriage Laws," *Pacific Citizen*, 15 September 1951.

72. Only the laws of Texas ("Marriage between persons of different color grounds for annulment") and Idaho and Utah ("Marriage between persons of different color is void") included in the list were conceivably applicable. "Miscegenation Laws of Various States of the Union," memorandum, 28 June 1954, Folder "AG 291.2 Race 1–1-54–6–30–54," Box 129, RG 407, Records of the Adjutant General's Office, Army-AG Decimal File, 1953–54, National Archives II.

73. Leon K. Walters, "A Study of the Social and Marital Adjustment of Thirty-Five American-Japanese Couples" (masters thesis, Ohio State University, 1953), 80–81. Another black-Japanese couple, while traveling through the American South, found that although

the wife was allowed to stay in "white" hotels, her husband was forced to sleep in their car. Spickard, *Mixed Blood*, 143.

74. Enoc P. Waters, "Kicked into Luxury," *Chicago Defender*, 10 September 1953.

75. "Looking and Listening . . . ," *The Crisis*, April 1952, 233.

76. Scott Kurashige, "The Many Facets of Brown: Integration in a Multiracial Society," *Journal of American History* 91, no. 1 (June 2004): 60, 67; Maya Angelou, *I Know Why the Caged Bird Sings* (New York: Random House, 1969), 204–205; Daniel Widener, "'Perhaps the Japanese Are to Be Thanked?': Asia, Asian Americans, and the Construction of Black California," *positions: east asia cultures critique* 11, no. 1 (Spring 2003): 166; Charlotte Brooks, "Ascending California's Racial Hierarchy: Asian Americans, Housing, and Government, 1920–1955" (Ph.D. diss., Northwestern University, 2002), 238 ("Little Tokyo's").

77. J. A. Rogers, "Rogers Says: Bill Favors Oriental Immigration at Price of Restricting Negroes," *Pittsburgh Courier*, 19 March 1949. The 1952 McCarran-Walter Act established an immigration quota of 100 per year for each British, French, and Dutch colony in the Caribbean. See, for example, "President Is Right," *Afro-American*, 5 July 1952; P. L. Prattis, "We Should Help Give the McCarran Act the Treatment It Deserves," *Pittsburgh Courier*, 17 January 1953; and Walter White, "Truman's Report on Immigration Exposes Bigotry and Weaknesses in McCarran Act," *Chicago Defender*, 7 February 1953.

78. Joseph D. Bibb, "After Pearl Harbor: If a Colored American Groans, He Is Branded As an Agent of Moscow," *Pittsburgh Courier*, 17 December 1949 ("Now, eight years after"); Claude A. Barnett to Dr. Harry V. Richardson, letter, 10 August 1954, Folder 5: "Race Relations—Asian-Americans (Including Hawaii), Correspondence, 1932–1960," Box 364, Claude A. Barnett Papers, Chicago Historical Society ("Is there any possibility").

79. Many white Americans held fast to their wartime hatred of the Japanese, but, as Caroline Chung Simpson has observed, "The 1950s transformation of the Japanese war bride from an opportunistic and ignorant alien seeking to penetrate the suburban affluence of white America to the gracious and hard-working middle-class housewife was an early exemplar for achieving the integrated future in America, a halcyon story of domestic bliss and economic mobility." Simpson, "'Out of an Obscure Place': Japanese War Brides and Cultural Pluralism in the 1950s," *differences: A Journal of Feminist Cultural Studies* 10, no. 3 (1998): 49–50. See also Robert G. Lee. *Orientals: Asian Americans in Popular Culture* (Philadelphia: Temple University Press, 1999), 162.

80. "The Truth about Japanese War Brides," *Ebony*, March 1952, 20.

81. "The Loneliest Brides in America," *Ebony*, January 1953, 17–18, 24.

82. Yuh, *Beyond the Shadow of Camptown*, 160, 212. Of course, not every Afro-Asian couple encountered hostility; a few experienced relatively smooth integration into their new communities. See, for example, William L. Worden, "Where Are Those Japanese War Brides?" *Saturday Evening Post*, 20 November 1954, 39.

83. "What Happened to the War Brides?" *Jet*, 17 January 1952, 20 ("unable to adjust"); Morrow, *What's a Commie Ever Done*, 118 ("because of the opposition"); Worden, "Where Are Those Japanese War Brides?" 133 ("most unhappy brides"); "The Loneliest Brides in America," *Ebony*, January 1953, 21; Edward A. Coble, letter to the editor, *Ebony*, April 1953, 8–9.

4. A Brown Baby Crisis

1. Otis Cary, ed., *Eyewitness to History: The First Americans in Postwar Asia* (New York: Kodansha International, 1995), 121–123.

2. LaCerda, *Conqueror Comes to Tea*, 23–24.

3. Alfred Smith, "Adventures in Race Relations," *Chicago Defender*, 4 January 1947.

4. "British Families Adopt Brown Babies: Illegitimate Tots Left Behind by Negro GIs Finally Find Homes," *Ebony*, March 1949, 22. For the figure of 70,000, see Michener, "GI Babies," 6.

5. Goedde, *GIs and Germans*, 111.

6. For a discussion of wartime African American condemnation of not only Nazi Germany but also the British Empire, see Von Eschen, *Race against Empire*, esp. chap. 2. For reasons of economy and scope I do not provide a detailed analysis of African American engagement with the brown baby crises of Germany and Britain. Nonetheless, a handful of examples are in order. Instances of favorable black coverage of European treatment of brown babies include "Survey Shows Most Europeans Want to Keep Tan Babics," *Afro-American*, 27 November 1948; "British Families Adopt Brown Babies: Illegitimate Tots Left Behind by Negro GIs Finally Find Homes," *Ebony*, March 1949, 19; "Fraulein Mothers Of 'Brown Babies' Love 'Em Fiercely," *Pittsburgh Courier*, 1 July 1950; and "Brown Babies Adopted by Kind Germany Families," *Jet*, 8 November 1951, 14–16. A notable exception is Allan Gould, "Germany's Tragic War Babies," *Ebony*, December 1952, 75–78. See also Yara-Colette Lemke Muniz de Faria, " 'Germany's "Brown Babies" Must Be Helped! Will You?': U.S. Adoption Plans for Afro-German Children, 1950–1955," *Callaloo* 26, no. 2 (2003): 352. For an analysis of the race and gender dynamics of American responses to the brown babies of Europe, see Brenda Gayle Plummer, "Brown Babies: Race, Gender, and Policy after World War II," in *Window on Freedom: Race, Civil Rights, and Foreign Affairs, 1945–1988*, ed. Plummer (Chapel Hill: University of North Carolina Press, 2003).

7. See, for example, discussions of the so-called "Brown Baby Plan," through which black-German children were adopted by African Americans, in Lemke Muniz de Faria, "Germany's 'Brown Babies,'" 342–362; Plummer, *Rising Wind*, 208; and Heide Fehrenbach, *Race after Hitler: Black Occupation Children in Postwar Germany and America* (Princeton: Princeton University Press, 2005), chap. 5. On Great Britain, see James L. Hicks, "How You Can Help 'Wild Oats' Babies," *Afro-American*, 27 November 1948, magazine section; "Dads of British War Babies Can Claim Tots," *Chicago Defender*, 21 February 1948; and "60 Tan Yank Tots to Be Brought Here," *Chicago Defender*, 29 May 1948. For information on the Bronx-based American Committee to Aid the Italian-Negro GI Babies, see Caroline Brescia, letter, 1 November 1946, Frame 349, Reel 8, Series A, Part 9, *Papers of the NAACP*.

8. Historian Christina Klein notes that early Cold War "middlebrow culture played a crucial role in cultivating a sense of political obligation to Asia. Middlebrow producers . . . imaginatively resolved the barriers to obligation that could not be so easily remedied in the political realm . . . [and] symbolically created . . . family ties with Asia." Klein, "Family Ties and Political Obligation," 37, 38. The author points specifically to the advertising strategies of the Christian Children's Fund (CCF) in American print media (44–50). My close perusal of more than half a dozen of the most popular black periodicals from 1945 through the mid-1950s uncovered no advertisements by the CCF or any similar group.

9. "Police Predict 14,000 GI Babies by June," *Pacific Stars and Stripes*, 10 March 1946.

10. Sgt. Charles Bull, " 'Babies' Story Not Confirmed," *Pacific Stars and Stripes*, 16 March 1946.

11. Darrell Berrigan, "Japan's Occupation Babies," *Saturday Evening Post*, 19 June 1948, 24, 118.

12. Elizabeth Anne Hemphill, *The Least of These: Miki Sawada and Her Children* (New York: Weatherhill, 1980), 92.

13. Goedde, *GIs and Germans*, 95. Historian Brenda Gayle Plummer notes that "the U.S. government in 1952 amended its policy to permit soldiers to recognize their children by German mothers. The recognition had to be voluntary and approved by the commander-in-chief of U.S. forces in Europe. After the peace treaty with West Germany went into effect, German women could bring suit to establish paternity and collect child support." Plummer, *Rising Wind*, 208.

14. William R. Burkhardt, "Institutional Barriers, Marginality, and Adoption among the American-Japanese Mixed Bloods in Japan," *Journal of Asian Studies* 42, no. 3 (May 1983)· 534; "Request for Procedure of Establishing Paternity of Child," 5 April 1948, Folder "291.1 #2, Marriage, Parentage & Nationality, 1949–51," Box 1260, RG 331, Records of the Supreme Commander for the Allied Powers (SCAP), Legal Section, Administrative Division, Decimal File, 1945–52, National Archives II. As of September 1952, the right to file paternity claims in Japanese civil courts against American personnel of the post-occupation "security forces" was still being debated. Kalischer, "Madame Butterfly's Children," 18.

15. Rohrer, "From Demons to Dependents," 128–129.

16. Stephen Murphy-Shigematsu, "Multiethnic Lives and Monoethnic Myths: American-Japanese Amerasians in Japan," in *The Sum of Our Parts: Mixed-Heritage Asian Americans*, ed. Teresa Williams-León and Cynthia L. Nakashima (Philadelphia: Temple University Press, 2001), 209; Spickard, *Mixed Blood*, 155–156; Sveinung Johnson Moen, *The Amerasians: A Study and Research on Interracial Children in Korea* (Seoul: Taewon Publishing, 1974), 36.

17. As one scholar notes, "The term *minjok* has no English equivalent. Its meaning is closer to *Volk* in German than 'race' in English." Won Moo Hurh, "Marginal Children of War: An Exploratory Study of American-Korean Children," *International Journal of Sociology of the Family* 2, no. 1 (March 1972): 13–14.

18. Ibid., 14; Hiroshi Wagatsuma, "Identity Problems of Black Japanese Youth," in *The Mixing of Peoples: Problems of Identity and Ethnicity*, ed. Robert I. Rotberg (Stamford, Conn.: Greylock Publishers, 1978), 128n1.

19. Although undated, the letter was likely sent in 1948 or 1949. Its location in an office file labeled "United States Army, 'Brown Babies in Europe,' 1945–49" suggests the low priority given Afro-Asian children by the NAACP. Masurao Hosokawa, letter, n.d., Frame 456, Reel 8, Series A, Part 9, *Papers of the NAACP*.

20. Berrigan, "Japan's Occupation Babies," 117; Frank Whisonant, "Brown Babies OK in Japan," *Pittsburgh Courier*, 2 December 1950.

21. Hemphill, *The Least of These*, 11, 80–81, 84; Junesay Iddittie, *When Two Cultures Meet: Sketches of Postwar Japan, 1945–55* (Tokyo: Kenkyusha Press, 1960), 148; Berrigan, "Japan's Occupation Babies," 117–118 ("The kindest thing"); Wagatsuma, "Mixed-Blood Children in Japan," 13.

22. Robert Thornton, letter to the editor, *Ebony*, December 1951, 8 ("orchids"); Cpl. Robert W. Sloan, letter to the editor, *Ebony*, December 1951, 8 ("many Japanese girls"); Frank Whisonant, "Brown Babies OK in Japan," *Pittsburgh Courier*, 2 December 1950 ("the city"). See also "Repair Toys for Japanese Orphans," photograph with caption, *Afro-American*, 14 January 1950.

23. The letter was filed under "United States Army, 'Brown Babies in Europe,' 1950–55." Thomas H. Pettigrew to the Executive Secretary of the NAACP, letter, 9 May 1951, Frame 521, Reel 8, Series A, Part 9, *Papers of the NAACP*.

24. Lois Austin, "Missing Yank's Mother Begs U.S. for His Children, Japanese Wife," *Chicago Defender*, 2 December 1950; "GI's Mother Wants Tots, Japanese Wife in America," *Afro-American*, 9 December 1950.

25. "Thousands in Tokyo Cheer Louis on Arrival for Three-Week Tour," *New York Times*, 15 November 1951; Ralph Matthews, "Louis Aids Japan Brown Babies," *New York Amsterdam News*, 22 December 1951; "Joe Louis Returns Home from Far East Tour," *Jet*, 27 December 1951, 55; "Louis Returns, Learns of California Bans," *Jet*, 3 January 1952, 65; "Backstage," *Ebony*, April 1952, 12; "The Week's Best Photos," *Jet*, 17 January 1952, 35; Hemphill, *The Least of These*, 97–98.

26. Ethel Payne, "Says Japanese Girls Playing GIs for Suckers: Says Fate That Awaits War Babies Is Tragedy of Yank Oriental Unions," *Chicago Defender*, 25 November 1950 ("crop of"); Waldo E. Williams, letter to the editor, *Chicago Defender*, 13 January 1951 ("What do you expect"); Rickie Solinger, *Wake Up Little Susie: Single Pregnancy and Race before Roe v. Wade* (New York: Routledge, 2000), esp. chaps. 2 and 6.

27. "War Babies of Japan: Shunned and Deserted, More than 2,000 Racially-Mixed Youngsters Face Tragic Future," *Ebony*, September 1951, 21 ("weaned"); "Victims of Loose Morals in Japan," photograph with caption, *Afro-American*, 3 February 1951 ("a succession").

28. "Starved, Mistreated and Abandoned, These Unwanted Babies Found Home in Japan," photograph with caption, *Afro-American*, 13 January 1951.

29. Milton A. Smith, "Unwanted Babies Find a Home in Japan," *Afro-American*, 6 January 1951 ("spindly legged"); Burkhardt, "Institutional Barriers," 526; "The Week's Best Photos," *Jet*, 13 December 1951, 33 ("full blooded").

30. "War Babies of Japan: Shunned and Deserted, More than 2,000 Racially-Mixed Youngsters Face Tragic Future," *Ebony*, September 1951, 15, 17–18, 21; Robert Thornton, letter to the editor, *Ebony*, December 1951, 8 ("will realize"); Catherine Daniels, letter to the editor, *Ebony*, November 1951, 6 ("they may grow up").

31. The 1945 War Brides Act made no provision for children, step-children, or adopted children to enter the United States with their married parents. "Ask House Group to Drop Race Restrictions in GI Brides Bill," *Pacific Citizen*, 19 February 1949. According to one historian, "Only 503 Japanese total had entered the country through normal immigration channels between the end of the war and June 30, 1947. The eighty-two entering in fiscal year 1947 . . . included only one minor child. Excluding private laws, only five Japanese children of American citizens received permission to enter the U.S. during fiscal 1950, and just eleven the next year." Rohrer, "From Demons to Dependents," 137.

32. Koshiro, *Trans-Pacific Racisms*, 199.

33. The figure of 10,000 mixed-race children was greatly exaggerated. "Britons Deny Plan to Ship Babies," *Afro-American*, 3 May 1947. See also "Adventures in Race Relations," *Chicago Defender*, 12 July 1947.

34. "Rep. Rankin's Objection Bars Entry for 3-Year Old Child," *Pacific Citizen*, 29 September 1951; "Rep. Rankin Drops Objection, Pass Bill to Admit Child," *Pacific Citizen*, 13 October 1951.

35. "Japanese Paper Says GIs Father 200,000 Babies," *Jet*, 28 February 1952, 17. Despite the subsequent availability of more precise figures, popular Japanese belief held that the total was or would eventually reach 200,000. See, for example, Iddittie, *When Two Cultures Meet*, 147; and Kalischer, "Madame Butterfly's Children," 15.

36. One American visitor encountered two children "with café-au-lait skin and tightly curled hair" in the isolated fishing village of Zenibako, where a regiment of black troops had been stationed for a short period following the war. Brown, *Over a Bamboo Fence*, 114.

37. Koshiro, *Trans-Pacific Racisms*, 164; Shibusawa, *America's Geisha Ally*, 41; Kalischer, "Madame Butterfly's Children," 15 ("half-breeds").

38. Koshiro, *Trans-Pacific Racisms*, 193.

39. "Japanese Paper Says GIs Father 200,000 Babies," *Jet*, 28 February 1952, 17. Another of Tokyo's largest newspapers joined in calling for the removal of the black-Japanese. See "Negro Japanese Babies Coming to U.S.," *Jet*, 6 March 1952, 14.

40. The article appeared in either the English-language *Japan Times*, available in both Japan and the United States, or the *Waseda Guardian*, an English-language university newspaper. Iddittie, *When Two Cultures Meet*, 147, 152–154.

41. Koshiro, *Trans-Pacific Racisms*, 170.

42. Murphy-Shigematsu, "Multiethnic Lives and Monoethnic Myths," 210–211; Hugh M. Smythe and Mabel M. Smythe, "Report from Japan: Comments on the Race Question," *The Crisis*, March 1952, 159.

43. Russell, "Race and Reflexivity," 13. Five years later, the *Dakko-chan* doll hit store shelves, immediately becoming the nation's top-selling toy and a common household item. It was "a highly caricatured jet black figure with big eyes and huge red lips, sold with a pole" up which the doll could be made to scurry. Millie Creighton, "*Soto* Others and *uchi* Others: Imagining Racial Diversity, Imagining Homogeneous Japan," in *Japan's Minorities: The Illusion of Homogeneity*, ed. Michael Weiner (New York: Routledge, 1997), 222.

44. Hiroshi Wagatsuma, "The Social Perception of Skin Color in Japan," in *Color and Race*, ed. John Hope Franklin (Boston: Houghton Mifflin, 1968), 154–155.

45. Richard L-G. Deverall, *The Great Seduction: Red China's Drive to Bring Free Japan behind the Iron Curtain* (Tokyo: International Literature Printing Co., 1953), 111.

46. Hemphill, *The Least of These*, 88.

47. The local board of education offered to provide the children with a separate classroom. Sawada opted to construct her own school on the Saunders Home grounds. Koshiro, *Trans-Pacific Racisms*, 178.

48. Hemphill, *The Least of These*, 94; Koshiro, *Trans-Pacific Racisms*, 189.

49. One indication of her success in this regard, as well as the lack of institutional support for Afro-Asians, may be found in a black newspaper's response to a query about contributing "foreign aid to the brown babies in Germany and Japan," published at the conclusion of Sawada's tour: "You may contact Mrs. Micki [*sic*] Sawada at the Saunder's [*sic*] Home. . . . For the German brown babies, contact your nearest child welfare agency." Letters to the editor, *Chicago Defender*, 29 November 1952.

50. "Negro Japanese Babies Coming to U.S.," *Jet*, 6 March 1952, 14; "Japanese 'Foster Mother' Arrives in U.S.," *Jet*, 25 September 1952, 15.

51. Miki Sawada to Walter White, letter, 30 June 1952, Frames 532–540, Reel 8, Series A, Part 9, *Papers of the NAACP*.

52. Hemphill, *The Least of These*, 120 ("the hard wall"); Michener, "GI Babies," 9.

53. Emphasis in the original. Miki Sawada to Roy Wilkins, letter, Frame 550, Reel 8, Series A, Part 9, *Papers of the NAACP*.

54. "Hope New GOP Congress Will Relax Ban on Jap-Negro Babies," *Jet*, 22 January 1953, 20–21 ("The UN"); Miki Sawada to Roy Wilkins, letter, Frame 551, Reel 8, Series A, Part 9, *Papers of the NAACP* ("These farmers").

55. Koshiro, *Trans-Pacific Racisms*, 190; Graham, "Those G.I.'s in Japan," 330; Lemke Muniz de Faria, "Germany's 'Brown Babies,'" 356; Christina Klein, *Cold War Orientalism: Asia in the Middlebrow Imagination, 1945–1961* (Berkeley: University of California Press, 2003), 174–175; Hemphill, *The Least of These*, 121.

56. Klein, *Cold War Orientalism*, 175.

57. See, for example, Hurh, "Marginal Children of War," 15, table 3, which indicates the large international adoption preference for white-Korean over black-Korean children from 1955 through 1966.

58. "How to Adopt Korean Babies," *Ebony*, September 1955, 31.

59. R. W. Kenney to Walter White, letter, 2 March 1955, Frame 615, Reel 8, Series A, Part 9, *Papers of the NAACP*.

60. Pearl S. Buck, "Should White Parents Adopt Brown Babies?" *Ebony*, June 1958, 26–28. By the late 1950s Buck had adopted seven children, including a German brown baby. For additional information on Buck and her early Cold War advocacy of international adoption, see Ellen Herman, *Kinship by Design: A History of Adoption in the Modern United States* (Chicago: University of Chicago Press, 2008), 210.

61. Claudette Debarre, letter to the editor, *Pittsburgh Courier*, 1 November 1952 ("thoroughly disgusted"); Ethel Payne, "Parents Wanted! Why Not Adopt a Baby?" *Chicago Defender*, 12 April 1952; Ethel Payne, "Why Not Adopt a Baby?" *Chicago Defender*, 3 May 1952; "Why Negroes Don't Adopt Children," *Ebony*, July 1952, 31 ("only 3,000"); Solinger, *Wake Up Little Susie*, 198; Alexander J. Allen, "A Commentary on a Study of Negro Adoptions," in David Fanshel, *A Study in Negro Adoption* (New York: Child Welfare League of America, 1957), 89 ("concept of an over-supply").

62. Hurh, "Marginal Children of War," 13–14; Moen, *The Amerasians*, 41, 69–70, 72 ("a great deal"); Katharine H. S. Moon, "South Korean Movements against Militarized Sexual Labor," *Asian Survey* 39, no. 2 (Mar.–Apr., 1999): 313; Murphy-Shigematsu, "Multiethnic Lives and Monoethnic Myths," 210; Spickard, *Mixed Blood*, 152–154.

63. Moen, *The Amerasians*, 82–84.

64. See, for example, Elmer R. Smith, "Japanese in the Americas: Race Relations in Brazil," *Pacific Citizen*, 26 April 1952; Elmer R. Smith, "Japanese in the Americas: Immigrants in Brazil," *Pacific Citizen*, 3 May 1952; and Yoko Sellek, "*Nikkeijin*: The Phenomenon of Return Migration," in *Japan's Minorities: The Illusion of Homogeneity*, ed. Michael Weiner (New York: Routledge, 1997).

65. Louise Young, "Rethinking Race for Manchukuo: Self and Other in the Colonial Context," in *The Construction of Racial Identities in China and Japan*, ed. Dikötter, 169.

66. Kalischer, "Madame Butterfly's Children," 15; Hemphill, *The Least of These*, 140–143; Wagatsuma, "Mixed-Blood Children in Japan," 13.

67. Era Bell Thompson, "Japan's Rejected," *Ebony*, September 1967, 54.

68. The number of American-Japanese stood at between twenty and thirty thousand, of whom perhaps 4,000 were Afro-Asian. Thompson, "Japan's Rejected," 44, 46; Wagatsuma, "Identity Problems," 120; Perry, *Beneath the Eagle's Wings*, 171–172; Spickard, *Mixed Blood*, 151; Koshiro, *Trans-Pacific Racisms*, 214. The number of black-Koreans was likely close to 2,000, but Korean census practices made a precise count impossible. Moen, *The Amerasians*, 68, 110; Hurh, "Marginal Children of War," 12–13.

69. Moen, *The Amerasians*, 61, 71; Murphy-Shigematsu, "Multiethnic Lives and Monoethnic Myths," 211; Wagatsuma, "Mixed-Blood Children in Japan," 11; "'Brown Baby' Olympic Hopeful from Japan," *Ebony*, October 1966, 58, 60. See also Perry, *Beneath the Eagle's Wings*, 172; Michael Charles Thornton, "A Social History of a Multiethnic Identity: The Case of Black Japanese Americans" (Ph.D. diss., University of Michigan, 1983), 35; and *Doubles: Japan and America's Intercultural Children*, VHS, directed by Reggie Life (Harriman, N.Y.: Transit Media, 1995).

70. Thompson, "Japan's Rejected," 42, 44, 46, 49–50.

71. John E. Adams, Holt Adoption Program, letter to the editor, *Ebony*, January 1968, 12 ("already hurt"); Evans Crosby, letter to the editor, *Ebony*, December 1967, 14 ("series of recent articles").

5. The Race of Combat in Korea

1. W. E. B. Du Bois, *In Battle for Peace: The Story of My 83rd Birthday* (New York: Masses and Mainstream, 1952), 179.

2. African American responses to intervention in Korea differed strikingly from those often highlighted in histories of black service in the turn-of-the-century Philippines. According to one historian, African Americans on the home front "displayed considerable sympathy for the independence movement among the Filipinos, whom they identified as 'our kinsmen' and 'our colored brothers,'" while black soldiers "were usually solicitous in their treatment of Filipino civilians and often identified with them racially." William B. Gatewood, Jr., *"Smoked Yankees" and the Struggle for Empire: Letters from Negro Soldiers, 1898–1902* (Urbana: University of Illinois Press, 1971), 12, 14. Another asserts that "during their stay in the Philippines, the black soldiers associated 'on terms of equality' with the local population." Foner, *Blacks and the Military*, 91. A third argues that because of African American ambivalence toward the Spanish-American War and its aftermath, "it became increasingly difficult to launch wars with soldiers of color in the vanguard." Gerald Horne, "Race from Power: U.S. Foreign Policy and the General Crisis of White Supremacy," in *Window on Freedom*, ed. Plummer, 49.

3. "25,000 in Korea! Truce Is Signed, Fighting Ends," *Afro-American*, 1 July 1953.

4. These individuals would have been assigned to American units around the globe, Korea included. "African Americans in the Korean War," http://korea50.army.mil/history/factsheets/afroamer.shtml. The war occurred within a four-year period during which roughly 220,000 black men were inducted through Selective Service, nearly 13 percent of the total and a clear instance of overrepresentation in the draft calls. Paul T. Murray, "Blacks and the Draft: A History of Institutional Racism," *Journal of Black Studies* 2, no. 1 (September 1971): 68; "Draft 3 Negroes to One White in Montgomery, Ala.," *Jet*, 13 November 1952, 5. Because the armed services were already desegregating by the start of the conflict, or, in the case of the army, began the process shortly thereafter, records on the precise number of black Korean War veterans remain incomplete.

5. A detailed analysis of the origins of the Korean War is beyond this book's purview. The war followed months of incursions by both North and South Korean forces. Suffice it to say that neither side accepted the division of their nation. As two scholars have observed, Korea was "a civil war fought between two domestic forces: a revolutionary nationalist movement, which had its roots in tough anti-colonial struggle, and a conservative movement tied to the *status quo*, especially to an unequal land system." Jon Halliday and Bruce Cumings, *Korea: The Unknown War* (New York: Pantheon Books, 1988), 10. For the definitive account of the war's deep-rooted causes, see Bruce Cumings, *The Origins of the Korean War, Volume 1: Liberation and the Emergence of Separate Regimes, 1945–1947* (Princeton: Princeton University Press, 1981), and Bruce Cumings, *The Origins of the Korean War, Volume 2: The Roaring of the Cataract, 1947–1950* (Princeton: Princeton University Press, 1990).

6. David Halberstam, *The Fifties* (New York: Villard Books, 1993), 66; Marilyn B. Young, "The Age of Global Power," in *Rethinking American History in a Global Age*, ed. Thomas Bender (Berkeley: University of California Press, 2002), 286; Barton J. Bernstein, "The Truman Administration and the Korean War," in *The Truman Presidency*, ed. Michael J. Lacey (New York: Cambridge University Press, 1989), 410, 413; Astor, *The Right to Fight*, 350.

7. The resolution recommended "that all Members providing military forces and other assistance" make them "available to a unified command under the United States." Only the final clause suggested any restrictions on American autonomy, proposing that the United States provide the Security Council with "reports as appropriate" on the course of the war.

Bernstein, "The Truman Administration," 410–411; I. F. Stone, *The Hidden History of the Korean War*, 2nd ed. (New York: Monthly Review Press, 1969), 78–79.

8. Besides the United States, the nations contributing land, air, or sea forces were Great Britain, Canada, Turkey, Australia, Thailand, the Philippines, France, Greece, New Zealand, the Netherlands, Colombia, Belgium, Ethiopia, South Africa, and Luxembourg. Fehrenbach, *This Kind of War*, 445–446; Bernstein, "The Truman Administration," 411.

9. Astor, *The Right to Fight*, 350; "Statistical Data on Strength and Casualties for Korean War and Vietnam," file number 2–3.7 AD.M, Historical Manuscripts Collection, U.S. Army Center of Military History, http://www.army.mil/cmh-pg/documents/237adm. htm; Linda Witt, Judith Bellafaire, Britta Granrud, and Mary Jo Binker, *"A Defense Weapon Known to Be of Value": Servicewomen of the Korea War Era* (Hanover, N.H.: University Press of New England, 2005), 67; Stone, *Hidden History*, 82; MacGregor, *Integration of the Armed Forces*, 430.

10. Fehrenbach, *This Kind of War*, 610; Susan D. Moeller, *Shooting War: Photography and the American Experience of Combat* (New York: Basic Books, 1989), 261; Albert J. Mayer and Thomas Ford Hoult, "Social Stratification and Combat Survival," *Social Forces 34, no. 2 (Dec. 1955)*: 155 (all quotes).

11. Robert T. Oliver, *Verdict in Korea* (State College, Pa.: Bald Eagle Press, 1952), 102–103; Brent Byron Watson, *Far Eastern Tour: The Canadian Infantry in Korea, 1950–1953* (Montreal: McGill-Queen's University Press, 2002), 56–57; Ralph Matthews, "How Uncle Sam Is Robbed of Millions in Pusan," *Afro-American*, 15 September 1951 ("cesspool"); Samuel King interview, "Korea: The Unfinished War" ("fathers").

12. Pfc. Leonard Turner, "First Army PX Opens in Pusan," *Pacific Stars and Stripes*, 28 August 1950; Fehrenbach, *This Kind of War*, 256. The American military's acceptance and promotion of an ethos of consumption, even on the front lines, continued through U.S. involvement in Vietnam. See Meredith H. Lair, " 'Beauty, Bullets, and Ice Cream': Reimagining Daily Life in the 'Nam" (Ph.D. diss., Pennsylvania State University, 2004).

13. Halberstam, *The Fifties*, 74; Moeller, *Shooting War*, 259. For an account of the ROK army's early reputation for unreliability and cowardice among Canadian servicemen, see Watson, *Far Eastern Tour*, 60–61.

14. "An Insult in Korea," *Pittsburgh Courier*, 2 September 1950; "Unification in UN Army: S. Koreans in Yank Ranks," *Pacific Stars and Stripes*, 25 August 1950; Watson, *Far Eastern Tour*, 62, 64, 68–69; Moeller, *Shooting War*, 261; Louis Baldovi, ed., *A Foxhole View: Personal Accounts of Hawaii's Korean War Veterans* (Honolulu: University of Hawai'i Press, 2002), xxiii, 61, 68.

15. Eric F. Goldman, *The Crucial Decade: America, 1945–1955* (New York: Alfred A. Knopf, 1956), 175 ("frantic retreat"); Moeller, *Shooting War*, 255; Cumings, *Origins of the Korean War, Volume 2*, 687, 690–691 ("fought a total war"). The most notorious American attack on Korean civilians occurred in July 1950 near No Gun Ri, in which at least 250 men, women, and children were killed or wounded. See, for example, "G.I.'s Tell of a U.S. Massacre in Korean War," *New York Times*, 30 September 1999; and Elizabeth Becker, "Army Confirms G.I.'s in Korea Killed Civilians," 12 January 2001. Reports on the war's disturbing aspects were freely available to stateside audiences. The author of an account published in *Life* and *Time* magazines described "the blotting out of villages where the enemy *may* be hiding; the shooting and shelling of refugees who *may* include North Koreans . . . , or who *may* be screening an enemy march upon our positions." Yet for all the conflict's ugliness, "our men in Korea are waging this war as they are forced to wage it *and*

as they will be forced to wage any war against the Communists anywhere in Asia." Emphasis in the original. John Osborne, "Report from the Orient: Guns Are Not Enough," *Life*, 21 August 1950, 77, 82. See also John Osborne, "The Ugly War," *Time*, 21 August 1950, 20–21.

16. Goldman, *The Crucial Decade*, 177.

17. During the brief American occupation after World War II, the military distributed language guides with phonetic spellings of phrases for Korea ("Han-Gook") and the United States ("Me-Gook"). Occupation personnel dropped the prefixes and applied the epithet to all Koreans, a practice adopted by combat forces five years later. Lee, *Orientals*, 190; Fradley H. Garner, letter to the editor, *New York Times*, 2 August 1950; Eric Larrabee, "Korea: The Military Lesson," *Harper's Magazine*, November 1950, 51.

18. Reginald Thompson, *Cry Korea* (London: Macdonald, 1951), 44 ("a dead Korean"); Walter Sullivan, "G.I. View of Koreans as 'Gooks' Believed Doing Political Damage," *New York Times*, 26 July 1950 ("a combination"); "GI's Warned Not to Use Word 'Gook,'" *Afro-American*, 2 September 1950 ("small minority"). In September 1950 the army issued a booklet advancing similar arguments. Six years later the Office of Armed Forces Information and Education produced *A Pocket Guide to Korea*, which again asked soldiers stationed there to avoid using the term. "New Weapons," *Pacific Citizen*, 23 September 1950; *A Pocket Guide to Korea* (Washington, D.C.: Office of Armed Forces Information and Education, 1956), 34–35.

19. As one historian has observed, "the use of American air power [in Korea] reprised many of the motives, methods, and results seen in the war with Japan (with Japan now providing the air bases)." Sherry, *In the Shadow of War*, 181. According to the journalist Tom Engelhardt, "For much of the war, the ratio of Communist to UN casualties stood somewhere between 20:1 and 14:1." Engelhardt, *The End of Victory Culture: Cold War America and the Disillusioning of a Generation* (Amherst: University of Massachusetts Press, 1995), 61–62.

20. Cumings, *Origins of the Korean War, Volume 2*, 917n146; John G. Westover, *Combat Support in Korea* (Washington, D.C.: Center of Military History, U.S. Army, 1987), 81 ("average good day"), 240 ("napalm mix"); "Tan Fliers over Korea," *Pittsburgh Courier*, 8 July 1950; "Negroes Well Represented in Far East Air Forces," *Cleveland Call and Post*, 8 July 1950; McCoy and Ruetten, *Quest and Response*, 233; Marilyn B. Young, "Korea: The Postwar War," *History Workshop Journal* 2001, no. 51 (Spring 2001): 113.

21. A journalist's conversation with one pilot is worth quoting at length for insights into how the Korean War, and wars in general, look from the air: "[The captain] had developed the most respect for napalm, simply because of the destructive power with which this jellied gasoline is endowed. He had no particular compunctions about using it against human beings, whom it is apt to turn into blazing torches. 'The first couple of times I went in on a napalm strike,' he told me, 'I had kind of an empty feeling. I thought afterward, Well, maybe I shouldn't have done it. Maybe those people I set afire were innocent civilians. But you get conditioned. . . . Besides, we don't generally use napalm on people we can see. We use it on hill positions, or buildings. And one thing about napalm is that when you've hit a village and have seen it go up in flames, you know that you've accomplished something.'" Kahn, *The Peculiar War*, 131–132.

22. Robert Chappel collection (AFC/2001/001/188), Veterans History Project; "Korean Christians Are Troubled in Spirit," *Christian Century*, 31 December 1952, 1515.

23. During World War II, the American military used approximately 14,000 tons of napalm, primarily across the Pacific Theater. Both totals pale in comparison to the 400,000 tons dropped on Southeast Asia during America's ten years of active fighting in Vietnam. Moeller, *Shooting War*, 265.

24. Stone, *Hidden History*, 312–313n ("The war was fought"), 114 ("The coolness"); Fehrenbach, *This Kind of War*, 254 ("The last time"); Thompson, *Cry Korea*, 94.

25. Fehrenbach, *This Kind of War*, 256; Cumings, *Origins of the Korean War, Volume 2*, 707.

26. Engelhardt, *End of Victory Culture*, 64.

27. Norman Bartlett, ed., *With the Australians in Korea*, 3rd ed. (Canberra: Australian War Memorial, 1960), 54; Callum A. MacDonald, *Korea: The War before Vietnam* (New York: Free Press, 1986), 216; John Dille, *Substitute for Victory* (Garden City, N.Y.: Doubleday, 1954), 129.

28. "Under the guise of military authority," it declared, "some men have shown an utter disregard for law and human decencies, committing violent, oppressive and otherwise objectionable acts upon members of the Korean population." "Misconduct of Troops," memorandum, 9 March 1951, Folder "250–1 #1 Morals and Conduct FEC Secret 1951," Box 747, RG 554, Records of General HQ, Far East Command, Supreme Commander Allied Powers, and United Nations Command, Adjutant General's Section, Operations Division, Secret General Correspondence, 1951, National Archives II.

29. Cumings, *Origins of the Korean War, Volume 2*, 747, 750–751, 753 (MacArthur quote); Engelhardt, *End of Victory Culture*, 64.

30. Oliver, *Verdict in Korea*, 101 ("Fifty-two"); Kahn, *The Peculiar War*, 28–29 ("just about as inert").

31. The physicist was Samuel Cohen. Cumings, *Origins of the Korean War, Volume 2*, 752.

32. Fehrenbach, *This Kind of War*, 500, 636; Cumings, *Origins of the Korean War, Volume 2*, 757; Keyes Beech, *Tokyo and Points East* (New York: Doubleday, 1954), 206 ("damndest war"); Halliday and Cumings, *Korea*, 159, 197 ("We'd be worried").

33. "The Savage, Secret War in Korea," *Life*, 1 December 1952, 25; William D. Dannenmaier, *We Were Innocents: An Infantryman in Korea* (Urbana: University of Illinois Press, 1999), 88; Paik Sun Yup, *From Pusan to Panmunjom* (McLean, Va.: Brassey's (US), 1992), 181–183.

34. Some of these Korean workers were compensated with items from the PX, which they in turn sold; others stole what they could, infuriating their GI employers. Kahn, *The Peculiar War*, 146, 169–170; Dudley J. Hughes, *Wall of Fire: A Diary of the Third Korean Winter Campaign* (Central Point, Ore.: Hellgate Press, 2003), 44, 60, 100; Dannenmaier, *We Were Innocents*, 68–69; Dille, *Substitute for Victory*, 129; Beech, *Tokyo and Points East*, 134.

35. Bowers, Hammond, and MacGarrigle, *Black Soldier, White Army*, 53–55; MacDonald, *Korea*, 224. A confidential August 1951 report from general headquarters revealed that the problem of drug abuse had "reached such proportions" that an alarming number of military personnel were "rendering themselves unfit for military duty." Check Sheet, 2 August 1951, Folder "250–1 #1 Morals and Conduct FEC Secret 1951," Box 747, RG 554, Records of General HQ, Far East Command, Supreme Commander Allied Powers, and United Nations Command, Adjutant General's Section, Operations Division, Secret General Correspondence, 1951, National Archives II. The folder also contains a December 1951 report listing six Japanese hotels accused of openly selling narcotics to soldiers on R&R.

36. Hughes, *Wall of Fire*, 44; Dannenmaier, *We Were Innocents*, 158 ("These days"), 123 ("their fields").

37. Sherry, *In the Shadow of War*, 181 ("meat grinder"); Halliday and Cumings, *Korea*, 11, 200; Fehrenbach, *This Kind of War*, 446; Cumings, *Origins of the Korean War, Volume 2*, 770, 919n23.

38. John E. Mueller, *War, Presidents, and Public Opinion* (New York: John Wiley & Sons, 1973), 147n13. What little evidence exists does suggest that southern blacks were less supportive of American intervention than southern whites. According to one study, "A significant minority apparently agreed with the relatively well-to-do Negro businessman and veteran of Korea, who wondered why 'we were so excited about saving such a crummy country and bunch of people.'" Alfred O. Hero, Jr., *The Southerner and World Affairs* (Baton Rouge: Louisiana State University Press, 1965), 522. On the other hand, in the spring of 1951 the *Cleveland Call and Post* asked six local black residents if the United States should pull its troops out of Korea. Five of them, including a factory worker, an insurance agent, and a housewife, answered no. "I don't think that any of us would want to see Communism spread throughout the world," one argued, "and that's what would happen if we left now." "The People Speak Out," *Cleveland Call and Post*, 18 May 1951.

39. Emphasis in the original. Goldman, *The Crucial Decade*, 176. See also Walter White, "Remember June 25, 1950; Date May Prove Important to All Negroes," *Chicago Defender*, 9 September 1950, which reprints the statement with slightly different wording.

40. Frank Whisonant, "'Go Back Home!' Seoul City Sue Tells Negro GIs: 'Koreans Are Colored, Too,' She Says," *Pittsburgh Courier*, 9 September 1950 ("we are all"); Bowers, Hammond, and MacGarrigle, *Black Soldier, White Army*, 78; "N. Koreans Use 'Blackface' Ruse to Confuse 24th Infantry," *Afro-American*, 12 August 1950; Bradford Laws, "How Can You Tell Friend from Foe Plagues Tanks [*sic*]: 'Red' Soldiers Use Black Face in War," *Afro-American*, 26 August 1950.

41. Philip S. Foner, ed., *Paul Robeson Speaks: Writings, Speeches, Interviews, 1918–1974* (Larchmont, N.Y.: Brunner/Mazel, 1978), 252 ("the Negro people"); Raphael Konigsberg, "Truman, Tell the Truth!" *California Eagle*, 7 July 1950 ("Will Americans"); John M. Lee, "The Peace Plot," *California Eagle*, 7 July 1950 ("to enforce"); Raphael Konigsberg, "In Honor of the American Revolution," *California Eagle*, 14 July 1950 ("irony of ironies"). See also "Jim Crow Fights in Korea," *California Eagle*, 1 September 1950.

42. Ellipses in the original. "Passing for White," *California Eagle*, 1 September 1950.

43. Diamond Kim, *California Eagle*, 21 July 1950. A much smaller group of conservative black leaders opposed American intervention as well. For a discussion of black Republican criticism of the Truman administration and the war, see Plummer, *Rising Wind*, 207.

44. J. H. Jenkins, letter to the editor, *Afro-American*, 15 July 1950 ("trigger-happy haste"); China Goodman, letter to the editor, *Chicago Defender*, 26 August 1950 ("white washed lies"); Mel Williamson, letter to the editor, *Afro-American*, 11 November 1950 ("crassest hypocrisy"); Roy C. Wright, letter to the editor, *Pittsburgh Courier*, 27 January 1951 ("No Negro"), "Men of 857th," letter to the editor, *Afro-American*, 4 August 1951 ("bring freedom").

45. "Negro Backing Urged: A. P. Randolph Asks Support of U.N. and U.S. in Korea," *New York Times*, 22 July 1950 ("Negroes throughout the country"); "There Are No Short Cuts," *Cleveland Call and Post*, 15 July 1950 ("only the most stupid"); "Korea: Background of the War," *Pittsburgh Courier*, 12 August 1950 ("national survival"). In July 1950, blues artist Andrew "Smokey" Hogg, a veteran of World War II, recorded "Classification Blues," expressing his desire to be classified 1-A (fit for military service) in order to fight in Korea: "I don't have a 1-A card, but I'm looking for my classification every day / We got to stop them Communists . . . from comin' this way." Rijn, *Truman and Eisenhower Blues*, 76.

46. "National Grapevine," *Chicago Defender*, 5 August 1950 ("putting color"); "Negro General for MacArthur," *Chicago Defender*, 15 July 1950; "24th Holds As Reds Step Up Pressure," *Chicago Defender*, 29 July 1950; "Let's Tell the World," *Afro-American*, 9 September 1950 ("the whole world").

47. "Is It a War of Color?" *Ebony*, October 1950, 94.

48. James E. Bryant, letter to the editor, *Ebony*, December 1950, 6 ("potent weapons"); Pfc. Thomas Felton, letter to the editor, *Ebony*, March 1951, 10 ("the fellows and myself"). The sole published dissent came from a resident of Los Angeles. In response to the magazine's dismissal of claims that the United States was bombing a nonwhite population, he asked if Koreans were now to be "classed as white people." Chester Jones, letter to the editor, *Ebony*, December 1950, 6.

49. "Tan Yanks' Action Cited: Consul Refutes Charge Korea Battle Race War," *Afro-American*, 29 July 1950.

50. Serious on-the-job industrial accidents were remarkably common at the time. During World War II, industrial workers were more likely to be injured or to die at work than those in uniform were to become casualties of Axis bullets and shells. Catherine Lutz, *Homefront: A Military City and the American Twentieth Century* (Boston: Beacon Press, 2001), 46.

51. See, for example, "High Court Rejects M'Gee Plea 3d Time," *New York Times*, 16 January 1951; "Blot on the Nation," *Chicago Defender*, 10 February 1951; "White Terrorists Run Amuck in Georgia Town," *Jet*, 24 January 1952, 6; Rufus Wells, "Hate Bomb Kills NAACP Secretary: Christmas Reunion with Korea Vet Marred by Tragedy," *Afro-American*, 5 January 1952; and "Dallas Night Club, Carolina Home Bombed," *Jet*, 24 January 1952, 3.

52. "War Heroes: More Negroes Win DSC in Korea than Received Coveted Award in Four Years of World War II," *Ebony*, May 1951, 15–18.

53. "The Last Days of a Navy Pilot," *Ebony*, April 1951, 15–16. See also "Democracy's Forward March . . . in Defense of Our Nation!" *Chicago Defender*, 28 April 1951.

54. "Second Negro in Korea Gets Medal of Honor," *Chicago Defender*, 16 February 1952; L. D. Reddick, "The Negro Policy of the American Army since World War II," *Journal of Negro History* 38, no. 2 (April 1953): 213. See also James L. Hicks, "Mother Given Hero Son's Bronze Star," *Afro-American*, 20 January 1951.

55. "Koreans Won't Like This," *Afro-American*, 26 August 1950 ("coined to indicate"); Lucius C. Harper, "Dustin' Off the News," *Chicago Defender*, 6 January 1951; "Is This White Chauvinism?" *The Crisis*, February 1951, 103 ("such phrases"); "Why Not All, Mac?" *Afro-American*, 23 September 1950 ("While he"); Artemus Brown, letter to the editor, *Pittsburgh Courier*, 27 January 1951 ("derogatory epithets").

56. Lipsitz, *Life in the Struggle*, 44; Frank Whisonant, "Wounded Tan GIs Await Second Crack at 'Reds,'" *Pittsburgh Courier*, 26 August 1950; "Tan GIs Pack Wounded List," *Pittsburgh Courier*, 21 October 1950; "African Americans in the Korean War," http://korea50.army.mil/history/factsheets/afroamer.shtml. *Ebony* noted in the spring of 1951 that although "the Army and Navy do not give any racial breakdown of casualties, pictures in a Chicago newspaper of 204 dead and missing in the Chicago area shows [*sic*] 44 of the casualties were Negro—more than 20 percent of the total although Negroes comprise only 10 per cent of the city's population." "The Last Days of a Navy Pilot," *Ebony*, April 1951, 15.

57. "GI Tells of Korean Atrocities," *Pittsburgh Courier*, 28 October 1950; "Horrors in North Korea," *Pittsburgh Courier*, 22 August 1953; Frank Whisonant, "Wounded Tan GIs Await Second Crack at 'Reds,'" *Pittsburgh Courier*, 26 August 1950 ("treacherous," "ruthless"); Bradford Laws, "Hills and Infiltration Main Korean Obstacles," *Afro-American*, 9 September 1950 ("crafty," "like monkeys"); James L. Hicks, "24th Quickly Learns New-Style Fighting: AFRO's Hicks Tells How Writers Fare in 'Filthiest Place in World,'"

Afro-American, 5 August 1950 ("fanatical"); "Negro GIs First Heroes," *Pittsburgh Courier*, 29 July 1950 ("slant-eyed"); "Fight or Die Is Army's Decision," *Afro-American*, 12 August 1950 ("Oriental Peoples"); Vincent Tubbs, "Korea Is Not the Place for a Modern War," *Afro-American*, 19 August 1950, magazine section ("There's something"); Rijn, *Truman and Eisenhower Blues*, 89 ("rice-eating").

58. Lyle Rishell, *With a Black Platoon in Combat: A Year in Korea* (College Station: Texas A&M University Press, 1993), 52 ("Running 24th," "Bugout Brigade"); William E. Alt and Betty L. Alt, *Black Soldiers, White Wars: Black Warriors from Antiquity to the Present* (Westport, Conn.: Praeger, 2002), 101 ("Bugout Boogie"); "The Unbunching," *Time*, 22 February 1954, 30; Nalty, *Strength for the Fight*, 258–259; Astor, *The Right to Fight*, 359–362; "National Grapevine," *Chicago Defender*, 9 December 1950 ("booted").

59. Bradford Laws, "Mows Down 30 Reds in One Day: GI Wipes Out Enemy Column," *Pittsburgh Courier*, 5 August 1950; "Eagle Eye GI Shoots 55," *Pittsburgh Courier*, 2 September 1950; Frank Whisonant, "Tan GIs Kill 200," *Pittsburgh Courier*, 2 September 1950.

60. "Sgt. Dudley: No. 1 Hero of Korean War," *Pittsburgh Courier*, 25 November 1950; "The Facts Are Eloquent," *Chicago Defender*, 13 January 1951 ("prodigious"); Bill Stapleton, "Fourth Squad, Third Platoon," *Collier's*, 13 January 1951, 9 ("quota"); "GI Kills Nine Reds to Save Life of White Georgia Officer," *Jet*, 2 April 1953, 16 ("single-handedly"); Douglass Hall, "God Took Sides with Me—Hero," *Afro-American*, 18 April 1953, magazine section ("used the same method").

61. Frank Whisonant, "One GI Mops Up Four Koreans," *Pittsburgh Courier*, 7 October 1950. The *California Eagle* was alone among major black newspapers to deplore the tendency of white and black media outlets to trumpet the number of enemy killed: "Every day we hear over the radio, or read in the big headlines of the number of Chinese 'Reds' that have been killed. The number is given gloatingly, as if the narrator were smacking his lips at the torture inflicted by our troops upon the people of another nation and another color." "The Korean War," *California Eagle*, 8 February 1951.

62. James L. Hicks, "Death of a City," *Afro-American*, 2 September 1950.

63. Vincent Tubbs, "Korea Is Not the Place for a Modern War," *Afro-American*, 19 August 1950; "Korean Assignment 'No Bed of Roses', Too Much Lacking," *Afro-American*, 29 July 1950 ("infamous sugar carts"); "Fight or Die Is Army's Decision," *Afro-American*, 12 August 1950 ("the real filth," "literal hell"); "Korean Vet Discovers U.S. Democracy Rising," *Afro-American*, 17 November 1951 ("filth and disease"); James L. Hicks, "24th Quickly Learns New-Style Fighting: AFRO's Hicks Tells How Writers Fare in 'Filthiest Place in World,'" *Afro-American*, 5 August 1950.

64. "Story of Korea Is Shocking Saga of a Nation Living in the Past," *Chicago Defender*, 23 December 1950. A reporter working for the Baltimore *Afro-American* and the *Cleveland Call and Post* had strikingly similar things to say about Korean poverty: "Over here in Korea, we correspondents have a saying that if the whole world was a pig, Korea would be the pig's tail—only we don't say tail. To begin with, Korea is the most dirty, the most stinking, the most filthy place on God's earth this writer has ever laid eyes on." James L. Hicks, "This Is Korea: Natives, Cows, Dogs, Chickens Live in Same Huts, Conditions Shocking," *Afro-American*, 30 September 1950; James L. Hicks, "First Hand Witness Tells of Korean Life and People: Korea—the Koreans Can Have It!, C–P War Correspondent Says," *Cleveland Call and Post*, 7 October 1950.

65. James L. Hicks, "This Is Korea: Natives, Cows, Dogs, Chickens Live in Same Huts, Conditions Shocking," *Afro-American*, 30 September 1950 ("more filthy"); "Story of Korea

Is Shocking Saga of a Nation Living in the Past," *Chicago Defender*, 23 December 1950 ("personal habits").

66. "Many sights in Korea will remind Americans [of] the West of home," explained one photograph caption, "like this woman carrying her child, who resembles an American Indian on a reservation." *Afro-American*, 29 July 1950. One correspondent maintained that the "country and concepts of the inhabitants are better suited to the skirmishes of cowboys and Indians." Vincent Tubs, "Korea Is Not the Place for a Modern War," *Afro-American*, 19 August 1950, magazine section. See also James L. Hicks, "How They Live in Old Korea," *Cleveland Call and Post*, 21 October 1950. For remarks by white Americans in this vein, see Cumings, *Origins of the Korean War, Volume 2*, 691, 901n65.

67. "Story of Korea Is Shocking Saga of a Nation Living in the Past," *Chicago Defender*, 23 December 1950 ("semi-primitive"); Milton A. Smith, "No Welcome Mat Out for U.S. in Korea," *Afro-American*, 26 December 1950 ("cruel"); Milton A. Smith, "Cruel People: 'Rather Be Negro in Ala. Than Korean in Seoul,' Says GI," *Chicago Defender*, 23 December 1950; Frank Whisonant, "Old Woman Sneaks behind UN Line, Fires on Our GIs," *Pittsburgh Courier*, 30 September 1950 ("You don't know").

68. Ralph Matthews, "Korean Newsman Forgave All until They Shanghaied His Pants," *Cleveland Call and Post*, 15 September 1951 ("denouncing all Koreans"); "What We Face in Korea," *Afro-American*, 15 July 1950 ("questionable value"); "An Insult in Korea," *Pittsburgh Courier*, 2 September 1950 ("Korean attitude"); L. Alex Wilson, "Reveals Facts about North Koreans' Alleged Contempt for Negro GIs," *Chicago Defender*, 10 March 1951 ("significant number"); J. A. Rogers, "Korean Vets, Fed Up with 'Useless War,' Want to Come Home and Forget," *Pittsburgh Courier*, 15 November 1952 ("don't want").

69. One twenty-two-year-old lieutenant from Virginia, for example, supervised more than seventy-five local workers. Milton A. Smith, "Va. Officer Feeds 15,000 Daily in Korea," *Afro-American*, 9 December 1950.

70. Ralph Matthews, "Meets a GI In Korea Who Does Not Gripe!" *New York Amsterdam News*, 22 December 1951.

71. Jose Garcia, letter to the editor, *Pittsburgh Courier*, 11 October 1952.

72. The 24th was one of the first African American units thrust into combat. For a list of several more, which together comprised thousands of black servicemen, see "Tan Troops on Move to Korea," *Pittsburgh Courier*, 15 July 1950.

73. Astor, *The Right to Fight*, 351; Bowers, Hammond, and MacGarrigle, *Black Soldier, White Army*, 79–80.

74. "'Let's Get This Mess Over and Go Home,'" *Pittsburgh Courier*, 5 August 1950. White servicemen exhibited similar cockiness in the early going, only to be surprised by the enemy's tenacity. "Before I came over here," explained a sergeant in early 1951, "I thought these Chinks and North Koreans . . . was crazy as hell—a bunch of gooks jumping the American Army after we'd just whipped the Japs and Germans. All I can say now is 'Kill them before they kill you.'" Kahn, *The Peculiar War*, 93.

75. Rishell, *With a Black Platoon*, 25, 29–32.

76. Bussey, *Firefight at Yechon*, 116–118.

77. Morrow, *What's a Commie Ever Done*, 4, 9.

78. Charles Berry collection, Veterans History Project.

79. The veteran described the incident immediately before launching into a recollection of American soldiers executing prisoners. Samuel King interview, "Korea: The Unfinished War."

80. Wilbert L. Walker, *We Are Men: Memoirs of World War II and the Korean War* (Baltimore: Heritage Press, 1972), x ("a strange war"); Tomedi, *No Bugles, No Drums*, 127 ("to kill"), 186 ("normal soldiers"); Samuel King interview, "Korea: The Unfinished War" ("like Indians"); "Wounded Clevelander Describes War on Korean Front as Heathen-Like," *Cleveland Call and Post*, 2 December 1950 ("tricky").

81. See, for example, Samuel King interview, "Korea: The Unfinished War"; "Without a Chance," photographs with caption, *Pacific Stars and Stripes*, 12 July 1950; "Barbarity on Hill 303," photographs with caption, *Pacific Stars and Stripes*, 19 August 1950; Frank Emery, "7 More Yank GIs Found Murdered by North Koreans," *Pacific Stars and Stripes*, 19 August 1950; and Don Whitehead, "Reds Massacre American Prisoners," *Pacific Stars and Stripes*, 23 October 1950.

82. Robert Chappel collection, Veterans History Project.

83. Tomedi, *No Bugles, No Drums*, 187. White servicemen made similar distinctions between North Korean and Chinese soldiers. According to one, "We quickly learned to have no sympathy for the North Koreans. They brought a viciousness to war that was unmatched by the Chinese." Dannenmaier, *We Were Innocents*, 47.

84. Morrow, *What's a Commie Ever Done*, 39, 41, 63–64.

85. Samuel King interview, "Korea: The Unfinished War."

86. George Cureaux, Jr., interview, "Korea: The Unfinished War."

87. Isaac Gardner, Jr., interview, "Korea: The Unfinished War."

88. Thompson's memoir was in part a rebuttal to allegations that black POWs received preferential treatment as a reward for, or successful inducement toward, collaborating with the enemy. Congressman Charles Rangel of New York, himself a veteran of the Korean War, applauded Thompson for "graphically detail[ing] truths . . . about P.O.W. treatment by third-world captors being color-blind." James Thompson, *True Colors: 1004 Days as a Prisoner of War* (Port Washington, N.Y.: Ashley Books, 1989), xii, xxv, xxvii–xxviii, 11, 25–26, 61, 108, 131. Of the twenty-three American prisoners who refused repatriation at the end of the war (two quickly changed their minds), three were black. "Case of the 23 Exiles," *Chicago Defender*, 8 October 1953.

89. Korea may also have heightened Afro-Asian tensions in an increasingly multiracial United States. Veteran Leroy Stewart, for example, grappled with the effects of his service on his personal life. "When I got back home I was angry," he explained. "In other words when I see, well I shouldn't use the word, Korean or Japanese   [here Stewart paused]. I was prejudiced towards them because we were in a war with them. . . . I had some buddies . . . killed and I dislike them for that." Leroy Stewart interview, "Korea: The Unfinished War."

90. Pvt. Matthew Holden, Jr. to Claude A. Barnett, letter, 9 July 1956, Folder 7: "Asia, Correspondence, 1942–65," Box 197, Claude A. Barnett papers, Chicago Historical Society.

Epilogue

1. Halliday and Cumings, *Korea*, 204; Sherry, *In the Shadow of War*, 196; Arthur A. Stein, *The Nation at War* (Baltimore: Johns Hopkins University Press, 1978), 35.

2. Sherry, *In the Shadow of War*, 182. One historian notes that the Korean War inaugurated a twenty-five-year period during which "Soviet-American competition took on a more militaristic flavor, and its heightened focus on the periphery gave the contest a more global, less Europe-centered context." Thomas J. McCormick, *America's Half-Century:*

United States Foreign Policy in the Cold War and After, 2nd ed. (Baltimore: Johns Hopkins University Press, 1995), 99.

3. Hogan, *A Cross of Iron,* 365, 371, 418.

4. Robert Fredrick Burk, *The Eisenhower Administration and Black Civil Rights* (Knoxville: University of Tennessee Press, 1984), 90. According to another study, "Official nonwhite unemployment stood at 4.5 percent in the last year of the [Korean] war, rose to 13 percent in the recession of 1958, and remained above 10 percent until the escalation of the war in Vietnam." Frances Fox Piven and Richard A. Cloward, *Poor People's Movements: Why They Succeed, How They Fail* (New York: Pantheon Books, 1977), 267.

5. P. L. Prattis, "The Horizon," *Pittsburgh Courier,* 23 September 1950 ("gravely alarmed"); Joseph D. Bibb, "Good Conduct," *Pittsburgh Courier,* 28 October 1950 ("golden opportunity"); "Job Market Easier," *Cleveland Call and Post,* 25 November 1950 ("best in years"); "Job Placements High," *Cleveland Call and Post,* 11 November 1950 ("extended period"); "FEPC Urgently Needed Now," *Afro-American,* 23 September 1950 ("pressing need").

6. Robert Chappel collection, Veterans History Project ("I appreciated"); Nichols, *Breakthrough on the Color Front,* 157 ("What worries"); Foner, *Blacks and the Military,* 202; Bogart, *Project Clear,* xxvi.

7. "Desegregation" may be more apt in this context than "integration," which implies a degree of equality of treatment, access to resources, and interracial affinity that varied considerably from one unit to the next. However, for reasons of style the two are used interchangeably. For the military's self-described "publicity blackout" on desegregation in East Asia and later Europe, see Morris J. MacGregor and Bernard C. Nalty, eds., *Blacks in the United States Armed Forces: Basic Documents,* vol. 12: *Integration* (Wilmington, Del.: Scholarly Resources Inc., 1977), 256. African Americans at home were generally better informed than their white counterparts of the ad hoc integration taking place in Korea in the early going.

8. "It is evident that integration in areas other than the Far East Command, particularly in the United States," wrote Secretary of the Army Frank Pace, Jr., to a stateside admirer in early 1952, "will present problems of greater magnitude and variety than those encountered in Korea and Japan." Frank Pace, Jr., to William F. Hellmuth, Jr., letter, 12 September 1951, Folder "291.2 Negroes June," Box 206, RG 335, Records of the Office of the Secretary of the Army, General Correspondence, Jan. 1951–Jan. 1953, National Archives II. Department of the Army officials evidently were instructed to provide this explanation verbatim. See, for example, "Army Integration Depends on Korea," *Afro-American,* 24 November 1951.

9. Ollie Harrington, "Dark Laughter," *Pittsburgh Courier,* 9 September 1950.

10. Mershon and Schlossman, *Foxholes and Color Lines,* 223; Astor, *The Right to Fight,* 392; McCoy and Ruetten, *Quest and Response,* 238; Foner, *Blacks and the Military,* 192; "Army Ends Segregation of GIs in West Germany," *Jet,* 26 June 1952, 13; "Army to End Segregation in Asia Command, Closing History of Its Last Negro Regiment," *New York Times,* 27 July 1951.

11. Nichols, *Breakthrough on the Color Front,* 189, 200 ("smoothly functioning"), 202.

12. "Defense Aid Says Armed Forces Jim Crow Dying Out," *Jet,* 30 October 1952, 6; "Good News from the Army," *Pittsburgh Courier,* 24 October 1953; Nichols, *Breakthrough on the Color Front,* 97, 201–204; Bogart, *Project Clear,* 279.

13. See, for example, "The Inquiring Reporter," *Afro-American,* 4 December 1948.

14. Leroy Stewart interview, "Korea: The Unfinished War." Another enlisted man, stationed with an all-black unit in the spring of 1951, balked at the prospect of serving with whites for similar reasons: "I would rather be with colored people all the time. . . . I am from Arkansas and it's just part of my training." Bogart, *Project Clear*, 51.

15. Bogart, *Project Clear*, 129 ("It might work"); Astor, *The Right to Fight*, 393 ("We knew then"). See also Cpl. Walter Langston, letter to the editor, *Ebony*, May 1953, 11.

16. "Yanks Bitter over Reports from U.S.A.," *Pittsburgh Courier*, 19 August 1950; Alex Rivera, Jr., "Rebel Flags Flood U.S.!" *Pittsburgh Courier*, 22 September 1951; Ralph Matthews, "Rebel Flags Flooding Korea," *Afro-American*, 1 December 1951. A November 1951 military inspection report on an integrating, previously all-black unit recorded three complaints by enlisted men of a Confederate flag flown above an officer's tent. Staff Report on the 999th Armored Field Artillery Battalion, 17 November 1951, Folder "Inspection File for 1951," Box 494, RG 338, Records of U.S. Army Operational, Tactical, and Support Organizations (World War II and Thereafter), I Corps, Inspector General Section, Investigation Files, 1944–53, National Archives II.

17. Walter White, "Confederate Flags! A Fad or Revival of Fanaticism," *Chicago Defender*, 6 October 1951.

18. Pfc. Raymond Brown, letter to the editor, *Chicago Defender*, 6 January 1951; Sgt. Paul L. Shaw, letter to the editor, *Ebony*, October 1951, 11. Shaw's remarks were prompted by an editorial that described a "military which . . . has a no-riot record to boast of. During the last war when segregation was the order of the day, any number of soldier outbreaks occurred regularly in Army camps as well as Navy bases. There have been none to speak of during the mobilization for the Korean war. The reason is simple: integration." "Why No Race Riots?" *Ebony*, May 1951, 100.

19. D. I. Whitfield, letter to the editor, *Ebony*, December 1954, 6.

20. Emphasis in the original. Cottrial Frazier, letter to the editor, *Ebony*, December 1954, 6.

21. "The Lesson of Korea," *Afro-American*, 8 August 1953 ("the first time"); "Race Hatred Propaganda Effect Noted," *Afro-American*, 29 August 1953 ("completely relaxed"); L. Alex Wilson, "Korea War Integrates U.S. Army," *Chicago Defender*, 30 July 1953 ("costly achievement").

22. Emphasis in the original. L. Alex Wilson, "Bombs, Brass, and Brotherhood: Integration Is Forced to Test by War in Korea," *Chicago Defender*, 3 February 1951.

23. Frank Whisonant, "Yokota Air Base Is Perfect Model of Race Harmony," *Pittsburgh Courier*, 25 November 1950 ("most peaceful"); "Integration. A Beneficial By-Product," *Chicago Defender*, 13 August 1953 ("no one likes").

24. Roy Wilkins, "Undergirding the Democratic Ideal," *The Crisis*, December 1951, 649–650. Walter White agreed: "The significance of desegregation in military units extends far beyond the boundaries of life within the armed forces. . . . The white youth who has shared a barracks, a tent, or a foxhole with a Negro youth . . . will find nothing surprising or disheartening in the fact that such a person has moved into the house next door to his own, or that his children are going to school with children of a different skin color." White, *How Far the Promised Land?* (New York: Viking, 1955), 102–103. See also Enoc P. Waters, "Adventures in Race Relations," *Chicago Defender*, 3 February 1951; and "General Ridgway Steps Forward," *Chicago Defender*, 11 August 1951.

25. According to one recent study, army integration—"widely assumed to have resolved all major racial problems in the American military"—became "a popular symbol of

enlightened governmental action." Mershon and Schlossman, *Foxholes and Color Lines*, 252–253.

26. Alan L. Gropman, *The Air Force Integrates, 1945–1964*, 2nd ed. (Washington, D.C.: Smithsonian Institution Press, 1998), 203n2. With little organized pressure from civil rights advocates for further reforms, it was another two years before President John F. Kennedy established the Advisory Committee on Equal Opportunity in the Armed Forces. McCoy and Ruetten, *Quest and Response*, 249.

27. Mershon and Schlossman, *Foxholes and Color Lines*, 262; MacGregor and Nalty, *Basic Documents*, vol. 12, 299; Charles C. Moskos, Jr., "Racial Integration in the Armed Forces," *American Journal of Sociology* 72, no. 2 (Sept. 1966): 141; Andrew J. Huebner, *The Warrior Image: Soldiers in American Culture from the Second World War to the Vietnam Era* (Chapel Hill: University of North Carolina Press, 2008), 185.

28. Gropman, *The Air Force Integrates*, 122–123; MacGregor and Nalty, *Basic Documents*, vol. 12, 331–332, 334 (all quotes).

29. Harold Bronson, letter to the editor, *Ebony*, August 1969, 23–24.

30. Norvel West, who found that enlistment offered "a way out of the ghetto," served long enough to see action in Vietnam as an officer. Curtis Morrow, who was dissuaded from marrying his Japanese girlfriend and contemplated killing Korean POWs, participated in air drops to assist the French in Vietnam from 1952 to 1954. Charles Berry, whose encounter with a young Korean suicide bomber convinced him to shoot first and ask questions later, retired in 1968 after serving in Vietnam. James Thompson, whose experiences in the World-War-II Pacific and a North Korean prison camp led him to ridicule "that Third World stuff," served on active duty for twenty-seven years and left the army a Vietnam veteran. Beverly Scott, who declared the North Koreans a "vicious" and "nasty" people, became a senior adviser to the Thai army in South Vietnam from 1963 to 1965 and then a member of the Army Inspector General staff in Vietnam until 1968. Norvel Phillip West interview, "Korea: The Unfinished War"; Morrow, *What's a Commie Ever Done*, 104, 106; Charles Berry collection, Veterans History Project; Thompson, *True Colors*, xxv; and Tomedi, *No Bugles, No Drums*, 247.

31. Era Bell Thompson, "The Plight of Black Babies in South Vietnam," *Ebony*, December 1972, 105–106, 108, 112.

32. ". . . . And Now a Domestic Baby Lift?" *Ebony*, June 1975, 134.

33. The celebrated retort "No Vietnamese ever called me a nigger," widely attributed to boxer Muhammad Ali, immediately springs to mind.

34. Huebner, *The Warrior Image*, 190–191.

35. According to a survey of black enlisted men and officers conducted by Terry in 1970, "37 per cent agreed that they were fighting a common Communist enemy with their white buddies in arms—the prevailing attitude among blacks three years ago." Wallace Terry II, "Bringing the War Home," *The Black Scholar* 2, no. 3 (Nov. 1970): 7–8. For a detailed analysis of the causes of heightened racial conflict in the military from 1968 to 1973, see James E. Westheider, *Fighting on Two Fronts: African Americans and the Vietnam War* (New York: New York University Press, 1997).

36. Westheider, *Fighting on Two Fronts*, 170.

37. Black Americans constituted nearly one quarter of army recruits in fiscal 2000, although by early 2005, as the occupation of Iraq entered its third year, that figure had fallen to just under 14 percent. Tom Philpott, "Study Shows 41% Drop in Number of Black Army Recruits since 2000," *Stars and Stripes*, European edition, 4 March 2005.

38. In 1995 three servicemen pleaded guilty in the abduction and rape of a twelve-year-old Okinawan girl, a notorious case that sparked an uproar throughout Japan and massive

protests against the presence of American bases. See, for example, Andrew Pollack, "One Pleads Guilty to Okinawa Rape; 2 Others Admit Role," *New York Times*, 8 November 1995. For a summary of similar recent incidents in Japan and Korea involving American servicemen of various racial and ethnic backgrounds, see Chalmers Johnson, *Nemesis: The Last Days of the American Republic* (New York: Henry Holt, 2006), 182–190; and Johnson, *Sorrows of Empire*, 92–93.

    39. Robert Chappel collection, Veterans History Project.

Selected Bibliography

Archival Material

Center for the Study of the Korean War, Independence, Mo.
National Archives II, College Park, Md.:
Record Group 107, Records of the Office of the Secretary of War.
Record Group 319, Records of the Army Staff.
Record Group 331, Records of the Supreme Commander for the Allied Powers (SCAP).
Record Group 335, Records of the Office of the Secretary of the Army.
Record Group 338, Records of the U.S. Army Operational, Tactical, and Support Organizations (World War II and Thereafter).
Record Group 407, Records of the Adjutant General's Office.
Record Group 554, Records of General HQ, Far East Command, Supreme Commander Allied Powers, and United Nations Command.

Oral History Collections

"Korea: The Unfinished War." Produced by American RadioWorks. St. Paul, Minn.: American Public Media, 2003.
Veterans History Project. American Folklife Center, Library of Congress, Washington, D.C.

Published Papers

Papers of the NAACP. Part 9: Discrimination in the U.S. Armed Forces, 1918–1955, Series A and B. Washington, D.C.: University Publications of America. Microfilm. 1982.

Published Government Documents

MacGregor, Morris J., and Bernard C. Nalty, eds. *Blacks in the United States Armed Forces: Basic Documents,* vol. 8, *Segregation under Siege.* Wilmington, Del.: Scholarly Resources Inc., 1977.
——. *Blacks in the United States Armed Forces: Basic Documents,* vol. 11, *The Fahy Committee.* Wilmington, Del.: Scholarly Resources Inc., 1977.
——. *Blacks in the United States Armed Forces: Basic Documents,* vol. 12, *Integration.* Wilmington, Del.: Scholarly Resources Inc., 1977.
Nalty, Bernard C., and Morris J. MacGregor, eds. *Blacks in the Military: Essential Documents.* Wilmington, Del.: Scholarly Resources Inc., 1981.
A Pocket Guide to Japan. Washington, D.C.: U.S. Government Printing Office, 1950.
A Pocket Guide to Korea. Washington, D.C.: Office of Armed Forces Information and Education, 1956.

Contemporary Periodicals

Afro-American (Baltimore)
California Eagle (Los Angeles)
Chicago Defender
Cleveland Call and Post
The Crisis
Ebony
Jet
New York Amsterdam News
Pacific Citizen (Los Angeles)
Pacific Stars and Stripes (Tokyo)
Pittsburgh Courier

Books and Articles

Allen, Ernest, Jr. "When Japan Was 'Champion of the Darker Races': Satokata Takahashi and the Flowering of Black Messianic Nationalism." *The Black Scholar* 24, no. 1 (1994): 23–46.
Alvah, Donna. *Unofficial Ambassadors: American Military Families Overseas and the Cold War, 1946–1965.* New York: New York University Press, 2007.

Anderson, Carol. *Eyes off the Prize: The United Nations and the African American Struggle for Human Rights, 1944–1955.* New York: Cambridge University Press, 2003.

Astor, Gerald. *The Right to Fight: A History of African Americans in the Military.* Cambridge, Mass.: Da Capo Press, 1998.

Bailey, Beth, and David Farber. *The First Strange Place: The Alchemy of Race and Sex in World War II Hawaii.* New York: Free Press, 1992.

Baker, Anni P. *American Soldiers Overseas: The Global Military Presence.* Westport, Conn.: Praeger, 2004.

Baldovi, Louis, ed. *A Foxhole View: Personal Accounts of Hawaii's Korean War Veterans.* Honolulu: University of Hawai'i Press, 2002.

Beech, Keyes. *Tokyo and Points East.* New York: Doubleday, 1954.

Bernstein, Barton J. "The Truman Administration and the Korean War." In *The Truman Presidency,* ed. Michael J. Lacey, 410–444. New York: Cambridge University Press, 1989.

Berrigan, Darrell. "Japan's Occupation Babies." *Saturday Evening Post,* 19 June 1948, 24–25, 117–118.

Biondi, Martha. *To Stand and Fight: The Struggle for Civil Rights in Postwar New York City.* Cambridge: Harvard University Press, 2003.

Blair, Clay. *The Forgotten War: America in Korea, 1950–1953.* New York: Times Books, 1987.

Bogart, Leo, ed. *Project Clear: Social Research and the Desegregation of the United States Army.* New Brunswick, N.J.: Transaction Publishers, 1992.

Bowers, William T., William M. Hammond, and George L. MacGarrigle. *Black Soldier, White Army: The 24th Infantry Regiment in Korea.* Washington, D.C.: Center of Military History, United States Army, 1996.

Brines, Russell. *MacArthur's Japan.* Philadelphia: J. B. Lippincott, 1948.

Brooks, Charlotte. "Ascending California's Racial Hierarchy: Asian Americans, Housing, and Government, 1920–1955." Ph.D. diss., Northwestern University, 2002.

Brown, Margery Finn. *Over a Bamboo Fence: An American Looks at Japan.* New York: William Morrow, 1951.

Burkhardt, William R. "Institutional Barriers, Marginality, and Adoption among the American-Japanese Mixed Bloods in Japan." *Journal of Asian Studies* 42, no. 3 (May 1983): 519–544.

Busch, Noel F. *Fallen Sun: A Report on Japan.* New York: D. Appleton-Century, 1948.

Bussey, Charles M. *Firefight at Yechon: Courage & Racism in the Korean War.* McLean, Va.: Brassey's (US), 1991.

Cohen, Lizabeth. *A Consumers' Republic: The Politics of Mass Consumption in Postwar America.* New York: Alfred A. Knopf, 2003.

Cohen, Theodore. *Remaking Japan: The American Occupation as New Deal.* Edited by Herbert Passin. New York: Free Press, 1987.

Creighton, Millie. "*Soto* Others and *uchi* Others: Imagining Racial Diversity, Imagining Homogeneous Japan." In *Japan's Minorities: The Illusion of Homogeneity,* ed. Michael Weiner, 211–238. New York: Routledge, 1997.

Crockett, Lucy Herndon. *Popcorn on the Ginza: An Informal Portrait of Postwar Japan.* New York: William Sloane Associates, 1949.

Cumings, Bruce. "Is America an Imperial Power?" *Current History* 102, no. 667 (Nov. 2003): 355–360.

——. *The Origins of the Korean War, Volume 1: Liberation and the Emergence of Separate Regimes, 1945–1947.* Princeton: Princeton University Press, 1981.

——. *The Origins of the Korean War, Volume 2: The Roaring of the Cataract, 1947–1950.* Princeton: Princeton University Press, 1990.

——. "Silent but Deadly: Sexual Subordination in the U.S.-Korean Relationship." In *Let the Good Times Roll: Prostitution and the U.S. Military in Asia*, ed. Saundra Pollock Sturdevant and Brenda Stoltzfus, 169–175. New York: New Press, 1992.

Dalfiume, Richard M. *Desegregation of the U.S. Armed Forces: Fighting on Two Fronts, 1939–1953.* Columbia: University of Missouri Press, 1969.

Dannenmaier, William D. *We Were Innocents: An Infantryman in Korea.* Urbana: University of Illinois Press, 1999.

DeRosa, Christopher S. *Political Indoctrination in the U.S. Army from World War II to the Vietnam War.* Lincoln: University of Nebraska Press, 2006.

Dikötter, Frank. "Introduction." In *The Construction of Racial Identities in China and Japan: Historical and Contemporary Perspectives*, ed. Frank Dikötter, 1–11. London: Hurst, 1997.

Dille, John. *Substitute for Victory.* Garden City, N.Y.: Doubleday, 1954.

Dower, John W. *Embracing Defeat: Japan in the Wake of World War II.* New York: W. W. Norton, 1999.

——. "Peace and Democracy in Two Systems: External Policy and Internal Conflict." In *Postwar Japan as History*, ed. Andrew Gordon, 3–33. Berkeley: University of California Press, 1993.

——. *War without Mercy: Race and Power in the Pacific War.* New York: Pantheon Books, 1986.

Ducksworth, Selika Marianne. "What Hour of the Night: Black Enlisted Men's Experiences and the Desegregation of the Army during the Korean War, 1950–1951." Ph.D. diss., Ohio State University, 1994.

Eichelberger, Robert L., with Milton Mackaye. *Our Jungle Road to Tokyo.* New York: Viking, 1950.

Engelhardt, Tom. *The End of Victory Culture: Cold War America and the Disillusioning of a Generation.* Amherst: University of Massachusetts Press, 1995.

Enloe, Cynthia. *Bananas, Beaches & Bases: Making Feminist Sense of International Politics.* Berkeley: University of California Press, 1990.

——. "It Takes Two." In *Let the Good Times Roll: Prostitution and the U.S. Military in Asia*, ed. Saundra Pollock Sturdevant and Brenda Stoltzfus, 22–27. New York: New Press, 1992.

Fehrenbach, Heide. *Race after Hitler: Black Occupation Children in Postwar Germany and America.* Princeton: Princeton University Press, 2005.

Fehrenbach, T. R. *This Kind of War: A Study in Unpreparedness.* New York: Macmillan, 1963.

Foner, Jack D. *Blacks and the Military in American History: A New Perspective.* New York: Praeger, 1974.

Gallicchio, Marc. *The African American Encounter with Japan and China: Black Internationalism in Asia, 1895–1945.* Chapel Hill: University of North Carolina Press, 2000.

———. "Memory and the Lost Found Relationship between Black Americans and Japan." In *The Unpredictability of the Past: Memories of the Asia-Pacific War in U.S.–East Asian Relations,* ed. Marc Gallicchio, 255–286. Durham, N.C.: Duke University Press, 2007.

Garon, Sheldon. *Molding Japanese Minds: The State in Everyday Life.* Princeton: Princeton University Press, 1997.

Gatewood, William B., Jr. *"Smoked Yankees" and the Struggle for Empire: Letters from Negro Soldiers, 1898–1902.* Urbana: University of Illinois Press, 1971.

Gayn, Mark. *Japan Diary.* New York: William Sloane Associates, 1948.

Gillem, Mark L. *America Town: Building the Outposts of Empire.* Minneapolis: University of Minnesota Press, 2007.

Goedde, Petra. *GIs and Germans: Culture, Gender, and Foreign Relations, 1945–1949.* New Haven: Yale University Press, 2003.

Goldman, Eric F. *The Crucial Decade: America, 1945–1955.* New York: Alfred A. Knopf, 1956.

Goluboff, Risa. " 'Let Economic Equality Take Care of Itself': The NAACP, Labor Litigation, and the Making of Civil Rights in the 1940s." *UCLA Law Review* 52 (June 2005): 1393–1486.

Graham, Lloyd B. "Those G.I.'s in Japan." *Christian Century,* 17 March 1954, 330–332.

Gropman, Alan L. *The Air Force Integrates, 1945–1964.* 2nd ed. Washington, D.C.: Smithsonian Institution Press, 1998.

Halliday, Jon, and Bruce Cumings. *Korea: The Unknown War.* New York: Pantheon Books, 1988.

Harries, Meirion, and Susie Harries. *Sheathing the Sword: The Demilitarization of Japan.* New York: Macmillan, 1987.

Hemphill, Elizabeth Anne. *The Least of These: Miki Sawada and Her Children.* New York: Weatherhill, 1980.

Hogan, Michael J. *A Cross of Iron: Harry S. Truman and the Origins of the National Security State, 1945–1954.* New York: Cambridge University Press, 1998.

Holt, Thomas C. "Marking: Race, Race-making, and the Writing of History." *American Historical Review* 100, no. 1 (Feb. 1995): 1–20.

Horne, Gerald. "The Asiatic Black Man? Japan and the 'Colored Races' Challenge White Supremacy." *Black Renaissance* 4, no. 1 (Spring 2002): 26–38.

———. "Race from Power: U.S. Foreign Policy and the General Crisis of White Supremacy." In *Window on Freedom: Race, Civil Rights, and Foreign Affairs, 1945–1988,* ed. Brenda Gayle Plummer, 45–66. Chapel Hill: University of North Carolina Press, 2003.

———. *Race War: White Supremacy and the Japanese Attack on the British Empire.* New York: New York University Press, 2004.

———. "Tokyo Bound: African Americans and Japan Confront White Supremacy." *Souls* 3, no. 3 (Summer 2001): 17–29.

Huebner, Andrew J. *The Warrior Image: Soldiers in American Culture from the Second World War to the Vietnam Era.* Chapel Hill: University of North Carolina Press, 2008.

Hughes, Dudley J. *Wall of Fire: A Diary of the Third Korean Winter Campaign.* Central Point, Ore.: Hellgate Press, 2003.

Hurh, Won Moo. "Marginal Children of War: An Exploratory Study of American-Korean Children." *International Journal of Sociology of the Family* 2, no. 1 (March 1972): 10–20.

Iddittie, Junesay. *When Two Cultures Meet: Sketches of Postwar Japan, 1945–55.* Tokyo: Kenkyusha Press, 1960.

Jefferson, Robert F. "Staging Points of African American Identity in the Southwest Pacific Theater and the Politics of Demobilization." *Contours: A Journal of the African Diaspora* 1, no. 1 (Spring 2003): 82–100.

Johnson, Chalmers. *The Sorrows of Empire: Militarism, Secrecy, and the End of the Republic.* New York: Henry Holt, 2004.

Kahn, E. J., Jr. *The Peculiar War: Impressions of a Reporter in Korea.* New York: Random House, 1952.

Kalischer, Peter. "Madam Butterfly's Children." *Collier's,* 20 September 1952, 15–18.

Kearney, Reginald. *African American Views of the Japanese: Solidarity or Sedition?* Albany: State University of New York Press, 1998.

Kelley, Frank, and Cornelius Ryan. *Star-Spangled Mikado.* New York: Robert M. McBride, 1947.

Klein, Christina. *Cold War Orientalism: Asia in the Middlebrow Imagination, 1945–1961.* Berkeley: University of California Press, 2003.

———. "Family Ties and Political Obligation: The Discourse of Adoption and the Cold War Commitment to Asia." In *Cold War Constructions: The Political Culture of United States Imperialism, 1945–1966,* ed. Christian G. Appy, 35–66. Amherst: University of Massachusetts Press, 2000.

Koshiro, Yukiko. *Trans-Pacific Racisms and the U.S. Occupation of Japan.* New York: Columbia University Press, 1999.

Kramer, Paul A. *The Blood of Government: Race, Empire, the United States, and the Philippines.* Chapel Hill: University of North Carolina Press, 2006.

Kurashige, Scott. "The Many Facets of Brown: Integration in a Multiracial Society." *Journal of American History* 91, no. 1 (June 2004): 56–68.

LaCerda, John. *The Conqueror Comes to Tea: Japan under MacArthur.* New Brunswick, N.J.: Rutgers University Press, 1946.

Lair, Meredith H. "'Beauty, Bullets, and Ice Cream': Reimagining Daily Life in the 'Nam." Ph.D. diss., Pennsylvania State University, 2004.

Lanning, Michael Lee. *The African-American Soldier: From Crispus Attucks to Colin Powell.* Secaucus, N.J.: Carol Publishing Group, 1997.

Latty, Yvonne. *We Were There: Voices of African American Veterans, from World War II to the War in Iraq.* New York: Harper Collins, 2004.

Lee, Robert G. *Orientals: Asian Americans in Popular Culture*. Philadelphia: Temple University Press, 1999.

Lemke Muniz de Faria, Yara-Colette. "'Germany's "Brown Babies" Must Be Helped! Will You?': U.S. Adoption Plans for Afro-German Children, 1950–1955." *Callaloo* 26, no. 2 (2003): 342–362.

Lipsitz, George. "'Frantic to Join . . . the Japanese Army': The Asia Pacific War in the Lives of African American Soldiers and Civilians." In *The Politics of Culture in the Shadow of Capital*, ed. Lisa Lowe and David Lloyd, 324–353. Durham, N.C.: Duke University Press, 1997.

——. *Rainbow at Midnight: Labor and Culture in the 1940s*. Urbana: University of Illinois Press, 1994.

Lubin, Alex. *Romance and Rights: The Politics of Interracial Intimacy, 1945–1954*. Jackson: University Press of Mississippi, 2005.

Lutz, Catherine, ed. *The Bases of Empire: The Global Struggle against U.S. Military Posts*. New York: New York University Press, 2009.

——. *Homefront: A Military City and the American Twentieth Century*. Boston: Beacon Press, 2001.

MacDonald, Callum A. *Korea: The War before Vietnam*. New York: Free Press, 1986.

MacGregor, Morris J., Jr. *Integration of the Armed Forces, 1940–1965*. Washington, D.C.: Center of Military History, United States Army, 1981.

Maier, Charles S. *Among Empires: American Ascendancy and Its Predecessors*. Cambridge: Harvard University Press, 2006.

McCoy, Donald R., and Richard T. Ruetten. *Quest and Response: Minority Rights and the Truman Administration*. Lawrence: University Press of Kansas, 1973.

Mears, Helen. *Mirror for Americans: Japan*. Cambridge, Mass.: Riverside Press, 1948.

——. "You in Tokyo." *New Yorker*, 23 November 1946, 84–93.

Mershon, Sherie, and Steven Schlossman. *Foxholes and Color Lines: Desegregating the U.S. Armed Forces*. Baltimore: Johns Hopkins University Press, 1998.

Michener, James A. "The Facts about the GI Babies." *Reader's Digest*, March 1954, 5–10.

Moeller, Susan D. *Shooting War: Photography and the American Experience of Combat*. New York: Basic Books, 1989.

Moen, Sveinung Johnson. *The Amerasians: A Study and Research on Interracial Children in Korea*. Seoul: Taewon Publishing, 1974.

Molasky, Michael S. *The American Occupation of Japan and Okinawa: Literature and Memory*. New York: Routledge, 1999.

Moon, Katharine H. S. "South Korean Movements against Militarized Sexual Labor." *Asian Survey* 39, no. 2 (Mar.–Apr. 1999): 310–327.

Morrow, Curtis James. *What's a Commie Ever Done to Black People? A Korean War Memoir of Fighting in the U.S. Army's Last All Negro Unit*. Jefferson, N.C.: McFarland, 1997.

Murphy-Shigematsu, Stephen. "Multiethnic Lives and Monoethnic Myths: American-Japanese Amerasians in Japan." In *The Sum of Our Parts: Mixed-Heritage Asian Americans*, ed. Teresa Williams-León and Cynthia L. Nakashima, 207–216. Philadelphia: Temple University Press, 2001.

Nalty, Bernard C. *Strength for the Fight: A History of Black Americans in the Military.* New York: Free Press, 1986.

Nichols, Lee. *Breakthrough on the Color Front.* New York: Random House, 1954.

Norgren, Tiana. *Abortion before Birth Control: The Politics of Reproduction in Postwar Japan.* Princeton: Princeton University Press, 2001.

Oliver, Robert T. *Verdict in Korea.* State College, Pa.: Bald Eagle Press, 1952.

Perry, John Curtis. *Beneath the Eagle's Wings: Americans in Occupied Japan.* New York: Dodd, Mead, 1980.

Plummer, Brenda Gayle. "Brown Babies: Race, Gender, and Policy after World War II." In *Window on Freedom: Race, Civil Rights, and Foreign Affairs, 1945–1988,* ed. Brenda Gayle Plummer, 67–92. Chapel Hill: University of North Carolina Press, 2003.

——. *Rising Wind: Black Americans and U.S. Foreign Affairs, 1935–1960.* Chapel Hill: University of North Carolina Press, 1996.

Porter, Bernard. *Empire and Superempire: Britain, America, and the World.* New Haven: Yale University Press, 2006.

Rijn, Guido van. *The Truman and Eisenhower Blues: African-American Blues and Gospel Songs, 1945–1960.* New York: Continuum, 2004.

Rishell, Lyle. *With a Black Platoon in Combat: A Year in Korea.* College Station: Texas A&M University Press, 1993.

Rohrer, Scott R. "From Demons to Dependents: American-Japanese Social Relations during the Occupation, 1945–1952." Ph.D. diss., Northwestern University, 2006.

Rosenberg, Jonathan. *How Far the Promised Land? World Affairs and the American Civil Rights Movement from the First World War to Vietnam.* Princeton: Princeton University Press, 2005.

Russell, John. "Race and Reflexivity: The Black Other in Contemporary Japanese Mass Culture." *Cultural Anthropology* 6, no. 1 (Feb. 1991): 3–25.

Schaller, Michael. *The American Occupation of Japan: The Origins of the Cold War in Asia.* New York: Oxford University Press, 1985.

Scipio, L. Albert, II. *Last of the Black Regulars: A History of the 24th Infantry Regiment (1869–1951).* Silver Spring, Md.: Roman Publications, 1983.

Sheldon, Walt. *The Honorable Conquerors: The Occupation of Japan, 1945–1952.* New York: Macmillan, 1965.

Sherry, Michael S. *In the Shadow of War: The United States since the 1930s.* New Haven: Yale University Press, 1994.

Shibusawa, Naoko. "America's Geisha Ally: Race, Gender, and Maturity in Refiguring the Japanese Enemy, 1945–1964." Ph.D. diss., Northwestern University, 1998.

——. *America's Geisha Ally: Reimagining the Japanese Enemy.* Cambridge: Harvard University Press, 2006.

Shukert, Elfrieda Berthiaume, and Barbara Smith Scibetta. *War Brides of World War II.* Novato, Calif.: Presidio Press, 1988.

Simpson, Caroline Chung. "'Out of an Obscure Place': Japanese War Brides and Cultural Pluralism in the 1950s." *differences: A Journal of Feminist Cultural Studies* 10, no. 3 (1998): 47–81.

Soh, C. Sarah. *The Comfort Women: Sexual Violence and Postcolonial Memory in Korea and Japan*. Chicago: University of Chicago Press, 2008.

Solinger, Rickie. *Wake Up Little Susie: Single Pregnancy and Race before Roe v. Wade*. New York: Routledge, 2000.

Spickard, Paul R. *Mixed Blood: Intermarriage and Ethnic Identity in Twentieth-Century America*. Madison: University of Wisconsin Press, 1989.

Stone, I. F. *The Hidden History of the Korean War*. 2nd ed. New York: Monthly Review Press, 1969.

Takemae, Eiji. *Inside GHQ: The Allied Occupation of Japan and Its Legacy*. London: Continuum, 2002.

Tanaka, Yuki. *Japan's Comfort Women: Sexual Slavery and Prostitution during World War II and the US Occupation*. New York: Routledge, 2002.

Terry, Wallace, II. "Bringing the War Home." *The Black Scholar* 2, no. 3 (Nov. 1970): 6–18.

Thompson, Era Bell. "Japan's Rejected." *Ebony*, September 1967, 42–54.

Thompson, James. *True Colors: 1004 Days as a Prisoner of War*. Port Washington, N.Y.: Ashley Books, 1989.

Thompson, Reginald. *Cry Korea*. London: Macdonald, 1951.

Thornton, Michael Charles. "A Social History of a Multiethnic Identity: The Case of Black Japanese Americans." Ph.D. diss., University of Michigan, 1983.

Tomedi, Rudy. *No Bugles, No Drums: An Oral History of the Korean War*. New York: John Wiley & Sons, 1993.

Van Staaveren, Jacob. *An American in Japan, 1945–1948: A Civilian View of the Occupation*. Seattle: University of Washington Press, 1994.

Von Eschen, Penny M. *Race against Empire: Black Americans and Anticolonialism, 1937–1957*. Ithaca: Cornell University Press, 1997.

Wagatsuma, Hiroshi. "Identity Problems of Black Japanese Youth." In *The Mixing of Peoples: Problems of Identity and Ethnicity*, ed. Robert I. Rotberg, 117–129. Stamford, Conn.: Greylock Publishers, 1978.

——. "Mixed-Blood Children in Japan: An Exploratory Study." *Journal of Asian Affairs* 2, no. 1 (Spring 1977): 9–17.

——. "The Social Perception of Skin Color in Japan." In *Color and Race*, ed. John Hope Franklin, 129–165. Boston: Houghton Mifflin, 1968.

Walker, Wilbert L. *We Are Men: Memoirs of World War II and the Korean War*. Baltimore: Heritage Press, 1972.

Watson, Brent Byron. *Far Eastern Tour: The Canadian Infantry in Korea, 1950–1953*. Montreal: McGill-Queen's University Press, 2002.

Weiner, Michael. "The Invention of Identity: Race and Nation in Pre-war Japan." In *The Construction of Racial Identities in China and Japan: Historical and Contemporary Perspectives*, ed. Frank Dikötter, 96–117. London: Hurst, 1997.

Westover, John G. *Combat Support in Korea*. Washington, D.C.: Center of Military History, U.S. Army, 1987.

Wildes, Harry Emerson. *Typhoon in Tokyo: The Occupation and Its Aftermath*. New York: Macmillan, 1954.

Young, Marilyn B. "Korea: The Post-war War." *History Workshop Journal* 2001, no. 51 (Spring 2001): 112–126.

Yuh, Ji-Yeon. *Beyond the Shadow of Camptown: Korean Military Brides in America.* New York: New York University Press, 2002.

Yup, Paik Sun. *From Pusan to Panmunjom.* McLean, Va.: Brassey's (US), 1992.

Index